THE Embassy
BOOK OF
WORLD SNOOKER

CLIVE EVERTON

THE Embassy
BOOK OF
WORLD SNOOKER

CLIVE EVERTON

BLOOMSBURY

First published in Great Britain 1993
Bloomsbury Publishing Limited
2 Soho Square
London W1V 5DE

Copyright ©1993 by Clive Everton

A CIP catalogue record for this book is
available from the British Library

ISBN 0 7475 1610 3

Designed by Bradbury and Williams
Typeset by Spectrum Typesetting
Limited, London
Printed by Cronion SA, Barcelona

CONTENTS

INTRODUCTION
6

The Embassy World Championship at the Crucible Theatre, Sheffield, has become snooker's Wimbledon, the climax each spring to the snooker year. It is an exhaustive examination of skill and psychological capacity, a 17-day marathon of the mind. It is incomparably the game's most prestigious title. Many other fine events, some with long-standing sponsors, are greatly valued elements of the circuit, but the sponsorship of the championship by Embassy in 1976, its move to the Crucible in 1977 and the BBC's decision, a year later, to cover comprehensively every day's play all emphasised a pre-eminence which remains unchallenged. The World Professional Billiards and Snooker Association's contracts with Embassy and with the BBC, the latter also encompassing the Grand Prix at Reading in October, the UK Open at Preston in November and the Masters at Wembley in February, are the commercial cornerstones of the professional circuit. Once the BBC had demonstrated that large numbers of the public liked watching championship snooker at length, ITV began to compete on this front and made its own contribution. Chiefly because eight- or nine-day world ranking events gave too many scheduling problems, ITV has now fallen by the wayside to leave BSkyB as the showcase for most of the circuit's other major events.

Snooker's status as a television sport would have amazed the game's pioneers. It has long been accepted that the game was invented in India in 1875 by a young subaltern, Neville Chamberlain, as an amalgam of various billiard table games, although it has recently become clear that some form of the game was being played in London clubs in the 1860s.

It continued for half a century as either a sociable way to pass an hour on the billiard table or, increasingly, as a gambling game which nurtured a new breed of player. Even when Joe Davis took the leading role in establishing the world professional snooker championship, it was only in the context of 'scraping and scratching to get a living', the lot of even the best billiard players of the 1920s.

Nor was it a smooth progression from Davis's first prize of £6.10s. in 1927 to the £175,000 Stephen Hendry pocketed in 1993. Snooker's first flowering, just before and after the 1939-45 war, appears modest in retrospect and was followed by a severe depression, in which even the world championship was not staged between 1957 and 1964.

A tentative revival was assisted by the BBC series *Pot Black*, which started in 1969, and by the emergence of Alex Higgins, an anti-hero who quickly became a box office attraction.

No box office take, though, would ever have been enough to transcend snooker's limited potentialities. In comparison with football pitches, athletics tracks and even tennis courts, the number of spectators who could obtain a worthwhile view of the action on a 12ft x 6ft snooker table is scarcely more than 1,500. Snooker would still have been widely played – there were three million players in the British Isles alone when television was scarcely acknowledging the game's existence – but its superstars would have been forever in limbo had the scene not been transformed by television and sponsorship.

And how it has been transformed! Before this rebirth fine champions like John Spencer and Ray Reardon were much nearer the ends of their careers than the beginnings. Nevertheless, Spencer's third and last world title made him the Crucible's first champion; Reardon's sixth and last made him its second. The other 1970s champion, Higgins, regained the title in an emotional finale in 1982.

The WPBSA's 'open house' policy on professional status, implemented in 1992, allowed for 542 entries in the 1993

Steve Davis, six times world champion on snooker's most famous stage

championship, whereas in 1931 there were only two. It is therefore unlikely that anyone will emulate the feat of Terry Griffiths, world champion at his first attempt in 1979, when his epic semi-final with Eddie Charlton provided one of the first of the gripping late-night finishes which sent the nation red-eyed to work next day. Cliff Thorburn, who has probably been responsible for more of these late nights than any other snooker player in history, became champion in 1980 and is still the only non-British Crucible champion. Even more memorably, he made the first 147 in championship history three years later.

Steve Davis bestrode the 1980s like a

colossus, winning six world titles and countless others, even if none of them is embedded so deeply in Britain's collective sporting memory as his defeat by Dennis Taylor, watched by 18.5 million BBC viewers, on the final black in 1985. Joe Johnson, an unregarded outsider, sustained a once-in-a-lifetime inspiration to win the title in dramatic fashion in 1986.

Stephen Hendry, save for John Parrott's world title in 1991, has dominated the 1990s so far, winning the game's blue riband three times. Jimmy White, whose engaging personality and dashing skills have made him a particular favourite, made the championship's second 147 break in 1992, but after four appearances in the final is still saddled with the description he detests: the greatest player never to win the title.

Few sports have expanded as spectacularly as snooker has. The administration of WPBSA, originally just a few players keeping the professional game alive under the guidance of Rex Williams, has had to cope, with varying degrees of success, with the responsibilities and issues arising from its position as a world governing body. Off-table disputes, usually generated by the pursuit of money or power, have proliferated.

Yet snooker is no nine-day wonder. Its tournament circuit, like that of any other sport, will always be subject to market fluctuations, but internationally it has grown out of all recognition and its great occasions – like a Crucible final – have become as much a part of the fabric of British sporting life as the FA Cup final or the Grand National. How Joe Davis, the father of professional snooker, would have loved to have been part of it all.

Snooker was initially a composite of various games, played on a billiard table as alternatives to the parent game, billiards. These were more sociable than billiards, not only because more than two could play, but because each player's turn at the table came round more quickly than would have been the case in billiards, even with moderately skilful exponents.

Pyramids, snooker's most obvious forerunner, was a game played with 15 reds, initially placed in a triangle, with the apex red on what is now the pink spot but which was then known as the pyramid spot. Each time a player potted a red, all his opponents paid him the agreed stake money per ball.

In life pool, each player was given a cue-ball and an object-ball (e.g. white on red, red on yellow), the second player's object-ball being the first player's cue-ball and so on. Each time a player's ball was potted, he lost a life and had to pay an agreed stake. When he had lost three lives he paid an extra sum for a 'star' (or extra life) and when that was gone he was 'dead'. The last remaining player scooped the kitty.

Black pool was a variant of pool with a black ball added. When a player had potted his allocated ball, he could attempt the black. If he was successful, each of his opponents paid him an additional sum and he could then attempt the nearest ball. Joe Davis spent many of his youthful hours playing a similar game, pink pool.

Black pool was the preferred game among the officers of the Devonshire Regiment stationed at Jubbulpore in 1875. During the rainy season, long afternoons in the officers' mess tended to be spent at the billiard table. A young subaltern, later Colonel Sir Neville Chamberlain, was inspired to devise a game with 15 reds and one each of yellow, green, pink and black. These new colours produced a game whose variety (and variety of monetary forfeits) immediately

caught on.

The concept of breakbuilding was much in the future, and even the point value of the balls was not established until a little later, but it has been generally accepted that it was in these casual beginnings that snooker had its origins.

"DO YOU KNOW BLACK POOL?"
"NO, BUT I ONCE SPENT THE NIGHT AT SOUTHPORT!"
Drawn by J. H. Thorpe

In an interview in 1938 with the novelist Compton Mackenzie, Chamberlain recalled that the Devons one afternoon received a visit from a young subaltern who had been trained at the Royal Military Academy, Woolwich. In the course of conversation, the subaltern happened to remark that a first-year cadet at Woolwich was referred to as a 'snooker', with the implicaton that this was the status of the lowest of the low. The original word for a cadet, the French *neux*, had been corrupted to 'snooker'.

Chamberlain told Mackenzie: 'The term was a new one to me, but I soon had the opportunity of exploiting it when one of our party failed to hold a coloured ball which was close to the corner pocket. I called out to him: "Why, you're a regular snooker."

'I had to explain to the company the definition of the word, and to soothe the feelings of the culprit I added that we were all, so to speak, snookers at the game, so it would be very appropriate to call the game snooker. The suggestion was adopted with enthusiasm and the game has been called snooker ever since.'

Chamberlain's claim was supported by many distinguished military figures, including Major-General W. A. Watson, Colonel of the Central India Horse for which Chamberlain left the Devons in 1876, Major-General Sir John Hanbury-Williams, Sir Walter Lawrence and Field Marshal Lord Birdwood, who recalled Chamberlain introducing snooker into the mess of the 12th Lancers at Bangalore.

Chamberlain was wounded in the Afghan war and then served with the Commander-in-Chief of the Madras Army. When he moved to the Hill Station at Ootacamund, snooker came to be recognised as the speciality of the Ooty Club, where the rules of the game were drawn up and posted in the billiard room. The Ooty Club epitomises the India of the Raj. Impeccable standards of dress and decorum were – and indeed still are – required and the billiard room is preserved as a shrine.

'The room itself is entered through a door properly fitted with a peephole, marked "Wait for stroke", so that you do not in ungentlemanly fashion cause distress at the table,' wrote Trevor Fishlock when he was the India correspondent of *The Times*. 'The room has ceiling beams and white walls hung with the skulls and heads of 19 beasts and with large pictures of the Defence of Rorke's Drift, the retreat from Moscow, the battle of Tel el-Kebir and the Charge of the Light Brigade. It has a handsome table over which, if you are fortunate, you may be permitted to lean and sight your cue almost as a kind of obeisance. The room's furnishings are redolent of leisured snookery evenings, joshing and cigar smoke, as the balls click, spin and glide across the faded baize. On the wall near the cue rack there are framed accounts and letters testifying to the origin of the game and its curious name.'

During the 1880s, rumours of this new game reached the ears of John Roberts Junior, not only the leading billiards player of his day but its foremost entrepreneur, who played everywhere, from mining settlements in the Australian outback to the Chicago Music Hall. On one of his many tours of India, he chartered some elephants to carry billiard tables to show to the Maharajah of Jaipur, who ordered half a dozen and created Roberts Court Billiards Player for life. With an annual salary of £500 with full expenses for coming to India one month a year, Roberts and his wife were housed in a palace of their own with 100 servants at their disposal. He gave tuition to the Maharajah and arranged entertainments, once bringing eight players from Britain for a tournament.

Roberts opened a billiard table factory in Calcutta and was dining with the Maharajah of Cooch Behar when Chamberlain was introduced to him. The Maharajah passed on the rules of snooker, which he had written down, and Roberts

John Roberts Junior, the foremost billiards player and impressario of his day

duly brought the game back to England.

While he had no clear view of what to do with the game, it had not escaped his attention that a set of 20 balls (blue and brown were added some years later) had commercial possibilities beyond those offered by the sets of three balls needed for billiards. Gradually snooker sets started to be sold and by 1910 the concept of breakbuilding was established, with reports of Tom Aiken, the Scottish professional billiards champion, making a break of 102 and other centuries being recorded by Cecil Harverson and Phil Morris.

Although snooker gained ground as a gambling game, there was no notable competition until 1916 when a prominent sportsman, Harry Hardy, suggested an amateur snooker championship in aid of war charities.

The rules of snooker, which had hitherto been subject to many local variations, were codified in 1919 by the Billiards

This 1869 painting by Henry O'Neil RA, which hangs in the billiard room at the Garrick Club, London, shows several club members of the day enjoying an evening on the billiard table. The game depicted is possibly an early form of snooker or, more likely, a form of life pool

Association and Control Club (later Council – BA&CC). The possibility of a drawn game was abolished through provision for the black to be re-potted at the end of a frame if the scores were equal and the free ball was introduced, although the penalty for going in off a red was still only one.

Low as the standard was in the amateur championship, it was not long before the provincial players, nurtured in money games, elbowed aside the leading exponents from London's traditional gentlemen's clubs. Even so, by 1925 the amateur championship record break was still only 27, until it shot up dramatically to 62 through W. L. Crompton of Blackpool.

Billiards remained far and away the dominant game, with snooker a mere sideshow. Nevertheless, there was a Midland professional snooker championship in 1921, in which Fred Lawrence beat Albert Cope 31-27 for the title, and a Welsh professional championship in 1922, in which J. S. Nicholls beat W. Davies 1032-777, the match being decided on the aggregate score of 18 frames. These were the days of billiards matches lasting a week, two sessions a day. A week's snooker match at Burroughes and Watts, Soho Square, featuring Arthur Peall and Joe Brady, two minor professionals, was tried as a curtain-raiser to the 1922-23 season, but interest was slight.

The Billiards Professionals Association (BPA), a forerunner of the Professional Billiards Players Association and thus of the present World Professional Billiards and Snooker Association, who declared their autonomy in 1971, was more enthusiastic about snooker's future than was the Billiards Association, a paternalistic amateur body who then governed the professional game as well. The BPA, an organisation more for markers and professionals attached to

clubs than for the big names of the day, organised a snooker tournament in 1923 in which Tom Dennis, who owned a billiard hall in Nottingham, made a 76 break.

When Dennis wrote to the BA&CC in August 1924, asking them to promote an open professional snooker championship, A. Stanley Thorn, the secretary, replied that the suggestion would receive consideration at an early date, but that it seemed a little doubtful whether snooker as a spectacular game was sufficiently popular to warrant the successful promotion of such a competition.

Meanwhile, George Nelson, a Leeds professional deeply involved in the promotion and trade aspects of the game, was publicly urging the BA&CC to wake up to snooker's potentialities. Bill Camkin, a Birmingham billiard trader, produced a book of rules under the auspices of the Midland Counties Billiards Association, imposing a minimum penalty of four points for a foul stroke, which was contrary to the then official rules.

As a proprietor of billiard halls, Camkin was well aware of the popularity of snooker and was friendly with Joe Davis, who had played the game since his youthful days of managing his family's billiard halls around Chesterfield. Together they decided to progress the idea of a professional snooker championship, and Davis wrote to the BA&CC, drafting the conditions under which the championship could take place. The association gave its consent, stipulating that the players should arrange their own venues and that the final would be at Camkin's in Birmingham. There was to be a five guinea entry fee and a five guinea sidestake. Half the entry fees were to be divided 60-40 between winner and runner-up, with the other half going to the BA&CC. Gate receipts were to be divided equally between the players after expenses.

'Joe was a great player before anyone else knew how to play the game,' Fred Davis, Joe's younger brother, was wont to remark in later life. He was certainly far too good for his rivals in the early championships, which attracted minimal publicity and, as Joe was feelingly to remark 50 years hence, little income.

Billiards was still very much the premier game, with snooker a sideshow which few were convinced would ever come to much as a public entertainment. Even Joe had his doubts.

There were ten entries for the initial world championship in 1927, for which Davis was the overwhelming favourite. He beat his first two opponents by roughly half the game and in the final disposed of Tom Dennis 20-11. He pocketed £6.10s. as his share of the gate receipts, but as the Billiards Association used the player's half of the entry fees to buy a trophy – the one that is still played for annually – there was nothing to come from that proposed source of prizemoney. Bill Camkin himself refereed the final, in which the highest break was Davis's 57. In one frame he had runs of 32, 34 and 35 in consecutive visits, which was thought to be exceptional at the time.

Davis, who had made a break of 96 in an exhibition in 1925, made his first public century, 100, during the following season at Manchester, when he was taking on local aspirants between sessions of a billiards match. He remained chiefly preoccupied with billiards but introduced snooker as a supporting attraction whenever he could.

The 1928 championship was played on a challenge basis, with Davis exempt until the other contenders had been reduced to one. He beat Fred Lawrence 16-13 at Camkin's to retain the title.

The championship made little headway in the next few years. There were only five entries in 1929, when Davis pushed the championship record up to 61 in beating Dennis 19-14 in the final, and only six in 1930, when Davis again superseded the championship best with a run of 79 in his 25-12 win over Dennis.

Snooker had by now become popular in Australia and New Zealand, mostly among the fraternity who liked to play for money. Murt O'Donoghue became the first player to clear the table from the opening stroke with a 134 in Auckland in 1928 and a little later he made breaks of 136 and 138. He hustled through the 1920s prior to building up a chain of 27 billiard clubs, became a wealthy man and never, he said, regretted his decision not to pursue the game competitively. His knowledge and skill were beyond dispute, and even in his seventies, with defective eyesight, he could demonstrate his skill at close quarters and was much respected as a coach. On 26 September 1934, playing in his own club at Griffith, New South Wales, he made snooker's first 147 break, in honour of which a special certificate, signed by 135 spectators, was later presented to him.

Meanwhile, the 1931 championship attracted only two entries, Davis defeating Dennis 25-21 in the latter's own room at the back of his pub in Nottingham. The score suggests that this was the toughest match Dennis ever gave Davis, for he led 6-4, 14-10, 17-15 and 19-16 before Davis took the next five frames to go in front 21-19. Fred Davis remembers attending the match as a spectator and Joe saying scornfully of Dennis: 'You could beat him couldn't you?' Since Joe had no great opinion of Fred's ability at the time, this was no great compliment.

It has been suggested that this may have been one of the occasions when Joe 'carried' an opponent into the later stages of the match, gate receipts being certain to be affected by an early finish, although the informed view was that no collusion was needed between the two players because Joe could raise his game sufficiently at

JOE DAVIS (1901-78)

Joe Davis took snooker by the scruff of the neck in the 1920s and 1930s and by the sheer force of his skill and personality hauled it into position as the premier billiard table game.

Without him, snooker would never have had a world professional championship. Without him, it would never have graduated from its early venues – a billiard hall in Birmingham, the backroom of a pub in Nottingham – to Thurstons, the billiards holy of holies in Leicester Square, and from there to larger public venues such as the Horticultural Hall, Westminster.

Without him, indeed, it would have been a different game; it was he who transformed it from a somewhat crude potting contest – 'the sort of game you play in corduroys and close' as an old billiards artist Rom Reece acidly put it – into the present sophisticated mixture of breakbuilding techniques and tactical complexities.

Originally, Joe was a billiards player. Born in 1901 in the Derbyshire village of Whitwell, he was 13 when he won the Chesterfield championship, the only amateur event in which he ever competed; at 25 he reached his first professional billiards final; and the whole of Chesterfield turned out at the station to welcome him when he came home world champion in 1928.

He approached the Billiards Association in 1926 to sanction a professional snooker championship. He won the event (it rated only three paragraphs in *The Billiard Player*) and retained it until he abdicated in 1946, by which time snooker had overtaken billiards in popularity.

This was because Joe, the Australian Walter Lindrum, the New Zealander Clark McConachy and another Englishman, Tom Newman, had achieved between them a unique sporting distinction: they had become so good at their game that they

had killed it as a public entertainment. Through their total mastery, notoriously of nursery cannons, they achieved such a degree of perfection in their play that it no longer seemed to bear much resemblance to the game of billiards that amateurs enjoyed in their own clubs. Having exhausted one game, it was time for them to try another.

Even after his retirement from world championship play, Joe continued to dominate the snooker scene. He was co-leaseholder of Leicester Square Hall, which succeed Thurstons as the home of the professional game, and he was chairman of the Professional Players Association: what he said went.

He continued to play brilliantly. He made the game's first official maximum in 1955 and in his entire career was beaten only four times on level terms, on each occasion by his brother, Fred. He won many tournaments conceding substantial handicaps and was unquestionably accepted as No. 1 long after he had ceased to play in the championship. During the Second World War, he toured theatres from the Palladium downwards with a variety act of intricate trick shots. Early television snooker revolved around him utterly. It was with him that the BBC negotiated.

It was always his priority to present snooker with a sense of dignity and status and no one took more pleasure than he in seeing the world professional championship become established at the Crucible Theatre, Sheffield, as one of sport's great annual spectacles.

He would have revelled in the glitter, drama and public attention of the modern game but it was, sadly, the tension of watching his brother, Fred, play Perrie Mans in the 1978 world semi-final which precipitated the heart-associated trouble from which he died in July 1978 at the age of 77.

will. Certainly it would have been beneath such a positive, even domineering personality to ask for a lesser player's co-operation.

The likely explanation is that Dennis was a little better than Joe gave him credit for. A three-frame deficit at such an advanced stage of the match would have been no laughing matter. It was entirely credible, though, that Joe should react to danger by raising his game and imposing his more positive personality when he needed to.

The great New Zealand billiards player, Clark McConachy, by no means such an accomplished snooker player, entered the 1932 championship – thus increasing the entry to three – and beat Dennis before losing to Davis. He was the first non-British entrant.

A future champion, Walter Donaldson, a Scot who managed billiard halls for the Davis family in the Chesterfield area, entered in 1933, losing 13-1 to Davis in the semi-final. One of the great billiards

players of the 1920s, Willie Smith, reached the final before losing to Davis by the comparatively respectable margin of 25-18.

From the dizzy heights of an entry of five in 1933, it was back to a mere two in 1934 when Davis defeated Tom Newman 25-23 in a match spread over three days at Nottingham and two at Kettering. Although Newman was a great billiards player, he was so inferior to Davis at snooker that it seems inconceivable that Davis could not have beaten him by a much wider margin had he wanted to.

Conrad Stanbury became Canada's first entrant to the championship in 1935, when Davis set a new championship record of 110. His lifetime best was still only 114, made in 1933, while Willie Smith, whom Davis beat 25-20 in the final, was stuck on 94 as his personal best even as war broke out.

Although a few players occasionally made centuries, standards were still low in comparison with today's. Tactical players with a good grounding in billiards almost invariably prevailed over those who placed most of their faith in potting. This tendency was even more pronounced in the amateur game.

In the mid-1930s snooker started to derive new impetus from the demise of professional billiards as a public entertainment. The top players had attained such standards that mammoth breaks and absence of dramatic conflict led the ordinary billiards enthusiast to desert the professional game as a spectator.

In the 1935-36 season, Thurstons, the home of the professional game in Leicester Square, decided to vary what had previously been an almost unrelieved diet of billiards by featuring week-long snooker matches. One reason for this was the presence of a credible Australian challenger in Horace Lindrum, nephew of the great billiards player, Walter Lindrum, who had made a break of 139 in Melbourne in March 1933. The Canadian, Clare O'Donnell, who eccentrically kept his chalk under his bridge hand when striking, did not prove to be of high quality, but there were a couple of other newcomers, Alec Brown, a former speedway rider, and Stanley Newman, a younger brother of Tom, who proved an

SPECTACLES

Necessity was the mother of invention for snooker spectacles. Although Fred Davis had made a promising start to his professional career, his championship debut in 1937 could hardly have been less auspicious. He was starting to suffer from myopia but was too self-conscious to tell anyone, even when the balls started to look like balls of wool. He lost 14-17 in the championship to W. A. Withers, a Welshman whom Joe Davis, furious at this affront to family honour, hammered 30-1 in the next round.

Joe's fury with his younger brother's performance persuaded Fred to consult an optician, who devised and fitted a then revolutionary design of swivel-lens spectacles. Fred's game immediately improved out of all recognition and in the following year, he reached the world semi-finals.

Swivel-lens spectacles remained the norm for players who needed assisted vision until 1984, when Dennis Taylor became the pioneer for a new style worn higher on the face and with a wider lens area.

asset to the overall standard.

With an attractive style and personality, Lindrum, still only 23, was an obvious threat to Davis and duly reached the final by beating Newman 29-2, making a break of 101. This final was certainly the greatest snooker match yet. Lindrum led 3-2, 6-4 and 11-9 before Davis, making breaks of 75 and 78, won four frames out of five on the third afternoon to lead 13-12. Yet Lindrum started the last day's play 26-24 ahead. Aided by a lucky snooker, he won the opening frame but then weakened and did not win another frame until Davis had achieved a winning lead at 31-27.

Thurstons was packed and it was abundantly clear that snooker had become the major game, a conclusion which was underlined when the *Daily Mail* switched their Gold Cup tournament from billiards to snooker.

Outside the world championship, both in billiards and snooker, it was customary for the champion to protect his reputation by conceding start. Virtually every match of any significance lasted a week, so the scope for surprise results, even among players of only marginally different standards, was much more limited than it

Horace Lindrum (left), the Australian challenger, shakes hands with Joe Davis prior to their 1937 world final

THE CUE

Alec Brown was a pre-war and immediately post-war professional whose father ran the billiard room at the Piccadilly Hotel, London. He made a few miniature ebony cues, about the size of a fountain pen, complete with tip.

Brown was playing at Thurstons on 14 November 1938, when the cue-ball finished so awkwardly marooned amongst a bunch of reds that he could not play it by any orthodox means. He removed the tiny ebony cue from his pocket, chalked its tip and nudged the cue-ball to play his shot.

When his opponent protested, Brown argued that he was within the rules. However, Charlie Chambers, resident referee at Thurstons, awarded a foul on the grounds that the implement was outside the spirit if not the letter of the law. This led the BA&CC to stipulate that a cue 'must be at least three feet in length and conform to the accepted shape and design'.

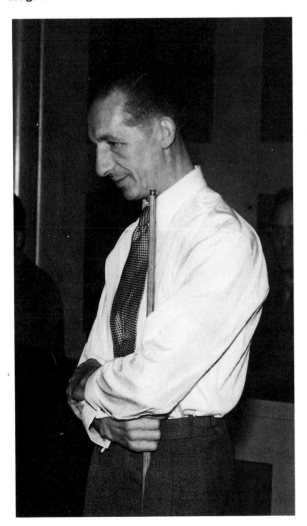

Alec Brown, whose use of the fountain pen cue caused the minimum length of the cue to be fixed at three feet

is today, when best-of-nines are the staple fare of most world ranking tournaments. With only a handful of professionals playing, handicapping made results less predictable and kept players in the game longer.

Davis customarily gave Lindrum seven start and as the back marker, off scratch, won the *Daily Mail* Gold Cup undefeated in a six-man round-robin, making five centuries. The event produced the first official total clearance, 133, by Sidney Smith. 'Thurstons doors locked' was a newspaper headline which epitomised snooker's new popularity.

Davis v Lindrum was big box office. With his black start, Lindrum won 39-36 in Manchester, when he made breaks of 141 and 135, and 74-69 in a fortnight's match – snooker's first – at Thurstons. Lindrum's break of 135 was accepted as a world record – the pockets being found to have conformed to standard size – only for Davis to equal the record later in the match.

Having run Davis to 32-29 in the 1937 world final, Lindrum did not compete in 1938 and lost to Alec Brown in the quarter-finals the following year. His early freshness and inspiration had burnt out, with the burden of the family name and reputation beginning to weigh heavily upon him. There was no doubt that he was a class player and could play to form in exhibitions, but in matches – at the point where winning or losing became the issue – he tended to fade.

So Davis continued to reign supreme, beating Sidney Smith in the 1938 and 1939 finals. But in 1940 a clear threat to his supremacy emerged in his brother Fred, 13 years his junior.

Joe had beaten Fred by the narrow margin of 17-14 in the 1939 semi-final, and at 36-35 in the 1940 final Joe achieved a winning lead with a century break. It was to be the last time they met in the championship.

WORLD CHAMPIONSHIP RESULTS

1927

FIRST ROUND: M. Inman beat T. Newman 8-5; T. Carpenter beat N. Butler 8-3

SECOND ROUND: T. A. Dennis beat F. Lawrence 8-7; A. Cope beat A. Mann 8-6; J. Davis beat J. Brady 10-5; Carpenter beat Inman 8-3

SEMI-FINALS: Davis beat Cope 16-7; Dennis beat Carpenter 12-10

FINAL: Davis beat Dennis 20-11

1928

FIRST ROUND: T. Newman beat F. Smith 12-6; A. Mann beat A. Cope 14-9

SECOND ROUND: Newman beat T. A. Dennis 12-5; F. Lawrence beat Mann 12-11

THIRD ROUND: Lawrence beat Newman 12-7

FINAL: J. Davis beat Lawrence 16-13

1929

FIRST ROUND: F. Lawrence beat A. Mann 13-12

SEMI-FINALS: J. Davis beat Lawrence 13-10; T. A. Dennis beat K. Prince 14-6

FINAL: Davis beat Dennis 19-14

1930

FIRST ROUND: F. Lawrence beat A. Mann 13-11; N. Butler beat T. Newman 13-11

SEMI-FINALS: J. Davis beat Lawrence 13-2; T. A. Dennis beat Butler 13-11

FINAL: Davis beat Dennis 25-12

1931

FINAL: J. Davis beat T. A. Dennis 25-21

1932

FIRST ROUND: C. McConachy beat T. A. Dennis 13-11

FINAL: J. Davis beat McConachy 30-19

1933

FIRST ROUND: W. Donaldson beat W. Leigh 13-11

SEMI-FINALS: J. Davis beat Donaldson 13-1; W. Smith beat T. A. Dennis 16-9

FINAL: Davis beat Smith 25-18

1934

FINAL: J. Davis beat T. Newman 25-23

1935

FIRST ROUND: W. Smith beat C. Stanbury 13-12

SEMI-FINALS: Smith beat A. Mann 13-4; J. Davis beat T. Newman 15-10

FINAL: Davis beat Smith 25-20

1936

FIRST ROUND: C. O'Donnell beat S. Lee 16-15; H. Lindrum beat H. Terry 20-11; J. Davis beat T. Newman 29-2; W. Smith beat S. Smith 16-15; C. Stanbury beat A. Mann 22-9

SECOND ROUND: Alec Brown beat Stanbury 16-15; Lindrum beat O'Donnell 19-6 *(retd)*; Davis beat Smith 22-9; S. Newman *wo*

SEMI-FINALS: Davis beat Brown 21-10; Lindrum beat S. Newman 29-2

FINAL: Davis beat Lindrum 34-27

1937

FIRST ROUND: W. A. Withers beat F. Davis 17-14

SECOND ROUND: J. Davis beat Withers 30-1; H. Lindrum beat S. Lee 20-11; W. Smith beat T. Newman 16-15; S. Smith beat Alec Brown 18-13

SEMI-FINALS: Lindrum beat W. Smith 20-11; J. Davis beat S. Smith 18-13

FINAL: Davis beat Lindrum 32-29

1938

FIRST ROUND: F. Davis beat Alec Brown 14-6 *(retd ill)*; S. Smith beat C. Stanbury 27-4; J. Davis beat S. Lee 24-7; W. Smith beat T. Newman 16-15

SEMI-FINALS: J. Davis beat W. Smith *(nrs)*; S. Smith beat F. Davis *(nrs)*

FINAL: J. Davis beat S. Smith 37-24

1939

FIRST ROUND: S. Smith beat S. Lee 21-10; W. Donaldson beat C. Falkiner 21-10; T. Newman beat A. Mann 19-12; F. Davis beat C. Stanbury 19-12

SECOND ROUND: J. Davis beat W. Smith 19-12; F. Davis beat Newman 20-11; Alec Brown beat H. Lindrum 17-14; S. Smith beat Donaldson 16-15

SEMI-FINALS: J. Davis beat F. Davis 17-14; Smith beat Brown 20-11

FINAL: Davis beat Smith 43-30

1940

FIRST ROUND: W. Donaldson beat Holt 24-7; J. Davis beat Alec Brown 20-11; F. Davis beat S. Lee 20-11; S. Smith beat T. Newman 22-9

SEMI-FINALS: J. Davis beat Donaldson 22-9; F. Davis beat Smith 17-14

FINAL: J. Davis beat F. Davis 37-36

1946

FIRST ROUND: J. Davis beat W. Donaldson 21-10; S. Newman beat S. Lee 19-12; F. Davis beat Alec Brown 24-7; H. Lindrum beat H. Holt 17-14

SEMI-FINALS: J. Davis beat Newman 21-10; Lindrum beat F. Davis 16-12

FINAL: Davis beat Lindrum 78-67

For the duration of the 1939-45 war, Joe Davis's snooker career continued uninterrupted as he played exhibitions for war charities and made a further reputation for himself by appearing on variety stages with a trick-shot act, played in front of a huge angled mirror. Fred Davis, having spent the war years in the Army, was demobbed in time to play in the first post-war world championship, which ran through the 1945-46 season.

However, Lindrum beat Fred in their semi-final at Oldham and therefore became Joe's opponent in the best-of-145-frames final, which was staged at the Royal Horticultural Hall, London. With full-house crowds of 1,200 per session, at prices ranging from five shillings to three pounds, the players came away with the unheard of sum of £1,500 each for their trouble. Joe never looked like losing and his 78-67 victory was assisted by six century breaks, the two highest of which, 133 and 136, were each, in turn, a new championship record.

That was Joe's cue to retire from championship play as 20 years' undefeated champion. This had long been a familiar ploy in the billiards world, in which the champion could either hold the promoters to ransom to defend the title or devalue the event by not playing in it. He could also thereby avoid risking his reputation.

Such an attitude seems barely conceivable now, but it had been common since the days of John Roberts Junior, who in the late nineteenth century grandly offered the Billiards Association a venue, a table and a trophy for their championship – but declined to play in it. Everyone knew he was the best player and that his personality was stronger than the game's administration. Joe had absorbed all these lessons, but his retirement from championship play was soon to devalue the championship itself. In less than ten years, professional snooker was to decline from

that peak of the 1946 final almost to the point of extinction.

Joe continued to play so well that it remained clear for almost another 20 years that he was still, apart from sporadic threats from Fred, the best player.

He was invariably the back marker in the handicap events which occupied most of the season. Usually sponsored by newspapers, notably the *News of the World* or the now defunct *Empire News* or *Sporting Record,* these were round-robins with each match of either three or six days' duration. Joe would play only the official reigning world champion on level terms; losing precious few matches and conceding seven or ten points per frame, he was only ever beaten on level terms by Fred – four times.

For Joe, it was the ideal situation to reign as the king in exile with Fred as champion, but it did not work out this way in 1947. Fred was confidently

Horace Lindrum in play during his 1946 world final against Joe Davis

expected, not least by Joe, to beat Walter Donaldson in the championship final, which was designed as the opening attraction for Leicester Square Hall in 1947.

However, in those days, Fred could seldom bring himself to practise in the summer while Donaldson, after years of struggle and obscurity, prepared himself single-mindedly for his great opportunity by locking himself away every day to practise in a friend's loft. Davis made the match's only three centuries but Donaldson, with a mixture of deadly long potting, relentless safety and a minimum risk policy in shot selection, inexorably ground out an 82-63 victory over the fortnight.

Through long-established if dubious conventions, this gave Donaldson the right to play Joe level. He held him to only two frames at halfway before being beaten 49-42, and Joe again beat Donaldson at the Kelvin Hall, Glasgow, where 1,800 saw one session and 10,000 attended during the week.

In the 1948 final, held only six months after the 1947 final, Fred deposed Donaldson by the ample margin of 84-61. But the match failed to produce a single century partly because, from the outset, Fred was determined to give nothing away in the safety exchanges, whereas the previous year he had taken risks and paid the penalty.

Much of the 1948-49 season was taken up by a professional handicap tournament at Leicester Square Hall, sponsored by the *Empire News*, whose sports editor, Harold Mayes, was responsible for the handicapping. Fred was his columnist while Joe wrote a column for the rival *News of the World*. In addition to the per frame handicaps, there was a sealed handicap. Fred beat Joe 36-35 level, the first time Joe had ever lost on level terms, but in a bizarre anticlimax, the sealed handicap revealed Joe to be in receipt of a

WALTER DONALDSON (1907-73)

Walter Donaldson was the first winner of the British Boys Billiards Championship in 1922. He turned professional the following year and won the Scottish Professional Billiards Championship in 1928.

Combining hard practice with moves to Rotherham and Chesterfield to manage billiard halls for the Davis family, he began to concentrate on snooker and first entered the world championship in 1933. Heavily defeated on that occasion by Joe Davis, he went away for no less than six years to work on his game before entering again in 1939.

Following five years' war service in the Eighth Army's desert and Italian campaigns, he returned home in 1946 to undertake a relentless programme of solo practice to regain his form. After Joe Davis's retirement had thrown the 1947 championship wide open, Donaldson, to the surprise of the snooker world, emerged to beat Fred Davis in the final. These two were also to meet in the next four finals, Davis winning the first two and the last and Donaldson the other.

Donaldson's strong points were his imperturbability and the general consistency which arose from plain ball striking, for he rarely used side in potting. This helped make his long potting the most consistently accurate the game had yet seen, but it limited his positional play and restricted the number of centuries he made.

His dour approach and thrust-out determined Scottish chin symbolised his approach to the game and indeed to life. He was a literal kind of man and he played a literal point-by-point type of game, making few concessions to the public. Though an excellent match player he was not in great demand for exhibitions and as professional snooker's appeal dwindled he acted out his disillusionment with the game by turning his billiard room at his Buckinghamshire home into a cowshed and breaking up the slates of his table to pave a path.

Donaldson about to embark on a practice session in a friend's loft

two-frame start and therefore the winner! This appeared to be an attempt by Mayes to score a point through his man conceding a start to Joe.

This was one of the periods when Fred was playing as well or perhaps even better than Joe, but neither this result nor his three subsequent wins over Joe on level terms made much impact with the public. The media, of which Joe was a shrewd manipulator, surrounded the undefeated champion with an aura of invincibility which nothing could shake.

Fred, meanwhile, won the world title again in 1949. Donaldson led him 45-39, before Fred levelled with a 6-0 session and from 60-57 romped away to a winning lead at 73-58, finishing on 80-65. Again, caution was the watchword, with several six-frame sessions taking more than three hours and Fred's 102 the only century.

Fred then beat Joe for a second time on level terms, 37-34 in a week's match, but

the result was widely attributed to Joe's tiredness from his recent trip to Bermuda.

The *Empire News* switched its sponsorship the following season to the world championship, with the *News of the World* taking over Leicester Square Hall for the £1,500 handicap tournament which filled most of the rest of the season. The daring step was taken of reducing matches from six to three days' duration, whereupon Fred declined to play on the grounds that three-day matches were an insufficiently true test of ability.

Joe won the tournament, the handicaps providing, for instance, for him to give Donaldson seven start, Lindrum 20. As Lindrum, Peter Mans and George Chenier were respectively the professional champions of Australia, South Africa and Canada, they quaintly conceded one point per frame to Sidney Smith and John Pulman.

This was nevertheless a season in which

Four world champions: (from left) Walter Donaldson, Joe Davis, Fred Davis and John Pulman

Joe Davis (on shot) and Sidney Smith pose prior to the commencement of a session at Leicester Square Hall

their presence gave professional snooker a promisingly cosmopolitan feel. Chenier made a particular impression with his plants and sets, a department of the game in which he was able to teach even the best of the British players a thing or two. He set a world record for a break with 144 – soon to be beaten by Joe with 146 – and reached the semi-finals of the world championship.

However, it was again a Fred Davis v Walter Donaldson final, with Donaldson springing a surprise by winning 51-46 to take the title for the second time. Fred's decision not to play in the *News of the World* tournament had left him short of match play, while Donaldson, who had not had a particularly good season, was at least match tight. Spectators were easier to please than they are now and packed the Tower Circus, Blackpool, for the nine days of the match, even though the highest breaks were only a 79 by Davis and 80 by Donaldson. There were several four-hour sessions.

As snooker reached a peak in popularity, another newspaper sponsor, the *Sporting Record,* provided the prizemoney for another professional handicap event. Joe

and Fred Davis were on scratch, but Lindrum took it as a personal affront that he was placed on +23 – receiving two points a frame from Sidney Smith – and declined to play, thus initiating a breach with Joe which was to last until shortly before his death in 1975. Joe won the tournament.

Storm clouds began to gather in the relationship between the professionals and the BA&CC when, in October 1950, the Professional Billiards Players Association applied to the BA&CC for permission to introduce the 'play again' in the *News of the World* tournament.

This eminently sensible rule gave a player the option of requiring his opponent to play again after he had committed a foul. It seems remarkable now that there was any opposition to what has become an accepted part of snooker, but the BA&CC, composed of amateur enthusiasts, either thought they knew better or discerned a threat to their authority. They agreed to the rule only on condition that any records set while it was in operation could not be eligible for official ratification. As discontent simmered, Fred Davis regained the world title in 1951 and Alec Brown, receiving a 30 start from Joe and lesser starts from everyone else, won the *News of the World* tournament with an unbeaten record. In the summer of 1951, during a tour of South Africa, Joe made breaks of 103, 128 and 134 in consecutive frames, the first time there had been such a hat-trick. All the time, though, the professionals' disenchantment was building inexorably to a breach with the BA&CC which was never completely healed.

The BA&CC declared that the world championship was primarily an affair of honour, which led to players deriving more prestige and more engagements.

John Pulman and
Fred Davis are
introduced for a
session of one of
their world finals at
Blackpool Tower
Circus

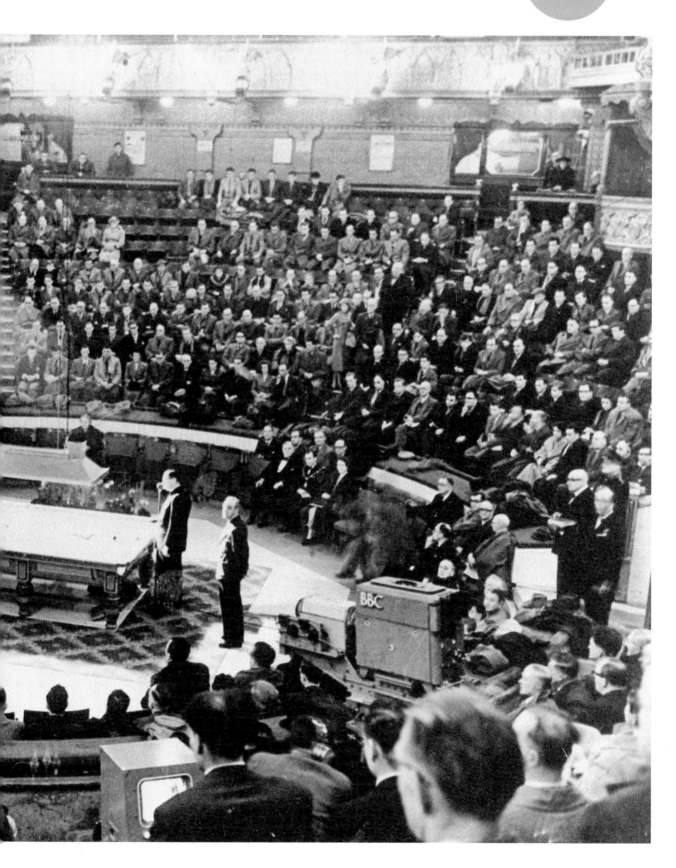

Rex Williams, newly recruited to the professional ranks as the 17-year-old English amateur champion

now, the professionals shrank from describing their own event officially as the world championship, even though this was how it was generally regarded. Fred beat Donaldson 38-35 to win it and also beat Joe 20-17 level in the *News of the World* tournament, but the professional game started to lose impetus. Although John Pulman, in five years as a professional, had made himself a force to be reckoned with and Rex Williams, an outstanding English amateur champion in 1951, appeared to be a hope for the future, in general there was not enough drama, not enough variety and not enough new faces to do more for snooker than merely keep it ticking over.

Fred beat Donaldson twice more in the 1953 and 1954 world (matchplay) finals and again beat Joe level 21-16 in the *News of the World* tournament of 1954, a year in which Joe twice made centuries in three consecutive frames. Commercially, though, professional snooker was petering out and Donaldson decided to retire to his Buckinghamshire farm.

The advent of television and the imposition of a new entertainment tax was making snooker a tough market in which to make a living. Leicester Square Hall's lease from the Automobile Association ran out, thus depriving the professional game of what had been its showcase for 54 years. Although Joe and Fred were still playing extremely well, they were dependent in those days on a public who would marvel at their skill, rather than be captivated by an intense battle with the outcome in doubt. Nobody cared very much what the results were in professional snooker.

Joe made his second 146 in the *News of the World* tournament and brought his career to a climax by compiling the game's first official 147 in an exhibition against the veteran Willie Smith at Leicester Square Hall on 22 January 1955.

The BA&CC shortsightedly refused to recognise the break, on the grounds that professionals were still playing under the

They published figures revealing that Fred Davis and Donaldson had shared £966 and £500 from the 1950 and 1951 finals, when the BA&CC's shares were just £100 and £58 respectively. But the argument was less about the ratio than the total, not to mention the negligible returns from the pre-final heats. The professionals decided to boycott the world championship, as staged under the auspices of the BA&CC, and institute their own event, the world professional matchplay championship. This immediately became, in the public's perception, the world championship because all the leading players, except Joe, played in it.

The BA&CC stubbornly organised their own event in which Lindrum, by now three blacks worse than the leading players, and the veteran New Zealander, Clark McConachy, were the only entries. Lindrum won a farcical match 94-49. He made his mother happy by having his name engraved on the famous trophy, but his fellow-professionals regarded him as a renegade.

In an age when established authority tended to be respected more than it is

play again rule, although it had obviously not cropped up in this particular frame. The rancour which followed was eventually glossed over when the BA&CC recognised the break in April 1957 and adopted the rule itself in January 1958.

In Donaldson's absence, Fred's opponent in the 1955 and 1956 world finals was Pulman, to whom Joe was still giving 14 start in the *News of the World* tournament, which went out into the provinces for the 1955-56 season. Both finals were close and

Pulman had a great chance to win in 1956, starting the last day 31-29 ahead, only to drop the afternoon session 5-1.

Fred now decided that the world championship was not worth playing in, and with the 1957 event in Jersey attracting only four entries, Pulman's victory there had a distinctly hollow ring. He was to hold the title unchallenged until 1964, for there was no promoter anywhere prepared to take the gamble of staging the game's premier event.

WORLD CHAMPIONSHIP RESULTS

1947
FIRST ROUND: H. Lindrum beat Albert Brown 39-34; S. Smith beat Alec Brown 43-28; W. Donaldson beat S. Newman 46-25; F. Davis beat C. McConachy 53-20
SEMI-FINALS: Donaldson beat Lindrum 39-32; Davis beat Smith 39-32
FINAL: Donaldson beat Davis 82-63

1948
FIRST ROUND: F. Davis beat Alec Brown 42-28; C. McConachy beat J. Pulman 42-29; Albert Brown beat S. Smith 36-35; W. Donaldson beat K. Kennerley 46-25
SEMI-FINALS: Davis beat McConachy 43-28; Donaldson beat Brown 40-31
FINAL: Davis beat Donaldson 84-61

1949
FIRST ROUND: W. Donaldson beat C. Stanbury 58-13; J. Pulman beat Albert Brown 42-29; S. Smith beat Alec Brown 41-30; F. Davis beat K. Kennerley 50-21
SEMI-FINALS: Donaldson beat Pulman 49-22; Davis beat Smith 42-29
FINAL: Davis beat Donaldson 80-65

1950
FIRST ROUND: Albert Brown beat J. Pulman 37-34; W. Donaldson beat K. Kennerley 42-29; G. Chenier beat P. Mans 37-34; F. Davis beat Alec Brown 44-27
SEMI-FINALS: Donaldson beat Brown 37-34; Davis beat Chenier 43-28
FINAL: Donaldson beat Davis 51-46

1951
FIRST ROUND: F. Davis beat J. Barrie 42-29; H. Lindrum beat Albert Brown 43-28; W. Donaldson beat K. Kennerley 41-30; J. Pulman beat S. Smith 38-33
SEMI-FINALS: Donaldson beat Lindrum 41-30; Davis beat Pulman 22-14 (retd ill)
FINAL: Davis beat Donaldson 58-39

1952
FIRST ROUND: Alec Brown beat R. Williams 39-22; Jack Rea beat J. Lees 38-32; Albert Brown beat J. Pulman 32-27 (records incomplete)
SEMI-FINALS: W. Donaldson beat Albert Brown 31-30 (records incomplete)
FINAL: F. Davis beat Donaldson 38-35

1953
FIRST ROUND: Albert Brown beat Alec Brown 35-26; J. Pulman beat Jack Rea 36-25; W. Donaldson beat Kennerley 42-19; F. Davis beat J. Barrie 32-29
SEMI-FINALS: Donaldson beat Brown (nrs); Davis beat Pulman 36-25
FINAL: Davis beat Donaldson 37-34

1954
FIRST ROUND: J. Pulman beat Jack Rea 31-30
SEMI-FINALS: W. Donaldson beat Alec Brown 36-25; F. Davis beat Pulman 32-29
FINAL: Davis beat Donaldson 39-21

1955
FIRST ROUND: J. Pulman beat R. Williams 22-15; Jack Rea beat H. Stokes (nrs)
SEMI-FINALS: F. Davis beat Rea 36-25; Pulman beat Alec Brown (nrs)
FINAL: Davis beat Pulman 37-34

1956
SEMI-FINALS: J. Pulman beat Jack Rea 36-25; F. Davis beat R. Williams 35-26
FINAL: Davis beat Pulman 38-35

1957
SEMI-FINALS: J. Pulman beat R. Williams 21-16; Jack Rea beat K. Kennerley 25-12
FINAL: Pulman beat Rea 39-34

THROUGH LACK OF PUBLIC SUPPORT NO CHAMPIONSHIP WAS ORGANISED BETWEEN 1957 AND 1964. AFTER A TRUCE WITH THE BA&CC A NEW SYSTEM WAS ADOPTED WHEREBY THE CHAMPION DEFENDED HIS TITLE AGAINST A SERIES OF SINGLE CHALLENGERS.

Between 1957 and 1964 there was no world championship and only the most sporadic and low-key professional competition. In part, this was the consequence of those years in which the professional game had grown ever more insular, with the short-sighted argument that there was little enough work for the handful of professionals there were without risking a further reduction by encouraging newcomers. High-quality English amateur champions like Pat Houlihan and Marcus Owen were mysteriously regarded as 'not the right type', at a time when professional snooker should have been going out of its way to infuse itself with new blood.

Professionals eked out a living by playing exhibitions in clubs, often on a fee/commission basis on behalf of charities like Guide Dogs for the Blind and the National Spastics Society, but even this was hard going. One winter, Fred Davis did not play at all.

Yet even in its darkest days snooker remained popular at amateur level. In Britain, the competitive structure was securely founded on the local leagues and county associations, while overseas those national associations which had originated to run billiards championships were running corresponding snooker tournaments. Northern Ireland started its amateur championship in 1927, Wales in 1930, the Republic of Ireland and Scotland in 1931, South Africa in 1937, India in 1939, New Zealand in 1945, Malta in 1947, Sri Lanka in 1948 and Australia in 1953.

Amateur standards rose slowly. In 1939, the English amateur championship break record was still only 69 by Kingsley Kennerley, primarily a billiards player, who turned professional without ever quite making the grade. Albert Brown, twice runner-up to Kennerley, turned professional with more success, but tactical players rather than breakbuilders tended

to dominate the amateur game.

Even when John Pulman won the 1946 English amateur title as an unknown from Exeter, his highest break of the competition was 25. Rex Williams played snooker of an altogether different quality in winning the title in 1951 at the age of 17, making a break of 74 and a string of 30s and 40s. He turned professional immediately, but made little impact on the professional game before it collapsed around him. In what should have been his prime years, he had hardly any tournaments in which to play.

The amateur game had its crowd pullers, notably Cliff Wilson, who in his youth was one of the greatest potters snooker has ever seen. Every time he played in the amateur championship at Burroughes and Watts, Soho Square, he could be guaranteed to fill the place. Although the womb-like amphitheatre held fewer than 200 people, it then seemed unthinkable that the primary amateur events could be held anywhere else.

No-one visualised what an asset to the professional game Wilson could have been. He settled for a hard life in the steelworks at Llanwern and was soon into a 15-year retirement, from which he emerged in the 1970s to win the world amateur title in 1978 and turn professional in the modern snooker boom.

Wilson's great Welsh rival, Ray Reardon, loved his forays to London for the English amateur championship and looked like winning it in 1956, when he led Tommy Gordon 7-3 at the end of the first day's play. With his first shot on the second day, Reardon's tip flew off; playing with a borrowed cue, he lost all five afternoon frames and Gordon won 11-9.

The scene was so dead that the BA&CC, clutching at straws, recognised a world open snooker championship which was played in Australia in 1960, although as entry was by invitation, it was anything but open. Fred Davis was in a class of his own and won it easily.

The advent of television had been one of the factors in snooker's commercial demise. Now television threw it a lifeline when ITV decided to stage a tournament in which four professionals played four amateurs over the best of five frames. When all four professionals lost in the first round, it was obvious that lack of competition had taken the edge from their games and they were dropped from ITV's next tournament. Amateur matches continued on ITV for a few years, until the *Sunday Times* revealed that the BA&CC – in dire financial straits and needing television fees, modest as they were, to ensure its survival – had put pressure on the players to prearrange certain matches and ensure that the fifth frame would be the decider.

In 1962, in the London area qualifying, Roland Foxley made a new English amateur championship break record of 85, which in the competition proper was abruptly superseded by Geoff Thompson, who broke the century barrier with 115.

A 106 by Gerry Povall in the 1956 South African championship had been the first century in a national amateur championship, and in December 1964 Thompson's world amateur break record fell to a 122 by a young Indian, Ratan Bader, in the West Bengal State championship. Bader, whose previous best had been 82 in practice and 50 in a match, never again made a century. Extraordinarily, at a time when amateur centuries were becoming common, his record remained intact until 1977.

A world amateur snooker championship was instituted in 1963, the idea first having been mooted by Sid Gillett, managing director of Thurstons South Africa in 1952. Australia had made a similar request shortly afterwards, only to have it 'deferred until some improvement in the BA&CC's finances takes place'.

JOHN PULMAN (1926-)

John Pulman won the 1946 English amateur snooker title as a 20-year-old unknown from Exeter and turned professional that year with the backing of a Bristol businessman, Bill Lampard, at whose house he stayed and in whose billiard room he practised intensively every day.

Although he won £400 in his first professional tournament, the *Empire News* event, his progress to the championship was gradual. He gave Fred Davis a close match in the 1954 semifinal and another in the 1955 final. Leading 31-29 starting the last day, he was on the brink of victory in the final the following year but Davis recovered to beat him and it was not

until 1957, when there were only four entries and Davis did not enter, that Pulman won the world title in Jersey.

He was unable to capitalise fully on his new status as champion as the game was entering an unprecedented depression and the championship became dormant until being revived on a challenge basis in 1964. Public interest was limited, but Pulman proved his qualities as a competitor by defending the title against a variety of opponents in a variety of venues until the championship was restored to a knockout basis in 1968-69.

When the established players were challenged by a wave of newcomers from the amateur ranks, Pulman stood up to the test better than any of his contemporaries, reaching the world final again in 1970.

Therafter, however, his standard gradually declined, even if glimpses of his former quality remained. In 1977 he made a great personal effort to achieve his best form for some years in reaching the world semi-final. His playing career was ended by a broken leg arising from a glancing blow from a bus and he became an ITV commentator in 1982 (right).

In 1958 the BA&CC announced its intention of inaugurating the event in London in 1959, but with both India and Australia opposing their choice of venue, the idea fell through until M. M. Begg, the Indian chairman, donated a cup and concluded arrangements for a tournament in Calcutta in 1963. The entry was small and restricted to those national associations who could afford to send a representative, a situation which was to change when government grants to sports bodies became the norm. Gary Owen, the 1963 English amateur champion, was sent by means of an appeal fund and easily won his four matches in the five-man round-robin to become the first world amateur champion.

By now there were only six active professionals: Joe and Fred Davis, Pulman, Jack Rea, Williams and Kennerley. Joe had no financial worries; Fred was comfortable, first at his hotel in Llandudno, then at his farm in Liss; Williams had a family printing business to fall back on. The others relied on exhibitions, a field in which Rea, with his repartee, imitations and jokes, excelled.

Williams, the youngest, most ambitious and most energetic, revived the world championship in 1964 on a challenge basis. He obtained the BA&CC's approval and recognition and the support of Burroughes and Watts, where the first match of this kind between Pulman and Fred was played. He took the lead in re-forming the professional association and promoted a four-man tournament at Blackheath, Staffordshire, which was won by Pulman.

Pulman beat Fred 19-16 for the revived professional title in 1964. Pulman was to retain his title through six more challenges over four years. One of the contests comprised a six-week tour of South Africa with Williams, but so disappointing was the sparse attendance one evening that they decided to flip a coin rather than play the match.

After the championship series, Williams made a 147 break in an exhibition in 1965, which was officially recognised as equalling Joe Davis's world record 147 in 1955.

Little notice was taken of any of Pulman's first five title defences and not very much more of his sixth, although this did at least have the merit of being against a newcomer from Australia, Eddie Charlton. There was no snooker coverage in the national press and in the snooker world itself the talk tended to be of a new generation of amateur stars, all with considerable breakmaking capacities.

Ray Reardon beat John Spencer 11-8 to win the 1964 English amateur title; Pat Houlihan beat Spencer 11-3 to win in 1965; Spencer beat Marcus Owen 11-5 in 1966.

Gary Owen, as defending world champion, and Spencer were nominated to represent England in the second world amateur championship in Karachi in 1966 and duly finished first and second respectively. Owen was awarded the MBE and the following year, still a Birmingham fireman, was offered a cue contract by Riley Burwat. Modest as this was, it meant he had to embrace professional status.

Spencer, returning from Karachi, expressed his dissatisfaction with the way the amateur game was run and said he would either turn professional or give up altogether. The National Spastics Society offered him a few engagements in the north and Pontins asked him to tour some of their northern camps in the summer.

The BA&CC, invited by Ken Shaw of Union Billiards South Africa to send a team of two for an England v South Africa test series, selected Ray Reardon, a Welshman, and Jonathan Barron, a Cornishman who had made a 107 break on ITV. The venture was well enough received for Shaw to promise Reardon a

South African tour if he were to turn professional. Reardon, pounding the beat on behalf of the City of Stoke constabulary, had grown accustomed as an amateur to charging a few pounds for exhibitions. A professional snooker career was no glittering prospect, but after ten years the beat was scarcely alluring either. He took the plunge.

In Australia Charlton, a former miner with competitive experience of soccer, cricket, athletics, boxing, tennis, surfing and speed roller skating, had turned professional in 1963 and won the Australian championship in 1964. As in Britain, there was a market for club exhibitions, although the competitive scene was not very active.

Charlton did, though, have a valuable supporter in Jack Chown, a wealthy Sydney enthusiast, who sponsored his challenge for Pulman's world title in a week's match at the Co-op Hall, Bolton, in 1968.

Pulman was at that time playing a great many club exhibitions under an agreement with John Player, the tobacco company, who were trying to reach the large market which clubs represented. They sponsored the Pulman v Charlton match, which was a close one until Pulman won nine of the 12 Thursday frames *en route* to clinching victory in the penultimate session at 37-28. Within a few days of this, Alex Higgins became the youngest-ever winner of the Northern Ireland amateur title at the age of 18.

Press coverage remained virtually non-existent, but John Player were sufficiently impressed by the number of full houses at Bolton to agree to sponsor the 1969 world championship, to an extent which enabled it to be restored to a knockout basis. They were also obtaining encouraging feedback from their two-year sponsorship of the British team championship, the second of which Higgins won virtually single-handed for Belfast YMCA.

As it was still to be several years before the professionals could accept the credibility of any match lasting much less than a week, the world championship ran through the 1968-69 season. Charlton did not compete this time but eight players did.

Pulman's title defence foundered at the first hurdle when he was beaten 25-18 by Spencer at Wryton Stadium, Bolton, a venue more commonly used for all-in wrestling. Gary Owen took a week's leave from the Birmingham Fire Brigade to beat Rea 25-17 at Stratford-upon-Avon Hippodrome. Williams outclassed Bernard Bennett 25-4 at Bennett's Castle Snooker Centre, Southampton, the earliest of the new-style snooker establishments which were to replace the dingy, disreputable billiard halls of old. Davis, with a consummate display of safety tactics, beat Reardon 25-24 in the concert room of Tunstall British Legion, Stoke, after a final session of five hours three minutes which finished at 1.33 a.m.

Owen then beat Davis and Spencer crushed Williams. Although Owen had had the better of his duels with Spencer and was considered the favourite for the final, Spencer beat him comfortably 37-24 at the Victoria Halls, London.

Spencer's long potting and prodigious screw shots, even when the cue-ball and object-ball were seven or eight feet apart, were a revelation, particularly when it is borne in mind that Crystalate balls were heavier and less manoeuvrable than the Super Crystalates which were to be introduced in 1973. Yet as well as he was potting, Spencer made only two 70s and three 60s in the entire week, Owen's 80 being the highest break of the match. Spencer's first prize of £1,780 was considered, in snooker terms, a fortune.

Coincidentally, BBC2, the only channel on which colour was then available, were at this time looking for low-budget programmes to which colour was intrinsic, so that sales of colour TV sets could be stimulated. Ted Lowe, who had maintained his contacts with BBC producers from the days when he used to commentate on Joe Davis v A. N. Other on Saturday afternoons, was able to say in all honesty that snooker had been enlivened by its recent influx of new professionals. Philip Lewis, a BBC producer, coined the name 'Pot Black' and the first programme under that name went out on 23 July 1969.

The BBC's hopes for *Pot Black* were not
immoderately high, but almost at once it
went to second place in the BBC2 ratings
and established that the potential viewing
public for snooker, properly presented, was
much greater than had been imagined.
Programmes were recorded in the BBC's
Birmingham studios, and although results
could not be taken too seriously, the
matches being of only one frame, the
exposure the game received and the
reaction to it was far-reaching in its
influence.

Yet it still seemed inconceivable that
championship snooker could ever become
a feature of television sport. How could it
be accommodated in the schedules? One
frame, once a week, was fine but
championship matches of 37 or 73 frames
were surely out of the question.
Professional snooker itself saw no way
round this impasse: how could
championships retain credibility if
matches were much shorter?

The 1970 world championship, again
sponsored by John Player, took place in
April according to the time-honoured
tradition of week-long matches. Reardon
eliminated Spencer in one semi-final,
Pulman beat Owen comfortably in the
other and after trailing 14-27 recovered to
33-34 in the final, again at the Victoria
Halls, before Reardon won the next three
frames to clinch the title.

Reardon held the championship less
than seven months, for in November that
year the event was staged again at various
venues in Australia, with nine competitors
from six countries, the most
internationally representative field there
had yet been. The double-elimination
system produced as semi-finalists Reardon,
Spencer, and two Australians, Charlton
and Warren Simpson.

Charlton had lost only once to Simpson
since 1964, but was involved in a minor
car accident on his way to the match, lost
the first three frames and never fully

recovered. Spencer, at the peak of his form, demolished Reardon in the other and treated Simpson similarly to regain the title, making three centuries in four frames on the second day of the match.

On his return from Australia with a then record first-prize cheque of £2,333 in his pocket, Spencer launched in January 1971 into the first Park Drive £2,000 tournament, a round-robin event in which he, Owen, Pulman and Williams played each other in club venues three times in seven-frame matches, before the top two played off for the first two prizes of £750 and £550.

The Park Drive event was not only snooker's first whiff of tournament sponsorship – outside the world championship – since the *News of the World* tournament, but marked the first involvement in the sport of West and Nally, a new London firm specialising in the rapidly developing world of sports sponsorship. Pitching for the Gallaher account, they included a snooker proposal of 18 one-night stands in clubs, with the best-of-seven-frames final on television – snooker's first attempt to bridge the gap between the best of 37 or more and *Pot Black's* single frame.

The involvement of West and Nally led to the first lengthy and level-headed appraisal – from the outside – of what snooker had to offer as a public entertainment and where its lamentably out-of-date methods of presentation had to be improved. Peter West, a television commentator of wide experience, had innumerable contacts in the sports and media worlds, while Patrick Nally was a bright, energetic ideas man. It was the first time snooker had had a high-powered, media-orientated outfit behind it and the company's role in the snooker boom in the 1970s has never been sufficiently acknowledged. There were four Park Drive £2,000 tournaments, of which Spencer won three and Reardon the

other. Reardon also won the Park Drive £600, a similar event specially devised for Yorkshire Television, making a break of 127, the highest so far seen on television.

Meanwhile, Alex Higgins had arrived in Lancashire and the area was buzzing with talk of this incredible Irishman who hardly seemed to aim and yet never seemed to miss. From the start, he was a promotable commodity. Receiving 14, he beat Spencer 23-18 and they played to packed houses in a series of £200 challenge matches.

As Gallahers had come into snooker, John Player had gone out, but interest in snooker had clearly picked up when the draw for the next world championship was made in February 1971. The idea was that the winner would take 60 per cent of the entry fees – £100 a man – and the runner-up the remaining 40 per cent, plus any income which could be generated from gate money, less expenses and the promoter's cut, at each match.

There were 16 entries and the event took a year to complete. In March 1971, Higgins began his long run to the title by beating Ron Gross 15-6 at the Brentham Club, Ealing. Gross, three times English amateur champion in the 1960s, was well past his best, as were other former English amateur champions like Houlihan, Maurice Parkin and Geoff Thompson who entered in the early 1970s. The upturn in the professional game, though, came at the right time for Graham Miles, who had won the Midland amateur championship twice and was just starting to develop into a quality player.

The championship wound a long, tortuous path to the semi-finals, Williams eliminating Reardon 25-23 in a quarter-final match that was played on five separate club tables in Scotland. Higgins, fresh from ending Rea's 21-year tenure of the Irish title by beating him 28-12, overcame him again in the championship 19-11 and then beat Pulman 31-23 in the quarter-finals. Charlton, so confident of

**Alex Higgins, world
champion at his
first attempt in
1972**

his physical stamina that he flew in from Australia only on the morning of their match at Bolton, beat David Taylor, the 1968 world amateur champion, 31-25.

Spencer, having beaten Fred Davis comfortably 31-21, embarked on a Canadian tour on which, playing with the livelier Canadian Vitalite ball and helped by the more generous Canadian pockets, made 29 centuries – 21 of them of 124 or over, including his first 147. He also made 60 breaks over 80 in 98 frames against Cliff Thorburn in their matches in Calgary and Edmonton.

It was a visit which opened Thorburn's eyes to a world beyond the pool rooms of Canada and the United States which had been his habitat for almost ten years, but it was also one which left Spencer exhausted. On his return he struggled past Charlton with great difficulty, 37-32, in their semi-final before winning the Park Drive £2,000 by beating Higgins 4-3, the very evening before they started their world final in the unpretentious concert hall of Selly Park British Legion, Birmingham.

Higgins had survived his semi-final against Williams only by winning the last of the 61 frames, casting away frames when he was in a winning position and winning them from losing positions with equal abandon.

Williams, potting steadily and demonstrating his two main strengths, his safety game and his immaculate positional play at close quarters, won nine consecutive frames to lead 12-6 and fell behind, 25-26, only during the penultimate session. Under extreme pressure at 29-30, Williams knitted together a difficult winning 61 and led 28-14 in the deciding frame before missing a blue from its spot into the middle pocket.

Although the cue-ball was only fractionally away from the side cushion, it was a shot no-one expected him to miss.

With automatic position on the five remaining reds, all in comfortably pottable positions, Williams would surely have clinched frame and match had the blue dropped. Had it done so, the next 20 years of snooker history might have worked out rather differently. As it was, Higgins responded with 32 and, after a tactical exchange, potted the green to assure himself of a place in the final.

Spencer was a clear favourite to retain the title, but the strain of his Canadian tour – as well as his match against Higgins the previous evening – had left him jaded and below form. Higgins, on the other hand, played with a sense of destiny and a sublime confidence to become, a few days before his 23rd birthday, the youngest-ever champion.

A miners' strike and consequent power failures contributed not only to the capacity attendances but to a bizarre interlude on the second evening when, with conventional lighting out of action and no heating in the room on that cold February night, the players agreed to continue under the dull and inadequate lighting produced by a mobile generator. Amazingly, the first three frames lasted only 35 minutes.

The hall bulged with a crowd accommodated on seats placed on stacked beer crates, a rough form of tiered seating, or hanging precariously from any point of vantage. Snooker was simply not used to the idea of the paying public being so keen to see a match. Even Fleet Street sports editors conceded that there was a degree of interest in the contest.

Not all the referees were up to such an important occasion and after two ghastly howlers, the unprecedented – and never repeated – step was taken of appointing 'linesmen', one sitting on either side of the table, to assist adjudication when the referee was in doubt or to settle appeals.

At 21-21, Higgins produced an inspired 6-0 Thursday evening session from which

Murt O'Donoghue (left), the first player to make a witnessed 147 break in 1934, pictured with Australia's most celebrated international competitor, Eddie Charlton

and for the later stages of the final to show on the second Saturday. There were public bars, public restaurants, a Ladbroke betting tent and carefully nurtured press coverage from every national newspaper. The television coverage was welcome, but at this stage the success of the promotion still depended heavily on gate money.

The publicity bandwagon, already rolling, gathered momentum with a Thames TV documentary *Hurricane Higgins* which took 25th place in the joint ITV/BBC ratings for the week. No public relations exercise, it none the less helped confirm Higgins in the minds of a great section of the uncommitted public as the only snooker player they had ever heard of. People were often hearing of him through his propensity for getting involved in disturbances and miscellaneous trouble, but there was no denying that he was box office. Many players had joined the professional ranks with rough social edges, but Higgins was alone in not even aspiring to social airs and graces. As the game's first authentic anti-hero he attracted huge support, much of it from those socially placed to care little for traditional or established values. His skill, dash, nerve and persona made him their champion against the rest of the world.

The publicity build-up for the 1973 championship in the last two weeks of April was centred round Higgins, not least because it was easy to write colourfully about him. He was seeded to meet Spencer in the final, but there was disappointment for those who expected a repeat of the 1972 final or their epic £1,000-a-side struggle at Radcliffe Town Hall, which Spencer had won 38-37, for both were semi-final losers.

Higgins, in fact, was pressed by Fred Davis in a quarter-final which uniquely included a stoppage for rain. Even in Manchester this was a bit thick, but the position was duly marked, the covers were put on and play ceased until the offending

Spencer never recovered. Spencer made the only two centuries of the match but Higgins, not to be denied, clinched the title early in the final session, 37-32, and snooker was never the same again.

His victory having convinced West and Nally of snooker's wider potentialities, they booked Belle Vue, Manchester, for the fourth Park Drive £2,000 final in which a crowd of 2,000 in October saw Spencer beat Higgins 5-3.

This crystallised Nally's burgeoning scheme to convert the world professional championship from an unwieldy event – lasting several months in different venues, with no continuity of interest and scant media attention – into a lavishly staged, Wimbledon-style spectacle with play taking place on eight tables in different arenas in the same large venue. With Park Drive as the sponsors, West and Nally promoted the 1973 championship at City Exhibition Halls, Manchester, condensing it into a fortnight, with £8,000 prizemoney and television coverage from BBC's *Grandstand* on the first Saturday

leak in the roof had been plugged. The
clash of styles between the impetuous,
brilliant Higgins and the calm, reflective
Davis – not to mention the element of
what many saw as Young Upstart v
Perfect Gentleman – reached 14-14, at
which point Davis missed a pink which
would have put him one up with two to
play. Higgins, having trailed 12-14, won
16-14, but this was the end of the road,
for Charlton won the opening session of
their semi-final 6-0 and ground out a 23-9
victory. The Higgins bubble had burst.

While this was happening, the other
semi-final seemed to be proceeding quietly
towards a routine win for Spencer, who led
Reardon 19-12. However, he missed an
easy black which would have put him
20-14 ahead, allowing Reardon instead to
pull back to only four behind and add the
three remaining frames of the penultimate
session to trail just 18-19.

Reardon's revival had coincided with the
end of the Charlton v Higgins match,
which brought a flood of spectators into
the hitherto half-empty arena where he
and Spencer were playing. This seemed to
get Reardon's adrenalin flowing and, after
innumerable thrills and vicissitudes, he
won 23-22. To have lost from so far in
front seemed to affect Spencer deeply. He
won many matches and many tournaments
and regained the world title in 1977, but
all without quite recapturing the easy
confidence and peak form of his greatest
years.

Reardon suffered merely a temporary
reaction when, next day, he lost the
opening session of the final 7-0, but
Charlton's dogged consistency proved no
match for Reardon's flair and wider range
of shots and after four sessions Reardon led
17-13, keeping in front to 27-25.

The eighth session broke the pattern
into which the match had settled. After
only a few minutes under the blinding,
newly installed television lights, much
more primitive than those of today, it was
obvious that Charlton could see but
Reardon could not. Three quick frames
went to the Australian before Reardon's
protests led to two of the largest
floodlights, which in any event were
needed only to illuminate the crowd, were
switched off. Further discussion took place
at the mid-session interval, during which
Reardon was able to compose himself. He
emerged to win four of the five remaining
frames of the day to lead 31-29 and forged
steadily ahead on the last day to finish
38-32.

Higgins went to Australia, where he was
thrown out of a hotel after wrecking his
room, and out of one club for calling the
popular veteran professional, Norman
Squire, 'an old no-hoper'. He was allowed
in again after writing an abject apology on
a piece of toilet paper. His projected tour
of India lasted only one day, for he so
offended the members of the Bombay
Gymkhana Club by his drinking, the
removal of his shirt and his insulting
behaviour that the BA&CC of India, his
hosts, put him on the next plane home. A
childish threat not to complete his
commitments in the 1972 *Pot Black* series
had not been carried out, but had been
punished by his omission from subsequent
series. Higgins made news wherever he
went, seeming bent on self-destruction in
his wild, uncontrollable and wilful way.

Reardon, in contrast, was the model
ambassador for snooker, touring India at
short notice to replace Higgins and
making 65 public centuries in a four-
month tour of South Africa.

West and Nally had set up two
subsidiaries: Snooker Promotions, whose
purpose was self-evident, and Mister
Billiards, selling equipment and pool
tables. With Ladbroke sponsorship, they
organised two gala dinner-snooker
evenings at the Café Royal in 1973 and
1974, and obtained a valuable new
sponsor, Norwich Union, whose
tournament at the Piccadilly Hotel

brought big-time snooker back to London and represented ITV's first serious attempt to network the sport since the days of black and white.

Reardon chose not to compete in the Norwich Union tournament, in which Spencer beat Pulman 8-7 for the £1,500 first prize after Pulman had recovered from 2-7.

Park Drive increased the prizemoney for the 1974 world championship but the vast, aircraft hangar-like hall at Belle Vue, Manchester, did not prove a successful choice of venue. This might not have mattered if the main box office attractions had not lost early but, as it was, Reardon retained his title with ease. Only Marcus Owen, who had turned professional after winning the English amateur title in 1973, extended him in a 15-11 quarter-final.

Spencer went out 15-13 in his first match to Perrie Mans, Charlton lost 15-13 to John Dunning and 61-year-old Fred Davis, just recuperating from his second heart attack, won the last three frames to beat Higgins 15-14. Reardon's opponent in the final was Graham Miles, who had sprung from obscurity by coming into *Pot Black* as a late replacement for Davis and winning it, not only that year but the following year. He came through to the final but proved no match for Reardon, who won 22-12.

Immediately after the tournament, Snooker Promotions presented to the WPBSA a schedule of their ambitious plans for an international tournament circuit. These were rejected so vehemently that West and Nally's interest in snooker was thereafter confined to the servicing of tournaments on behalf of sponsors they had obtained. What they had achieved for snooker became a matter not for gratitude but for envy, jealousy and distrust. The 1975 world championship was awarded to Eddie Charlton Promotions, Park Drive disappeared from snooker, and the

niggling and internecine strife, which had disfigured the game in the past, disfigured it again. Although this development delayed the creation of a full tournament circuit, good things were still happening to snooker. Immediately after the 1974 championship, a Pontins Festival of Snooker was held at Prestatyn, its initial success making it a permanent feature of the calendar. Pontins knew snooker was popular because Spencer, Reardon, and from time to time other professionals, were regularly spending their summers playing exhibitions around the camps. *Pot Black* was going strong on BBC2 and Ted Lowe suggested to Sir Fred Pontin that

The 14-year-old Jimmy White receives the first prize for the Pontins junior tournament from Sir Fred Pontin

there might be scope for a week featuring a professional event, comprising the eight *Pot Black* professionals, and an Open, in which amateurs received 25 points per frame.

It was an event which emphasised the snooker world's intimate, democratic qualities. The holidaymakers mixed for the week with the stars of their sport, some of them earning a chance for glory and cash against the big names, all of them having the opportunity to watch top-class matches and talk snooker as much as they liked. To a degree unparalleled in the snooker world, it brought the snooker family closer together.

Reardon beat Spencer 10-9 to win the professional event and Doug Mountjoy, then only an unpredictable if talented amateur, took advantage of his 25 start to win the Open, beating both Reardon and Spencer.

Until extensive television coverage altered the face of the sport, the Pontins tournaments remained among the most important in the calendar. Though they no longer have this status, the Spring Festival at Prestatyn still holds its own special place in the schedule.

Some of the larger snooker centres with match arenas staged events which were then substantial, and in November 1974 Spencer retained the Norwich Union Open by beating Reardon 10-9.

Despite packed houses and abundant television coverage, Norwich Union then withdrew from snooker, but within a few months West and Nally introduced another sponsor and another event which still remains in the calendar. The first Benson and Hedges Masters was held at the West Centre Hotel, Fulham, before its removal the following year to the New London Theatre and later still to the Wembley Conference Centre, its home since 1979. The deciding frame of that first final required an extra black which Spencer potted to beat Reardon 9-8 for the

£2,000 first prize.

Since Spencer and Reardon were clearly the two top players, there was uproar when the seedings for the 1975 world professional championship, played at various venues all over Australia, placed Reardon, at No. 1, and Spencer, at No. 8, to meet in the quarter-finals. The fact that the draw was made contrary to WPBSA conditions was allowed to pass, although it did not escape the attention of the *cognoscenti* that Reardon, Spencer and Higgins were all in the opposite half of the draw to the promoter, Charlton.

The quarter-final was one of the best matches Reardon and Spencer played, countless frames turning on a single half chance or being won from 50 or 60 behind. Reardon trailed 16-17 but eventually won 19-17 and then from 10-10 beat Higgins 19-14 in the semi-final. In the opposite half, Dennis Taylor made his first significant impact on the championship by reaching the semi-finals, but had to endure a choppy plane trip from Sydney to Brisbane on the morning of his match against Charlton and never recovered from a poor start.

It was an extraordinary final. Reardon led 16-8 before Charlton strung together the next nine frames to lead 17-16; then it was 22-20 to Reardon until Charlton overtook him to 28-23. At 24-29, Reardon potted a crucial pink to keep in the match at 25-29 when failure would have left Charlton six up with seven to play.

In the following frame, Charlton missed a frame-ball brown, which would have put him five up with six to play, and lost the frame by going in off the black. Reardon extended his winning streak to seven to lead 30-29, before the excited crowd in the Nunawading Basketball Stadium saw Charlton equalise at 30-30. The Australian held the initiative in the decider, but Reardon fashioned a break of 62 to win the £4,000 first prize and take his third consecutive world title.

WORLD CHAMPIONSHIP RESULTS

1964
J. Pulman beat F. Davis 19-16; J. Pulman beat R. Williams
40-33

1965
J. Pulman beat F. Davis 37-36; J. Pulman beat R. Williams
25-22 (matches); J. Pulman beat F. Van Rensberg 39-12

1966
J. Pulman beat F. Davis 5-2 (matches)

1968
J. Pulman beat E. Charlton 39-34

1969
FIRST ROUND: J. Spencer beat J. Pulman 25-18; R. Williams beat
B. Bennett 25-4; G. Owen beat Jack Rea 25-17; F. Davis beat
R. Reardon 25-24
SEMI-FINALS: Spencer beat Williams 37-12; Owen beat Davis
37-24
FINAL: Spencer beat Owen 37-24

1970 (APRIL)
FIRST ROUND: David Taylor beat B. Bennett 11-8
QUARTER-FINALS: J. Pulman beat Taylor 31-20; G. Owen beat
R. Williams 31-11; R. Reardon beat F. Davis 31-26; J. Spencer
beat Jack Rea 31-15
SEMI-FINALS: Pulman beat Owen 37-12; Reardon beat Spencer
37-33
FINAL: Reardon beat Pulman 37-33

1970 (NOVEMBER)
ROUND-ROBIN: J. Spencer beat P. Mans 20-17; beat N. Squire
27-10; beat J. Pulman 23-14
R. Reardon beat Mans 22-15; beat E. Charlton 21-16; beat
Spencer 21-16
W. Simpson beat G. Owen 19-18; beat Pulman 21-16; beat
Mans 19-18
Charlton beat Squire 27-10; beat Mans 26-11; beat Owen
23-14
Owen beat P. Morgan 26-11; beat Squire 26-11
Morgan beat Simpson 21-16
SEMI-FINALS: Spencer beat Reardon 34-15; Simpson beat
Charlton 27-22
FINAL: Spencer beat Simpson 37-29

1972
FIRST ROUND: J. Pulman beat J. Dunning 19-7; A. Higgins beat
Jack Rea 19-11
QUARTER-FINALS: J. Spencer beat F. Davis 31-21; E. Charlton
beat David Taylor 31-25; Higgins beat Pulman 31-23;
R. Williams beat R. Reardon 25-23
SEMI-FINALS: Higgins beat Williams 31-30; Spencer beat
Charlton 37-32
FINAL: Higgins beat Spencer 37-32

1973
FIRST ROUND: P. Houlihan beat Jack Rea 9-2; D. Greaves beat
B. Bennett 9-8; G. Miles beat G. Thompson 9-5; P. Mans beat
R. Gross 9-2; W. Simpson beat M. Parkin 9-3; C. Thorburn beat
Dennis Taylor 9-8; David Taylor beat J. Dunning 9-4;
J. Meadowcroft wo K. Kennerley scr
SECOND ROUND: F. Davis beat Greaves 16-1; Miles beat
J. Pulman 16-10; E. Charlton beat Mans 16-8; G. Owen beat
Simpson 16-14; R. Reardon beat Meadowcroft 16-10;
R. Williams beat Thorburn 16-15; J. Spencer beat David Taylor
16-5; A. Higgins beat Houlihan 16-3
QUARTER-FINALS: Higgins beat F. Davis 16-14; Spencer beat
Williams 16-7; Charlton beat Miles 16-6; Reardon beat Owen
16-6
SEMI-FINALS: Charlton beat Higgins 23-9; Reardon beat Spencer
23-22
FINAL: Reardon beat Charlton 38-32

1974
FIRST ROUND: B. Bennett beat W. Simpson 8-2; B. Werbeniuk
beat G. Thompson 8-3; J. Meadowcroft beat K. Kennerley 8-5;
M. Owen beat M. Parkin 8-5; P. Mans beat I. Anderson 8-1;
J. Pulman beat S. Lee 8-0; J. Dunning beat David Taylor 8-6;
P. Morgan beat C. Thorburn 8-4
SECOND ROUND: Mans beat J. Spencer 15-13; Dunning beat
E. Charlton 15-13; M. Owen beat G. Owen 15-8; A. Higgins
beat Bennett 15-4; G. Miles beat Morgan 15-7; R. Williams
beat Pulman 15-12; F. Davis beat Werbeniuk 15-5; R. Reardon
beat Meadowcroft 15-3
QUARTER-FINALS: Williams beat Mans 15-4; Reardon beat Owen
15-11; Miles beat Dunning 15-13; Davis beat Higgins 15-14
SEMI-FINALS: Miles beat Williams 15-7; Reardon beat Davis
15-3
FINAL: Reardon beat Miles 22-12

1975
FIRST ROUND: W. Simpson beat R. Mares 15-5; J. Pulman beat
P. Tarrant 15-5; David Taylor beat R. King 15-8; I. Anderson
beat L. Condo 15-8; Dennis Taylor beat P. Mans 15-12;
G. Owen beat D. Greaves 15-3; B. Werbeniuk beat
J. Meadowcroft 15-9; C. Thorburn beat P. Morgan 15-6
SECOND ROUND: R. Reardon beat Simpson 15-11; J. Spencer
beat Pulman 15-10; A. Higgins beat David Taylor 15-2;
R. Williams beat Anderson 15-4; Taylor beat F. Davis 15-14;
G. Owen beat J. Dunning 15-8; E. Charlton beat Werbeniuk
15-11; Thorburn beat G. Miles 15-2
QUARTER-FINALS: Reardon beat Spencer 19-17; Higgins beat
Williams 19-12; Taylor beat G. Owen 19-9; Charlton beat
Thorburn 19-12
SEMI-FINALS: Charlton beat Taylor 19-12; Reardon beat Higgins
19-14
FINAL: Reardon beat Charlton 31-30

It was with a sense of incredulity that the snooker world learned, out of the blue, in October 1975 that Embassy were to sponsor the 1976 world championship. It had been five years since the professionals had had anything to do with the Billiards and Snooker Control Council, the domestic amateur governing body, but its vice-chairman, Maurice Hayes, was handling exhibition bookings for several players, including Higgins, and had promoted a few small tournaments.

He approached Embassy to sponsor not only the championship but a series of subsidiary events. While there was nothing wrong with any of these ideas, it soon became apparent that Hayes's organisation, Q Promotions, was not really up to carrying them out as envisaged. For all the difficulties and sketchiness of organisational structure, there was a sense that snooker was a product which could be marketed into shape for much wider consumption – but no-one was quite sure how to do it.

Ray Reardon playing out of a snooker during the Benson and Hedges Masters at the New London Theatre

The snooker business was looking up worldwide. Terry Haddock and the late Al Selinger, two prominent figures in the Canadian trade, were instrumental in putting together a Canadian Open which ran during the annual Canadian National Exhibition in Toronto in September. The first of these was won by Higgins, who took the $5,000 first prize by beating Pulman 15-7 in the final. The promising Leicester junior, Willie Thorne, showed his class by beating Spencer in reaching the semi-finals and on the strength of this was invited by Ted Lowe into the eighth series of *Pot Black*. As a result, he turned professional.

The spread of the motorway system encouraged the growth of amateur open tournaments and sponsors like Double Diamond, Canadian Club and Joe Coral kept the scene bubbling by supporting amateur events of national scope. In general, the exhibition market was in decline as it became clear that the public wanted to see matches and tournaments.

The Benson and Hedges Masters was switched in its second year to a plush new venue, the New London Theatre. Snooker was not really suitable for presentation in a traditional proscenium arch theatre, but this was an age when theatre in the round, ideal for snooker, was growing in popularity. Reardon beat Miles 7-3 for the £2,000 first prize, the final being shown, as the first Masters final had been, on BBC's *Grandstand* the following day. In this way, snooker was still making inroads as a television sport, even if live coverage was still considered too dangerous to attempt, owing to the unpredictability of the frames, both in length and in dramatic quality. The inaugural Benson and Hedges Irish Masters was staged at the national boxing stadium in Dublin, in front of RTE's cameras, with Spencer beating Higgins 5-0 for the £600 first prize.

But just as snooker seemed to be getting somewhere with the media, the fiasco of the draw for the 1976 world championship provided a chilling reminder of how haphazard its organisation still was.

The BBC, having shown some of the 1973 and 1974 championships on Saturday afternoons, were keen to do so again, and to stimulate prior interest agreed to Hayes's suggestion that they cover the draw on the early evening magazine programme, *Nationwide*. The plan was for Higgins to be in Lime Grove, Spencer in Manchester and Dennis Taylor in Birmingham, where they would each perform a few trick shots and comment on the draw.

Higgins arrived at Lime Grove ten minutes before the deadline, but Spencer claimed to know nothing of the plan. Taylor was still playing in a tournament in Portsmouth and neither he nor Miles, his substitute, who was stuck in a traffic jam at Newbury, could reach Birmingham in time. The BBC took a poor view of snooker's failure to meet its side of the bargain, having been offered peak viewing publicity.

EMBASSY WORLD CHAMPIONSHIP

The first Embassy World Championship could have hardly have begun in lower key. There were two qualifying groups – at the Park House Hotel, Blackpool, and the Prince of Wales Hotel, Southport. The former was won by David Taylor, an 8-7 winner over the Irish veteran Jack Rea in the qualifying round, and the latter by Jim Meadowcroft, who beat Thorne 8-5.

There were also two curtain-raising events to the championship proper which, asking for trouble it clearly seems with hindsight, Hayes had decided to split between two venues, Middlesbrough Town Hall and Wythenshawe Forum, Manchester.

The curtain-raiser at Wythenshawe was a 16-man amateur tournament, which was won by John Virgo. Middlesbrough, something of a bastion of male chauvinism at the time, staged a women's championship in which Ann Johnson, a Cheltenham probation officer, made a break of 40, at the time the highest ever made by a women in competition.

The overall standard illustrated only too clearly that even the best women players could not sustain women's snooker as a public entertainment. Vera Selby, a Newcastle art teacher, won the first prize of £500, dropping only one frame in the entire event, despite her highest break being only a modest 23.

Any theory that the curtain-raisers would forestall problems occurring during the championship was exploded on the first day at Middlesbrough, when officials spent the morning buying up almost every yard of black cloth which could be found in the town to hang over the hall's enormous windows, through which the sun would otherwise have streamed on to the players.

Although Reardon, not the easiest player to please in terms of playing conditions, knew nothing of this difficulty, he was soon disturbed by movement near the entrance and a constant stream of human traffic to and from bar, toilet and refreshment areas. Spectators were often careless in lighting cigarettes in a player's line of sight and had to be forbidden to bring drinks into the match arena, a restriction which did nothing to increase attendances. The defending champion trailed John Dunning, a sound and solid Yorkshireman, 4-2 at the first interval, but found his form in the second session and won impressively 15-7.

Dennis Taylor, a world semi-finalist the previous year and now a seasoned professional, saw off Gary Owen 15-9. Owen, making his last world championship appearance, seemed to have lost all heart for the game and was fully

three blacks worse than he had been in winning his two world amateur titles. Taylor was nevertheless no match for Reardon who, with 'some of the best snooker I've ever played', beat him 15-2 to reach the semi-finals.

As the No. 4 seed, Rex Williams had been expected to play Reardon at that stage, but Meadowcroft beat him 15-7 in the first round, Perrie Mans beat the fifth seed, Graham Miles, 15-10 and then beat Meadowcroft 15-8 to become the first South African ever to reach the world quarter-finals.

Although Mans was one of the best potters snooker had ever seen, his cue-ball control was poor and in these two matches he made only two half-century breaks. He was nevertheless a keen competitor with an awkward safety game. Perhaps his own obliviousness to his limitations was an advantage in that it left his confidence undiminished.

His limitations were drastically exposed, however, when Reardon beat him 20-10, with 133 the highest break of his impressive performance. Reardon was generous enough to offer and Mans not too proud to accept a half-hour tutorial on the table afterwards on what the champion considered to be his incorrect shot selections.

Meanwhile, there had been teething problems at Wythenshawe, where a goodly number of press people had arrived on the first day, only to find that there were no phones with which to communicate news to the outside world. Another detail which had been overlooked was the size of the pockets, which varied according to the manufacturer's whim.

Charlton made a 137 total clearance in beating Pulman 15-9 and enquired whether this was a world championship record. The records revealed that Spencer had made a 139 at Manchester in 1973, although the official record still stood to Williams with his 142 against Pulman in

Alex Higgins awaits the outcome of a shot during his 1976 world final with Ray Reardon (seated) at Wythenshawe Forum, Manchester

their world championship series in South Africa in 1965. It also transpired, on examination, that no fewer than five of the six pockets on this table were considerably easier than standard, partly because of a rounded pocket drop.

Raper and Sons, the firm supplying the tables, were unhelpful in their response to criticism and, rather than leave matters as they were, an Embassy man roused from his bed a fitter employed by a rival firm to make the necessary adjustments overnight.

Higgins reached the final with three

dramatic wins. He had to take the last three frames to beat Cliff Thorburn 15-14. Having led 14-12 in the next round against Spencer, he was again taken the full distance before reaching the semi-finals against Charlton, who had beaten Fred Davis 15-13.

Higgins led Charlton 5-1 but Charlton pulled up to 12-13 before Higgins again moved four ahead at 16-12. Charlton fought his hardest and produced his best in constantly recovering from situations in which he was down but not quite out.

When Higgins led 19-16, Charlton needed to win the remaining four frames. He won two of them but Higgins took the third on the black to win 20-18 and reach his first world final since taking the title at his first attempt four years earlier.

Only a few shots had been played in the final before it became obvious that the players could not see properly, the glare and dazzle from the television lights being altogether unacceptable. As Reardon fumed, Higgins led 4-2 at the first interval. In what was to become a familiar pattern, Reardon headed straight for the tournament office at the end of the session and insisted that the lights were adjusted. He then won six of the next seven frames to lead 8-5.

The table was not of a quality appropriate to a world final. It was practically impossible to pot a ball along the left-hand side cushion, almost as impossible to miss one along the right-hand side cushion to which any ball attempted slowly clung like a leech. There was something peculiar, too, about the cushions, so that it was virtually impossible to swing the cue-ball round off three cushions behind the green from the break-off shot. Reardon's mood grew blacker and his jokes more barbed as Higgins won the session 5-1 to lead 10-9. Straight to the tournament office went Reardon to complain bitterly about the table, and attempts were made during the interval to put it right.

Worse was to follow in the evening when the referee, Bill Timms, judged that Higgins had failed to escape from a snooker. Uproar reigned, but Timms was adamant. 'I'll have to accept it, but you're wrong,' said Higgins and Reardon, who had thereby been awarded a free ball, gave his view of the decision by merely asking Higgins to play again.

There were many mistakes from both players but Reardon was shrewd enough to play a cautious and limited game, by means of which he won four frames in succession before his 87 break in the last frame of the day gave him a 15-11 lead at the halfway mark.

Higgins recovered to 15-13 by winning the first two frames on the third day, and had handy leads in each of the next three only to lose them all – the last after leading by 31 points with only the colours remaining.

Reardon, 18-13 ahead, also led 70-0 in the last frame of the session, to which Higgins replied with 32 and laid a couple of snookers from which Reardon failed to escape. The second of these prompted referee Timms to award a free ball, a decision which aroused the disagreement of Reardon and those situated behind the shot.

As it happened, Reardon still won the frame to lead 19-13, but during the interval he made his now familiar journey to the tournament office. There was less than universal surprise when it was announced that Timms was ill and that John Williams would take over as referee for the evening session.

Reardon extended his lead to 24-15 at close of play, as Higgins, his display both wild and demoralised, conceded several frames with reds still on the table. The final day's play was little more than a formality, with Reardon taking three of the first four frames to win with a session and a half to spare.

1976 EMBASSY WORLD CHAMPIONSHIP

FIRST ROUND: R. Reardon beat J. Dunning 15-7; Dennis Taylor beat G. Owen 15-9; P. Mans beat G. Miles 15-10; J. Meadowcroft beat R. Williams 15-7; E. Charlton beat J. Pulman 15-9; F. Davis beat B. Werbeniuk 15-12; A. Higgins beat C. Thorburn 15-14; J. Spencer beat David Taylor 15-5

QUARTER-FINALS: Reardon beat Taylor 15-2; Mans beat Meadowcroft 15-8; Charlton beat Davis 15-13; Higgins beat Spencer 15-14

SEMI-FINALS: Reardon beat Mans 20-10; Higgins beat Charlton 20-18

FINAL: Reardon beat Higgins 27-16

In the aftermath of the first Embassy championship, Reardon beat Davis 10-9 to win the Pontins Professional. This triumph, together with his Masters and world titles, gave him £9,000 from the season's leading three first prizes, easily top of the embryo money list. Doug Mountjoy, one of a new breed of full-time amateurs, won the Pontins Open for the second time in three years. He had just won the Welsh amateur championship for the second time and was much too good to be given 25 start by anyone.

Higgins beat Reardon 6-4 for the £1,000 first prize in the Canadian Club Masters, which was recorded for later transmission by Yorkshire Television, who also screened their pro-celebrity series featuring such diverse participants as Fred Trueman, Arthur Mullard and Frankie Vaughan.

Q Promotions predictably crashed, with several clubs instituting legal action after suffering financial loss when players booked for exhibitions failed to appear. Hayes vanished abruptly, and a year or so later was sighted driving a taxi in Canada. There were many pieces to be picked up.

The WPBSA hoped that Embassy would take up the option to repeat their sponsorship, although no-one could be confident of this after all the difficulties of the 1976 championship. As it happened, Nick Hunter, the BBC Manchester producer who had been responsible for the Wythenshawe coverage, had become convinced that snooker could be shown on television at a length hitherto undreamed

Nick Hunter, BBC's executive producer in charge of snooker as it exploded as a television sport

of. Mike Watterson, an English amateur international who had aspirations as a snooker entrepreneur, decided he would like to promote the championship when his wife, Carol, returned from an evening at the Crucible to say that as a theatre in the round it would be an ideal venue. He guaranteed a £17,000 prize fund to the WPBSA and Embassy, noting this development and that Hunter had persuaded the BBC to cover not only the final but also the semi-finals, renewed their sponsorship.

There was a great deal of interest in snooker: the equipment firms were doing well; professionals were busier and more numerous; amateur activity had completely outgrown its administration. Yet all these developments seemed to occur independently.

Where there should have been overall coherence, there was all too often, on the professional side, an unseemly, every-man-for-himself scramble for the rewards the game could now offer. The WPBSA, which was held together largely by Rex Williams and its devoted secretary, Mike Green, exerted a measure of control over the world championship but, largely because it comprised professional players each of whom had his own interests to consider, it failed (or lacked the muscle) to guide development in all but the most immediate matters. Alliances, formal or otherwise, were formed within the professional ranks and decisions on many issues appeared to hinge on inter-personal politics and short-term profit rather than any long-term vision.

Mike Watterson, snooker's leading promoter in the late 1970s and early 1980s, whose inspiration it was to take the Embassy World Championship to the Crucible

One of the WPBSA's mistakes was to approve a so-called world professional matchplay championship in Melbourne in November 1976. Charlton beat Reardon to win it and thereafter seldom discouraged the Australian public from referring to him as the world champion. Financially, the players did well out of it, but the indiscriminate application of the word 'world' to such a tournament was a disservice to the game. Even BBC's *Grandstand* and ITV's *World of Sport* announced that 'snooker has a new world champion' as 'Eddie Charlton has beaten the reigning champion Ray Reardon'.

There had at least been good reason for the world matchplay championships of the 1950s, because the professionals considered, erroneously, that the Billiards Association and Control Council had a copyright on the world championship itself. The matchplay championship was clearly in those days the real thing and the 'official' championship match between Horace Lindrum and Clark McConachy equally clearly bogus. There was no justification for the 1976 event other than money.

On the amateur front, snooker had progressed, in little more than a decade, from having no international contact at amateur level to an established world amateur championship which many national associations eagerly sought to stage. In the British Isles there was an established home international series which, though dominated by England and Wales, gave Scottish and Irish players a measure of top-class matchplay which had previously been unavailable to them. International contacts of all sorts had been fostered, and British standards in depth were by the mid-1970s much higher than ever before, while other nations were also producing some of the best players in their history.

The world amateur title had remained an English monopoly. After Gary Owen's

wins in the inaugural championship in Calcutta in 1963 and in Karachi in 1966, David Taylor brought the title back from Sydney in 1968. Jonathan Barron, a Cornishman who never seriously considered turning professional, won in Edinburgh in 1970 and Ray Edmonds, who did not turn professional until he was slightly past his peak, won consecutive titles in Cardiff in 1972 and Dublin in 1974.

Mountjoy gave Wales its first amateur champion in Johannesburg in November 1976 and, having submitted a post-dated application, immediately became a professional. In his first professional tournament, Mountjoy illustrated how narrow the gap between top amateur and professional standards had become when he beat Pulman, Davis, Higgins and Reardon, 7-6 on the final pink, to win the Benson and Hedges Masters in February 1977.

As a 14-year-old London prodigy, Jimmy White made a break of 103 in

Cliff Wilson was a youthful prodigy but turned professional only after a lengthy mid-career retirement

winning an opening-night tournament at the Pot Black Snooker Centre, Wandsworth, one of many new clubs opening in a new wave of snooker interest. Cliff Wilson emerged from a 15-year retirement to regain the Welsh amateur title he had won 21 years earlier. Terry Griffiths, having won the Welsh amateur title in 1975, won the first of two consecutive English amateur championships – which Welshmen were then allowed to enter. Patsy Fagan, thought to be 'not the right type', because a couple of his managers had taken him round the country playing money matches, was accepted as a professional by the WPBSA after two rejections. A fresh-faced young Essex businessman, Barry Hearn, was revitalising Lucania, the down-at-heel chain of snooker halls he had acquired in 1976. One day, he was called from his office below its Romford hall to watch a ginger-haired youth practising with an air of eerie concentration. His name was Steve Davis.

EMBASSY WORLD CHAMPIONSHIP

There was little recent form to indicate that John Spencer would be the Crucible's first world champion. Following his two world titles in 1969 and 1970 he had lost a few close matches, suffered a few surprise defeats and lost form to the extent that he only just rated the eighth and last seeding position.

There were enough new professionals to kick up a fuss about the inequality of 14 players being exempted and 11 more playing off for the remaining two qualifying places. At a stormy EGM of the WPBSA, whose constitution then permitted one man one vote, an 11-10 majority was obtained in favour of only eight players being excused the qualifying competition.

This was held at Hounslow Civic Centre and Fisher's Snooker Centre, Acton. A surprise was on the cards when Jack Rea led Mountjoy 9-8, and although Mountjoy

came through to win 11-9, there were nevertheless signals that the hectic pace of his new life as a professional was starting to take the edge from his game – and thus from his prospects of uniquely holding the world amateur and professional titles simultaneously.

From the first day, the Crucible felt the ideal venue for the championship, whose success lay not only in an attendance of over 20,000 for the fortnight, or record prizemoney or record television coverage, but also in the quality of organisation and spectator amenity. It was a fortnight which showed what snooker was capable of and what it might aspire to. Remembering the chaotic elements of the 1976 championship, it seemed almost incredible that 1977 could be so very different.

The pre-planning had included some patient work by BBC's Nick Hunter to arrange tests for special lighting which could accommodate the demands of television without creating problems for the players. This resulted in the best lighting there had yet been for a televised event, and with few modifications it is now accepted as standard. Indeed, many of today's players actually prefer this form of illumination to that which was then and still remains the norm in today's clubs.

There were some splendid first-round matches. Pulman, a stone lighter and without a drop of alcohol having passed his lips since New Year's Eve 113 days earlier, displayed some of the best form he had shown for at least five years as he put out Fred Davis 13-12, in a match which reproduced the refined skills of their title battles of a decade or more earlier.

Going into the final session, Pulman led 11-6 and was two up with three to play, but eventually needed a 54 break in the deciding frame to qualify for the quarter-finals.

John Virgo twice led Spencer by three frames, but from 8-8 after two sessions

Spencer won 13-9. Dennis Taylor made the highest break of the match, 76, to clinch a 13-11 win over the tenacious Perrie Mans.

The most riveting match, though, produced a 13-12 win for Mountjoy over Higgins. Having recovered from 10-12 to 12-12, Higgins looked the winner when he rolled an almost straight pink slowly towards the middle pocket. He was 36 in front and that pink and the easy red to follow would have left Mountjoy needing snookers.

Reprieved, Mountjoy took the last two reds and the colours to the pink before missing a middle-pocket doubled black for the match. The black finished about 18 inches from the baulk pocket, with the cue-ball about a foot from the top cushion. As Higgins got down to attempt it, a voice from the back of the hall insisted, quite irrelevantly, on a scorecheck as there was a discrepancy of one point between the two scoreboards.

Higgins, obviously distracted, missed the black. It went safe but Mountjoy's answering safety shot left Higgins another death-or-glory cut into the top pocket. He missed it again. The black looked as if it was going to finish over the middle pocket but actually finished an inch or so past the middle pocket jaw, with the cue-ball also just off that side cushion, about two feet behind it. Mountjoy struck the black smoothly along the side rail to the baulk pocket for victory.

This match had drained most of Mountjoy's reserves of nervous energy. He trailed Dennis Taylor 10-7 in their quarter-final, won two black-ball games to make it 9-10 and potted the black, which would have tied the 20th frame if the cue-ball had not flashed into a middle pocket. Thus leading 11-9, Taylor went to 12-9 and achieved victory at 13-11.

Reardon was the clear favourite to win the championship but sufficient adrenalin never seemed to run through his veins as

he went out tamely to Spencer 13-6, in the quarter-finals. Pulman beat Graham Miles 13-10 at the same stage, leading all the way but never by much, and Cliff

Thorburn beat Eddie Charlton 13-12 in the first of many late-night Crucible finishes in which they were to become involved. The deciding frame lasted 62 minutes; the final session took five and half hours.

Spencer trailed Pulman 3-7 in the semi-finals, but as the match wore on, he proved much the steadier as he won the last five frames of the third session and the first of the fourth to lead 13-9. Converting this to 15-10, he came to the final session needing only two of the seven frames for victory. However, like an old warhorse reacting to the whiff of gunshot, Pulman won the first three to recover to 15-16 and then trailed only 16-17. With Spencer needing a snooker, the match looked likely to run its full distance, but somehow he extracted the necessary penalty points and cleared the colours to win 18-16. This proved to be Pulman's last effort as an authentic contender.

Thorburn and Taylor both felt the pressure of trying to clinch an appearance in their first world final as their semi-final proceeded to 16-16. Thorburn missed a simple blue which would have put him two up with three to play, but at 16-16 he reappeared from the mid-session interval to compile a meticulous 111 clearance, potting his only black at the very end, and clinched his 18-16 victory by taking an 80-0 lead.

Spencer's experience and doggedness carried him to a 25-21 win over Thorburn in the final. Thorburn had led 15-11 until Spencer won the next four frames to level at 15-15, and it was 18-18 going into the last day's play. Spencer rose at 7.30, not a familiar hour for him, for an hour's stroll in the park to clear his mind for the 11 o'clock session. He won the first three

1977 EMBASSY WORLD CHAMPIONSHIP

FIRST ROUND: R. Reardon beat P. Fagan 13-7; J. Spencer beat J. Virgo 13-9; G. Miles beat W. Thorne 13-4; J. Pulman beat F. Davis 13-12; E. Charlton beat David Taylor 13-5; C. Thorburn beat R. Williams 13-6; Dennis Taylor beat P. Mans 13-11; D. Mountjoy beat A. Higgins 13-12

QUARTER-FINALS: Spencer beat Reardon 13-6; Pulman beat Miles 13-10; Thorburn beat Charlton 13-12; Taylor beat Mountjoy 13-11

SEMI-FINALS: Spencer beat Pulman 18-16; Thorburn beat Taylor 18-16

FINAL: Spencer beat Thorburn 25-21

frames to lead 21-18 and at 21-20 made an important 67 break to reopen a two-frame gap. Thorburn closed to 21-22 but faded thereafter as Spencer took the next three frames for the title.

Not the least remarkable element of Spencer's success was that he achieved it with a cue he had used for less than two months prior to the championship. This exploded two myths: first, that it takes months or even years to become accustomed to a new cue, a view supported by most professionals using the same cue for their entire careers; second, that top-class snooker could not be played with a two-piece cue, hitherto considered suitable only for the smaller American pool tables.

Both finalists, in fact, used two-piece cues. As Canadians, long under American influence, had always done so, it would have been surprising if Thorburn had used anything else, but for Spencer, so near the championship, to discard the 'old faithful' cue with which he had recorded all his successes, in favour of what was regarded in the British game as little better than a new-fangled gimmick, was looked upon with incredulity. What only Spencer himself knew was that his old cue, broken into four pieces in a car accident shortly before the 1974 Norwich Union Open, had never, despite the masterly cue surgery of Cliff Curtis, played quite the same after it had been pinned together. Gradually losing confidence in it, he had laboured on indecisively until, on a visit to Canada, he picked a two-piece out of stock. Still he hovered, until five century breaks during a week's tour of Cornwall, convinced him that he could use it in the championship. All the same, a few months after becoming champion he discarded it in favour of another two-piece model made in Japan.

Fifteen years later, of course, two-piece cues are just as common at championship level as one-pieces, and it may not be long before one-pieces are regarded as archaic.

The week following the 1977 championship, Spencer beat Pulman 7-5 for the Pontins professional championship and Higgins won the Pontins Open from 864 entries, conceding Terry Griffiths 21 and beating him 7-4.

The match of the week was the junior final in which 17-year-old Tony Meo beat the 15-year-old Jimmy White 3-2. Meo potted the black to win and in his excitement stopped the cue-ball with his hand before it came to rest. This should have given White frame and match, but fortunately for Meo the referee did not have his wits about him.

Fred Davis was awarded the OBE, following Joe's award in 1963, and Williams resigned as WPBSA chairman after a heated disagreement with Watterson, over the degree to which a championship promoter should keep the WPBSA informed of his plans. Williams, who also felt that the other players were leaving him to shoulder too much of the burden of responsibility, was replaced by Peter Reeve, a Bristol businessman who was friendly with several of the leading players, but who died in office the following year.

Meo made his first 147 break at the age of 17 and Steve Davis made his first at his home club, Plumstead WMC. A woman brushed past him as he was potting the brown, but otherwise the maximum came, Davis felt, 'with almost no bother at all'. BBC Wales demonstrated its interest in snooker by agreeing to cover a match for the revived Welsh professional championship, sponsored by William Hill and won by Reardon, who beat Mountjoy 12-9 for the title. This was the start of a BBC Wales commitment to the top Welsh snooker event – now a world ranking tournament, the Regal Welsh Open – which remains to this day.

The Canadian Open, won by Thorburn in 1974, Higgins in 1975, and Spencer in 1976, again went to Higgins, who beat Reardon 9-7 and Spencer 17-14 in the last two rounds. The setting was not at all reminiscent of the Crucible. Owing to an administrative difficulty, the tournament was accommodated not in one of the CNE's permanent buildings but, as the only alternative to cancellation, in a large tent. A steel band, a non-stop dance band and a circus, all within earshot, not to mention a plague of flies in 100 degree temperatures and sunlight in the afternoon sessions, fully tested the concentration of competitors. Several times a day the earth reverberated as a man was shot out of a cannon in the next tent.

On the amateur front, first prizes of £300, £400 or £500 began to become common. Amidst the boom, fringe operators, middlemen, managers, or simply people who wanted to carve out some distinctive niche within the snooker world, hustled endlessly. One- or two-man maintenance and equipment firms proliferated, some of them lasting long enough to dent the complacency of the established firms.

The BBC, already committed to *Pot Black* and the final of the Benson and Hedges Masters, agreed to cover the final of the inaugural UK championship, which was sponsored by Super Crystalate balls,

from the Tower Circus, Blackpool in December 1977. Momentously, BBC's schedulers agreed to daily coverage of the Embassy World Championship, which was to be held at the Crucible in the spring.

Blackpool in the depths of winter did not provide the crowds which had supported the spring world finals of the 1950s but there were some lively matches. Reardon went out 5-4 to Jim Meadowcroft in his first match; Spencer was a 5-3 loser to Mountjoy; but the surprise champion was Patsy Fagan, who beat John Virgo 9-8 in the semi-final – after trailing 5-8 and by 60 in the following frame – and Mountjoy 12-9 in the final.

That Fagan could win a major tournament in the same way that Mountjoy had won the Benson and Hedges Masters earlier in the year proved once again that outstanding amateurs could quickly mature into successful professionals. There were no wholesale applications for WPBSA membership because, for any but the top dozen, there was less money available than for regular winners on the amateur circuit.

While there was a growing awareness of snooker's potentialities as a television sport, the WPBSA was not as yet much involved in negotiations, which tended to be left to individual promoters. Mike Barrett, taking a busman's holiday from the boxing world, staged the Dry Blackthorn Cup for ITV at the Wembley Conference Centre and Fagan, direct from his UK success, beat Spencer and Higgins to take the £2,000 first prize from this four-man event.

There still tended to be plenty of time between tournaments, though, and there was nothing of note after Higgins' 7-5 victory over Thorburn for the £3,000 first prize in the Benson and Hedges Masters at the New London Theatre, until the 1978 championship took the stage at the Crucible.

EMBASSY WORLD CHAMPIONSHIP

The BBC's decision to give the 1978 championship extensive daily coverage enabled them to present a portrait of an event, rather than simply a few glimpses of its later stages. It was the single most influential decision ever made in the history of snooker, broadening its commercial horizons for ever.

Despite the erosion of the conventional wisdom that the viewing public would accept snooker only in small doses, broadcasting live snooker was still felt to be very risky, for a given frame might be dull, or precious transmission time might be wasted through one player trying to obtain an unlikely number of snookers.

This danger was partly obviated by the innovation of two-table coverage, giving a choice of material. With a complex outside broadcast operation involving many video machines, the transmissions were an astute mix of live and recorded action, the latter encompassing either the finest play or the most significant frames from the available matches.

Frank Keating wrote of the final in the *Guardian*: 'It was the weekend that snooker finally managed its coming out party at the grand old age of 103. On BBC's *Grandstand* the very raving climax of the soccer season took second place to the hushed clink of the ivories at the appropriately named Crucible in Sheffield. As Ray Reardon, the dignified ex-cop with the Silvikrin hairdo and equally glittering cufflinks, finally pulled away from his challenger, all our producer dared to do was stick up little captions over the green baize saying: "Spurs up, West Ham lose".'

While Nick Hunter, who was to remain executive producer of BBC's coverage until 1989, was confident that snooker would make an impact through intensive television exposure, even he was unprepared for a success story of such magnitude.

Near midnight on the first Monday

there was an audience of five million for the recorded highlights. Two days later, six million watched. By the end of the championship fortnight it was seven million, and BBC2 had taken the unprecedented step of clearing the decks for live coverage of the final on Thursday and Friday afternoons, with live coverage of the final five o'clock session on the last day to continue – pushing back all programmes originally scheduled – until a result was reached.

Hard-core snooker men enthused that this was the first time snooker had ever been covered seriously. It was partly a question of time. A snooker match takes a long time to play and has to be in progress a while before the players' wills, styles and personalities start to interact. It takes time for tension, the most interesting ingredient of a match, to build up.

It was not only what happened on the table which television captured so well, but the immediate personal reaction of the players both before and after key shots or even as they sat out breaks from their opponents.

To some degree, this had been done before, but in *Pot Black,* for example, there was insufficient time for authentic tension to accumulate. Although players wanted to win, they knew full well that one frame was no true test and were therefore not so very disappointed when they lost. It was entirely different for a match to last long enough for players to have to reach deep into psychological resources, to live on a cliff edge of tension for hours on end, so that they felt utterly and completely drained at the end of it.

The 13-12 losers at Sheffield – Higgins, Thorne and Thorburn on this occasion – all looked, despite the brave face they put on it, desolate and shattered. They had given their all – for nothing.

By joining the action at several stages of the match, rather than just at the end, the viewer was able to participate in the

tension as it built up, becoming much more involved. The uncommitted public also gained the unmistakable impression that this was the Real Thing, the Big One, the One That Really Mattered, the one in which players dig down beyond their ordinary limits to their deepest reserves, where all their emotional resources and securities are cashed in.

The public took to snooker's top professionals in a big way. As John Burrows put it in the *Sunday Telegraph:* 'An ability to play snooker in mature years was, it used to be said, a sure sign of a misspent youth. How wrong can you be? Those who watched the world

Perrie Mans, Embassy World Championship runner-up in 1978

championship in Sheffield must have been impressed at the cool, pleasant sportsmanship. Not for Reardon, Charlton, Davis, Mans et al. kisses to the crowd after potting a black or histrionic gesticulation when missing one. There was only professionalism and a desire to get on with the game in the right spirit. I'd say snooker is a better character builder than many another sports.'

John Spencer became the first of four Crucible champions whose title defence did not survive their first match on their return to Sheffield the following year. Even when he trailed Perrie Mans 9-7 going into the final session, his chances were still widely fancied. He opened with a total clearance of 138, enough to earn the £500 break prize, but Mans, unshaken, went on playing his own game and when Spencer started to miss picked off the four frames he needed for victory.

Ray Reardon, 2-7 adrift to Doug Mountjoy, eventually beat him 13-9, but Alex Higgins fell at the first fence to Patsy Fagan. That match came to an unbelievably exciting climax when Fagan, two down with three to play, won one frame on a tie-break black, another on the black and the decider on the pink to prevail 13-12. There was pandemonium. The crowd could hardly believe it. Television viewers talked about it for days.

'It's a long time since I've cried,' said Willie Thorne, who missed a black to a baulk pocket which would have completed a 13-9 win over Eddie Charlton. Agonisingly, he lost not only this frame but the remaining three as well, as Charlton went through 13-12. Charlton went one better in the quarter-finals, beating Cliff Thorburn from four down with five to play.

'At 12-9, I was 40 in front,' Thorburn recalled years later. 'I was on the side cushion and I played a red sticking out from a pack of four. I missed it and Eddie cleared up.

A bespectacled Fred Davis in his prime (left) and, wearing contact lenses, still competing at the highest level at the age of 64

'The next game, I trapped him so that he was tight on the baulk cushion, just out from the baulk pocket. He couldn't get safe and he couldn't get on anything. He just rolled the red in, smooth as silk, and put me in trouble. I got out of it and put him in the same situation that he'd been in before. But he just rolled that red in as well, pocket weight.

'The whole thing just got worse and worse. The feeling came over me like a tidal wave that I was going to lose. I felt I just couldn't do anything about it. To go from having a chance to win the championship to losing in a situation like that has got to intensify your self-doubt.'

Reardon, rising to practise at 8 a.m. in an attempt to overcome his aversion to morning sessions, beat Bill Werbeniuk 13-6, and there were other comfortable quarter-final victories for Mans over Graham Miles and for Fred Davis over Fagan.

The Crucible's capacity crowds responded warmly to Davis's puckish personality and refined skills as psychologically he commanded the stage, with Fagan diverted into a supporting role. It was some compensation, albeit belated, for all the years that even snooker's top players had been forced to spend in the wilderness.

In many ways the star of the championship, Davis also starred in the BBC's 'musical item', set to the Beatles' 'When I'm 64'.

When he took the opening session of his semi-final against Mans 5-2, he looked set for a place in the final. But the South African demonstrated again and again his exceptional quality as a single-ball potter, winning innumerable frames either by building up a lead with a series of fragmentary contributions interspersed by safety, or by counterpunching near the end with the last two or three reds and all the colours.

Mans led 8-6 after two sessions, 13-8 after three and 16-12 going into the final session, a deficit which left Davis needing to win six of the remaining seven frames. He pulled back to two behind and a daring blue, doubled into a middle pocket, brought him within one ball of 15-16 but, extraordinarily, he missed a straight corner-pocket pink from its spot to allow Mans to pot pink and black to go three up with four to play.

At 16-17 Davis was still in contention but Mans, having made only seven breaks over 30 in 33 frames, made his highest of the contest, 60, to become the first South African ever to reach the final.

Reardon, trailing Charlton 12-9 after three sessions of the other semi-final, afterwards confessed that he infringed his strict self-imposed regime by sinking some eight double gins and getting to bed at 3 a.m. before appearing for the following morning's session.

'The previous day I'd felt wonderful and couldn't hit a ball. This time I felt tired and listless and played marvellously,' he said after the 7-0 session whitewash took him to 16-12 *en route* to his 18-14 victory.

In the final, Mans maintained his inspiration to split the first 20 frames 10-10. Reardon was pretty deadly at close quarters and once in round the black spot rarely lost position, whereas Mans used the blue heavily and the baulk colours frequently too. Having led only 12-11 going into the fourth session, Reardon emerged with an 18-14 lead. This was reduced to 18-17 before he responded with a superb 100, the final turning point of the match, as he took seven frames out of eight to win 25-18.

The championship had a tragic sequel. Joe Davis, intensely absorbed in Fred's semi-final, was taken ill during the mid-session interval of the final session.

'He was playing every shot for Fred. He was swinging this way and that,' said the former women's world champion Joyce Gardner, who was sitting with him in the arena. When Fred missed the pink which would have brought him back to 15-16, Joe 'almost fell off his seat'.

Ashen faced, exhausted and complaining of pains in his back, Joe was taken back to his hotel and spent all the following day in bed before he was driven back to his London home. On arrival, he fell flat on the pavement on getting out of the car. He remained there for 25 minutes until he was moved to St Mary's, Paddington. A six and a half hour operation got him over the crisis but he died a few weeks later from a chest infection when he was convalescing in the country. He at least had the satisfaction of seeing the game which he had pioneered at a peak of popularity and the championship he had founded established as one of Britain's great annual sporting spectacles.

1978 EMBASSY WORLD CHAMPIONSHIP

FIRST ROUND: **P. Mans beat J. Spencer 13-8; G. Miles beat David Taylor 13-10; P. Fagan beat A. Higgins 13-12; F. Davis beat Dennis Taylor 13-9; E. Charlton beat W. Thorne 13-12; C. Thorburn beat P. Houlihan 13-8; B. Werbeniuk beat J. Pulman 13-4; R. Reardon beat D. Mountjoy 13-9**

Quarter-finals: **Mans beat Miles 13-7; Davis beat Fagan 13-10; Charlton beat Thorburn 13-12; Reardon beat Werbeniuk 13-6**

Semi-finals: **Mans beat F. Davis 18-16; Reardon beat Charlton 18-14**

Final: **Reardon beat Mans 25-18**

Terry Griffiths, winner of two English amateur titles but excluded from an attempt at the 1978 world amateur championship because of his early defeat in his own national championship, the Welsh, had turned professional, but was struggling to obtain the two exhibition bookings a week, at £70 each, that he needed to keep his head above water in his new career.

His first professional match had provided one of the most astonishing reversals in the history of the game. In the qualifying competition of the UK Championship, which had a prestigious new sponsor in Coral, the bookmaking group, he led Rex Williams 8-2 only to lose 9-8. Less than six months later he was to win the Embassy World Championship at his first attempt.

Meanwhile, his fellow-Welshman, Cliff Wilson, won the world amateur title in Malta, beating Kirk Stevens 8-2 in the semi-finals, then Joe Johnson, later to become Embassy world champion, 11-5 in the final. He was invited to play in the Benson and Hedges Masters, but withdrew when the professionals threatened a boycott unless he also turned professional. Ironically he did turn professional the following year.

Another Welshman, Doug Mountjoy, won the Coral UK but the surprise of the tournament was David Taylor, who had made a negligible impact on the professional game since winning the world amateur title in 1968. During the summer he had claimed a world record for compiling three consecutive total clearances, 130, 140 and 139 in an exhibition at Butlins Holiday Camp, Minehead — all the more remarkable a feat for being performed in far from ideal conditions, in ordinary room lighting with no shade over the table and sun shining through the windows.

In his first match at Preston Guild Hall, which has remained the UK's venue ever since, he ousted defending champion Patsy Fagan 9-7, going on to beat John Virgo and Alex Higgins on his way to the final. He and Mountjoy were level at 7-7 at the end of the first day's play, but Mountjoy won five of the first six frames on the resumption, before sealing his 15-9 victory with a break of 120.

In the opposite half of the draw, Willie Thorne recorded his best tournament result to date by overcoming the reigning world champion, Ray Reardon, 9-6, only to go out 9-1 to Graham Miles, whose break of 139 in the clinching frame stood as a record for the event until Thorne's 140 in 1985. Another sign of the changing of the old order was the 9-8 defeat of John Spencer by Roy Andrewartha, a time and motion study expert from Wallasey in his second season as a professional.

Mountjoy beat Andrewartha and Miles comfortably to leave himself relatively fresh for the final. His first prize was £3,500, a significant increase on the £2,000 Fagan had taken the previous year.

Some sports departments in ITV could see, as clearly as did the BBC, that snooker possessed unrealised potential. Unfortunately, progress was obstructed by the internecine strife endemic to the organisation's federal structure. Thames, for instance, contracted to cover a new tournament at the Fulcrum, Slough, devised and promoted by Ray Davies and sponsored by Holsten, the lager brewers. Unfortunately, Thames could not persuade other regions to take coverage and, in effect, to share their costs for this full-scale outside broadcast. Wishing neither to pay overtime nor to have more than one crew on call, they decided to cover only selected parts of each match, which was a sure recipe for disaster.

By the time Spencer and Thorburn arrived together but late for their quarter-final, most of the spectators had dispersed in the belief that there would be no further play until the evening session. The promoter, however, decided that the first three frames should be played forthwith, so in front of a handful of spectators and without the television crew, who were on a meal break, Spencer compiled the first 147 maximum break seen in tournament play.

Great was the chagrin of Thames when their highlights programme went out that evening without one of the great moments in tournament history. The lesson was clear: every ball of every frame must be covered, and so it has been by both BBC and ITV ever since.

In fact, it transpired that the table's pockets had not been tested against the official templates, and as the unanimous opinion was that the middle pockets in particular were much easier than standard, in all probability the break would not have qualified as a record anyway.

The whole incident showed that the WPBSA was prepared at this stage to leave almost everything to promoters and television companies. Apart from controlling membership – and thus entry into professional tournaments – and exercising some influence in the conduct of the world championship, the association allowed a commercial free-for-all. While it was understandable that the players were more interested in playing than in committee work, their inaction merely allowed situations to develop which were all the more difficult to sort out later.

The Holsten tournament itself was played to a novel but never repeated format, in which aggregate scores rather than frames determined the outcome. This produced a thrilling first-round finish when Spencer, trailing Fagan by 91 going into the last frame, won the match with a break of 109. In contrast, Spencer's opening quarter-final salvo – including his maximum – left him leading Thorburn 372-1 by the time the television cameras began recording the remaining three academic frames. The event reverted to the orthodox system for the semi-finals and final, in which Spencer beat Miles 11-7 for the £3,500 first prize.

The sponsors marked Spencer's 147 with an *ex gratia* payment of £500. Had he made this break at the Benson and Hedges Masters a few weeks later, it would have been worth £10,000. As it was, a new venue for the Masters, Wembley Conference Centre, provided the setting for Mans to score a surprise victory without making a 50 break in the entire competition. He beat a very subdued Higgins 8-4 in the final.

In a spontaneous, unco-ordinated way, the tournament schedule was growing more crowded. Mike Barrett, the boxing promoter, sold a four-man event to London Weekend Television, the *Daily Mirror* Champion of Champions, in which Reardon beat Higgins 11-9 for the £2,000 first prize at Wembley Conference Centre.

ATV, the forerunner of Central, screened a Grandmasters, sponsored by State Express and won by Miles; Anglia's first snooker venture, the Tolly Cobbold Classic, was won by Higgins. ITV's snooker thus remained a series of localised efforts rather than co-ordinated network coverage.

Reardon beat Spencer 9-6 at the Royal Exchange Theatre, Manchester, to win the £3,000 first prize in the Forward Chemicals Tournament. This was a revival of the four-man leagues played at club venues with a showpiece final, which had been so popular with the Park Drive events in the early 1970s. Higgins beat Fred Davis for a £750 first prize in an open tournament at the Castle Club, Southampton, the type of event which soon would be unable to generate the kind of prizemoney to attract leading professionals. The Benson and Hedges Irish Masters moved to an impressive new venue, the bloodstock sales ring at Goffs, Co. Kildare, where Mountjoy beat Reardon 6-5 in the final.

Ray Reardon (in play) and John Spencer, the two greatest players of the 1970s, in opposition at the Crucible

In February 1979, the world professional matchplay championship, due to be staged less than two weeks later by Eddie Charlton Promotions in Melbourne, was cancelled to howls of outrage from the leading players, who had reserved four of their most lucrative exhibition weeks of the season to play in the event. These players were already in Bombay to compete in India's first professional tournament, won by Spencer, and it did not make them feel any better that they had to remain there until their fixed-date air tickets, geared to subsequent participation in Melbourne, came into play.

Few tears were shed over the demise of this ill-judged carbon copy of the world championship – certainly not by the BBC, by Embassy or by the world championship promoter Mike Watterson. It was difficult to resist the conclusion that the promise of $35,000 in prizemoney deflected the WPBSA (i.e. the players) from even considering any effect it might have on the overall development and credibility of the game. The WPBSA were slow to realise that it was time to order itself more like the Professional Golfers Association and develop some overall vision of the development of the game, rather than jump at any promotional offer which came along.

Meanwhile, three young players were

making significant progress.

When Steve Davis beat Tony Meo 7-6 to win the Pontins Open in the week following the 1978 Embassy World Championship, Rex Williams remarked: 'Davis is the best young prospect I have ever seen. He has such a good cue action – he hits the ball so straight and keeps dead still – that he is bound to keep improving.'

Barry Hearn, his manager, was looking for the moment for him to turn professional, which came when he was offered a place in *Pot Black*, to be recorded in December. He immediately applied for professional status and was thus in time to enter the 1979 world championship.

Meo had beaten Higgins in reaching the final of the Canadian Open in September 1978, before losing 15-17 to Thorburn, and in the same month Jimmy White won the £800 first prize from 338 entries in the Pontins amateur tournament, beating the 1975 English amateur champion, Sid Hood, 7-6 in the final. Later in the season, White beat Dave Martin 13-10 to become, at 16 years 10 months, the youngest ever English amateur champion.

EMBASSY WORLD CHAMPIONSHIP

That Terry Griffiths should win the Embassy World Championship at his first attempt was more than an amazing personal triumph: it was a confirmation that the old order was changing.

Although those who had been at or near the top for the previous ten years were by no means finished, it was now clear that they were finding the going very much harder, not least because the standard had been pushed up through intense competition and there were therefore fewer opportunities to coast through matches.

'Terry winning this has been the greatest achievement the game's ever known,' said Fred Davis. 'The only thing you could really compare it with was Higgins in 1972, but the game was nothing like as big then and the championship was broken up over a whole season, not concentrated into a fortnight as it is now. For someone like Terry with no experience of a series of long matches to come through and win is just incredible.'

Griffiths himself went into the championship only with the modest objective of qualifying. He beat Bernie Bennett 9-2 and Jim Meadowcroft 9-6 to be sure of £1,000, of going to Sheffield and of paying off what he owed on his car.

'With no immediate worries, I felt I had everything to gain and nothing to lose.' The ideal state of mind for a snooker player.

He quietly fancied his chances in the first round against Perrie Mans; respecting him for having reached the final the previous year, he none the less noted that his inability to make breaks of a size to win a frame in one or even two visits was evidence of a lack of genuine class.

His own inexperience of long matches, the most common factor in distinguishing top amateurs from professionals, led to his fading towards the end of the middle session as Mans recovered determinedly from 4-10 to 7-10. The South African also won the first frame of the final session, but Griffiths came back to win three in a row and prevail 13-8.

Memorably, Griffiths then beat Higgins 13-12. Higgins made consecutive centuries, 105 and 112, in the second and third frames and, with 45, looked well on the way to becoming the first player in the history of the championship to make three in three frames. However, when he missed unexpectedly, Griffiths cleared with 63 to win on the black.

Without this and the 61 clearance which had given him the opening frame on the black, Griffiths's position would have been even more dire at the first interval than it was at 2-6. In the evening he won the last three frames of the day to level at 8-8.

The following morning they swapped frame for frame before Griffiths clinched the decider with a break of 107. The brilliance of Higgins and the deadly counterpunching of Griffiths made this contest possibly the best of its kind the championship had yet seen. Higgins missed his chance at 11-11 while leading 55-0 and in perfect position on the black, he missed to let Griffiths in for a winning clearance to the pink of 67.

In contrast to the cut and thrust of this match, Griffiths's 19-17 semi-final win over Charlton was achieved only after the most protracted of struggles, in which sheer endurance and the ability to keep his concentration and self-belief were factors fully as important as pure skill.

Charlton eroded Griffiths's lead of 10-4 with a slow tempo, long bouts of safety, no risks, and few mistakes when he was in. Charlton went ahead 16-15 and 17-16, but it had taken him two days to get a frame in front from six behind and his reserves were dwindling. So were the Welshman's. 'If Eddie had won the next frame, that would have put him two up with three to play and I don't think I could have won from there.'

Favoured by one or two kindly rubs of the green, including fluking the last red out of a snooker and fluke doubling the brown from the baulk cushion to the

middle pocket, Griffiths levelled at 17-17, made a 69 break to win the following frame and from 0-48 cleared with 97 to reach the final. It was 1.40 a.m. The final session had lasted five hours 25 minutes.

Dennis Taylor, twice a losing semi-finalist, reached the final from the other half. Steve Davis, making his Crucible debut, had extended him to 13-11 without appearing to have either the experience or the self-confidence to win, and the quarter-finals had brought the Irishman a 13-8 victory over Ray Reardon, the defending champion fading in the final session at just the sort of juncture where he had customarily grown strong.

John Virgo established himself as a top-class player by beating Cliff Thorburn 13-10 and from 8-1 down against Bill Werbeniuk recovered to 13-9 to reach the semi-finals, Werbeniuk having removed Spencer 13-11 in the first round. Going into the final session against Virgo 5-11 adrift and with defeat looming, he won the first four frames – equalling the championship record with 142, the highest break yet made at the Crucible, in the process – before Virgo took the two frames he needed.

Virgo in turn was too inconsistent to cope with Taylor in the semi-finals. With a jackpot prize for a 147 maximum now a feature of the championship, Virgo was within sight of a £10,000 payout when he took 12 reds, 11 blacks, before failing at the 12th black.

The final was best of 47 frames, spread over three days, as opposed to the 35 frames over two days it became the following year. Griffiths led 5-2 after one session and 8-7 after two, but the end was still so far distant that, dog tired from the Charlton match, he ground along in low gear on the second day, concentrating simply on keeping the match on relatively level terms prior to the real business of the run in.

Having trailed 9-11 and 12-14, Griffiths needed to win the last frame of the penultimate day to level at 15-15, having missed a simple pink which, with black to follow, would have given him the previous frame after needing two snookers.

On the last morning, Griffiths crucially won the opening frame on the black and opened the gap to two by winning the second frame with breaks of 64 and 44. The gap narrowed to one but Griffiths won a scrappy 50-minute frame to restore it to two and made it three with the aid of a break of 71.

This opened the floodgates as Griffiths began to cue with the fluency he had shown earlier in the tournament, running through the remaining three frames of the morning and the first two of the evening to complete his seven-frame winning streak to the title.

'I didn't really feel I was playing for the championship until the last day,' said Griffiths. 'Once I saw the winning post, Dennis did seem to fade a bit. I was playing against the grain on Friday, not really enjoying it, though I always thought that if I could stay with Dennis until the last day I'd have a good chance on the run in.'

The BBC had doubled the screen time they had devoted to the championship the previous year and in Griffiths created a new television hero as millions shared his battles, watched him grow tired, became familiar with his mannerisms and were emotionally involved in his aspirations.

1979 EMBASSY WORLD CHAMPIONSHIP

FIRST ROUND: E. Charlton beat D. Mountjoy 13-6; B. Werbeniuk beat J. Spencer 13-11; J. Virgo beat C. Thorburn 13-10; F. Davis beat K. Stevens 13-8; Dennis Taylor beat S. Davis 13-11; A. Higgins beat David Taylor 13-5; T. Griffiths beat P. Mans 13-8; R. Reardon beat G. Miles 13-8

QUARTER-FINALS: Charlton beat Davis 13-4; Taylor beat Reardon 13-8; Virgo beat Werbeniuk 13-9; Griffiths beat Higgins 13-12

SEMI-FINALS: Griffiths beat Charlton 19-17; Taylor beat Virgo 19-12

FINAL: Griffiths beat Taylor 24-16

I t did not take Griffiths long to realise that his life had changed irrevocably.

'Terry loves the game as only an amateur or someone who hasn't been a professional very long can love it,' said Reardon. 'As you get older, become more successful, you get pressure from all sorts of directions which reduces your enjoyment of the game itself.'

It did not take long for these pressures to make themselves felt. On his first day as champion, Griffiths spent ten hours at the Annual General Meeting of the WPBSA, where the minnows out-voted the mighty on the proposal that only the champion and runner-up (Griffiths and Taylor) should be excused the qualifying rounds of the 1980 championship.

The mighty were outraged and the Professional Snooker Association Limited swiftly emerged as a potential rival governing body to the WPBSA. At first, PSA Limited appeared to be simply a souped-up version of the International Snooker Agency, a management agency run by Del Simmons, a colourful character from the club and car trades, who founded ISA, with Reardon and Spencer as the other directors.

However PSA's very choice of name hinted at deeper ambitions and the leading players joined it to a man. There were hawks like Reardon who believed that too little of the game's new money was finding its way to the players. There were doves like Griffiths who nevertheless, to protect their own interests, did not wish to be on the weaker side. Hawks and doves alike were dissatisfied with the WPBSA's limited effectiveness and efficiency.

PSA's chief function became the exertion of pressure on the WPBSA to do better, with the implied threat of setting up a rival association if matters did not work out to their satisfaction. Almost immediately, the new exemption system was thrown out in favour of extending the final phase of the Embassy World Championship from 16 to 24 players, with only the last eight places depending on the outcome of the qualifying competition.

Meetings of PSA and WPBSA, often held on the same day, even in the same room, usually with most of the same people present, gradually produced a working arrangement which was generally accepted as fair. PSA's proposal to introduce voting and non-voting categories of membership within WPBSA was accepted.

It was resolved that only the 21 players who had reached the last 16 of the world championship in the preceding three years would be entitled to vote and that the top ten in the rankings would automatically constitute the committee.

This second decision, which made Higgins a member of the board before which he was so often subsequently to appear on disciplinary matters, was soon abandoned as unworkable, on what appear to be the obvious grounds that prowess on the table often bore no relation to the capacity to make the kind of decisions which were now being demanded of a governing body.

Subsequent modifications extended voting rights to players who had appeared in the top 20 in the world rankings in the preceding three years, plus elected officers of the association. Full voting rights now reside with the top 40 in the last two world rankings, plus members of the board. Non-players became eligible for board membership, although it was still mandatory for the board of ten to have a majority of players over non-players. As the ranks of the professional game expanded, a player came to be defined as one who had at least once been ranked in the top 128.

Money, as ever, was a highly emotional subject. PSA, believing that Mike Watterson's profits from promoting the championship were now excessive, wanted all key contracts with television and sponsors to go through the WPBSA. Watterson, denying that his profits were excessive, was reluctant to see this happen, visualising this move, in essence, as one of commercial acquisitiveness by the players at his expense.

The eventual outcome was that on 5 September 1981, PSA Limited was wound up and the WPBSA, reconstituted as a limited company, came to organise the game and negotiate contracts in the manner normally expected of governing bodies. Simmons was taken on board as contracts negotiator.

In principle, it is hard to argue that anyone other than the governing body should hold a sport's key television and sponsorship contracts but, in practice, in such a close-knit sport as snooker, the seeds were sown for a ruling élite to do more or less as they liked.

While events were meandering to this conclusion, the uneasy fear lingered that television and sponsors might, through disillusionment, find themselves some other sport. But the quality of snooker entertainment which was actually appearing on the screen was – and always

would be – the sport's best safeguard.

Griffiths confessed that the game's political struggles worried him more than any other single factor, and he also found it terribly hard to cope with the deluge of offers, contracts and commitments which descended upon him. His gruelling schedule and snooker's internal problems blunted his appetite for the game, although the full effects of this were not apparent until the defence of his title fell due the following spring.

The players who were best off were those who left their political and commercial thinking to others. Steve Davis, who was already leaving his to Barry Hearn, won the 1979 Pontins Spring Open giving 30 start, having won it the previous year receiving 30. After beating Jimmy White 7-3 in the final he observed, with a clear appreciation of one of the paradoxes so beloved of snooker psychologists: 'I think it would have been closer if Jimmy hadn't had so much start.'

Amateur tournaments, open or invitation, sprang up everywhere. Motorways made it easier for amateurs to get to more events and a combination of rising unemployment and increasing

Patsy Fagan using the dreaded rest

amateur prizemoney hastened the creation of a new breed of full- or nearly full-time amateurs. At the Warners Open at Hayling Island, Tony Meo celebrated his acceptance as a professional by the WPBSA by beating White 5-2 for the £1,750 first prize. Joe Johnson, Cliff Wilson and Mike Hallett were also among the new intake.

The curtain-raiser to the 1979-80 season was the Canadian Open in Toronto, where Thorburn won the $6,000 first prize by beating Griffiths 17-16 after leading 10-3. In contrast to the cloistral calm of the Crucible, the tournament was held, as usual, in the heat of high summer amidst the annual jamboree of the Canadian National Exhibition, whose other attractions included a funfair, a cattle show, lumberjacking and, in the same building as the snooker, a fashion show with electric organ accompaniment and a display featuring police sirens.

The BBC, again delighted with their viewing figures for the championship, and with the UK and Masters finals also an annual feature of their schedules, decided they could do with a slightly different type of tournament. So Watterson devised a World Cup for national teams of three, obtained a sponsor in State Express, and nine days' coverage was devoted to it. Wales, represented by Griffiths, Reardon and Mountjoy, won first prize, but the abiding memory for television viewers was provided by Fagan. Since winning the 1977 UK title and reaching the 1978 world quarter-finals, he had slipped quickly downhill as a result of a mystifying mental block, possibly set in motion by a car accident. Whatever the cause, his total inability even to strike the cue-ball when forced to use the rest provided some agonising viewing as he vainly struggled to break what a psychologist called 'a vicious circle of anxiety'.

Various ITV companies continued to respond to snooker's potential with locally shown events, Higgins winning the Padmore/Super Crystalate tournament on ATV, promoted by Watterson, and Spencer the Wilson Classic on Granada.

BBC Wales, delighted with so much Welsh success at top level, annually covered the Welsh professional championship, sponsored by Bulmers, and won in 1980 by Mountjoy.

Virgo won the 1979 Coral UK and a first prize of £4,500. He recovered from 0-5 to beat Tony Meo 9-6 in his first match and held off the rapidly improving Steve Davis 9-7 in the quarter-finals, before beating Dennis Taylor 9-4 in the semis.

The event was then restricted to UK-based players but, stretching a point, Werbeniuk, a Canadian, was allowed to compete because he was spending most of the year in Worksop. He recovered from two down with three to play to beat both John Spencer and Ray Edmonds, before going out 9-3 in the semis to Griffiths, who had beaten Higgins 9-7 in the quarters with a four-frame winning streak from 5-7.

Virgo played to a standard he has seldom since sustained in taking a 7-1 lead in the final and was 11-7 ahead after two of the three sessions. In order to tailor the final for BBC's *Grandstand*, the concluding session was scheduled for noon rather than the 1.45 start which had pertained for afternoon sessions throughout the week. Virgo, having failed to check the timetable, was alerted in his hotel room some 15 miles away only a few minutes before noon. Despite a rapid drive to the Guild Hall and sprinting the last half mile on foot because of traffic queues into the main car park, he was 31 minutes late. Under the rules as they then were, he had to forfeit two frames.

Griffiths pleaded for the rule to be waived but to no avail. So, accruing two frames by forfeiture and two on the table, he levelled at 11-11. At the mid-session

John Virgo, now co-host of the BBC gameshow *Big Break*, on his way to winning the 1979 Coral UK Championship

10-9 to win the Benson and Hedges Irish Masters.

With the annual pilgrimage to Sheffield looming close, Higgins won two events within a week – a new British Gold Cup at Derby Assembly Rooms and the Tolly Cobbold Classic at the Corn Exchange, Ipswich.

The Gold Cup was yet another tournament which Watterson brought into the circuit. Obtaining the sponsorship of three trade concerns, Riley, Strachan and Super Crystalate, he devised a format of four-man groups playing best-of-three-frames matches with the group winners meeting in the concluding knockout. The tournament was not televised, although its potential was recognised the following year when ITV gave it four days' coverage on the network, with sponsorship increased from a modest £12,500 from the trade consortium to £30,000 from Yamaha Organs.

Higgins, needing to beat Griffiths 3-0 in his last match to win his group, did so with breaks of 135 and 134, the first time anyone had made breaks of 130-plus in consecutive frames in tournament play. While the other groups were being decided, he played in Ipswich, where his 5-4 final win over Dennis Taylor was marred by an altercation with his opponent and the referee. Their complaints, added to those already on file from sources as various as referees and exhibition organisers, led to the WPBSA fining him £200.

After his victory over Taylor, Higgins was driven through the night back to Derby, but it was 6 a.m. before he was in bed. At 11 a.m. he beat Meo 4-0 in the semi-finals and after an hour's nap in the afternoon, demolished Reardon 5-1 in the final in the evening. Taylor made up for losing the Ipswich final by dispossessing Higgins of the Irish title he had held since 1972, his challenge at the Ulster Hall, Belfast being successful 21-15.

interval, Griffiths suggested that the prizemoney be split, but while Virgo acknowledged the spirit in which the offer was made, he declined it. When Griffiths looked set for victory with a 13-12 lead, Virgo managed to give an amazing tale one final twist by taking the last two frames relatively comfortably for what remains the most prestigious title of his career.

On the crest of a wave, Virgo then beat Thorburn 17-13 to win the £3,000 first prize in an international tournament in Bombay, the last of its kind to be held in India until 1992 because of difficulties over exchange control regulations.

Griffiths had felt that there would have been something inappropriate in winning the UK title with the aid of forfeited frames, but he was fully focused for his first attempt at the Benson and Hedges Masters, in which he completed his 9-5 win over Higgins in the final with a 131 total clearance. He also beat Mountjoy

EMBASSY WORLD CHAMPIONSHIP

Cliff Thorburn's capture of the world title was a triumph of the trier, a welcome reminder that strength of character and day in, day out dedication can earn the highest prizes for a player upon whom nature has not bestowed the prodigious natural talent of some of his rivals.

Kirk Stevens, the man in the white suit, was twice a world semi-finalist at the Crucible

'He's a grinder,' commented Higgins, beaten 16-18 in their gripping final. 'But he grinds you real hard, believe me.'

The final could hardly have offered a clearer contrast in styles between Higgins, quick, edgy, impulsive, and Thorburn, measured, calm and calculating. So gripping was the television coverage that when it was interrupted to show the life-or-death drama of the SAS resolving the siege at the Iranian Embassy, many viewers telephoned irately to demand that the snooker be restored to their screens.

The newly instituted first-round matches at the Crucible produced dramatic 10-9 wins for Higgins over Meo and for Werbeniuk over Thorne. Kirk Stevens, appearing at the Crucible for the second time, made a break of 136 which, but for a failure at the final black, would have been a new championship record.

Steve Davis, improving rapidly and defeating one top player after another in challenge matches in his home-match arena at Romford Lucania, always looked likely to press Griffiths in the first match in defence of his title, but it could hardly have been predicted that he would win the first seven frames with a display of text book snooker.

From 6-10 after two sessions, the defending champion displayed his best form of the match to win the first four frames the following morning to level at 10-10, but a fatally over-ambitious attempt to pot the last red past a blue blocking a pocket left the red in the jaws. From this Davis compiled a 34 clearance to win on the black. His confidence restored, Davis made it 12-10 with a break of 116 and, despite a few late alarms, clinched victory in the following frame.

'What are his strengths?' Griffiths was asked afterwards.

'His strengths? I've spent the last three days trying to find a weakness.'

Another former world champion, John Spencer, made a first-match exit at the Crucible for the third consecutive year, beaten 13-8 by Stevens. John Virgo led Eddie Charlton for most of their match, but was brittle and edgy when he should have been steady as Charlton went through 13-12.

Thorburn began his title attempt with a 13-10 win over Mountjoy, winning two frames on the pink and one on the black from 10-10. The 18th frame of this contest lasted 69 minutes, 21 of them spent on a duel on the brown, first with the black jammed behind it in the jaws and then, after Thorburn had knocked in the black, with the cue-ball either touching or almost touching the brown.

Dennis Taylor, the previous year's runner-up, went out 13-10 to Jim Wych, a left-handed Canadian whose first entry to the championship had already included wins over Rex Williams in the qualifying competition and John Pulman in the first round at the Crucible. Relaxed, almost jovial from his narrow escape against Meo, Higgins disposed of Mans 13-6 to reach the quarter-finals.

Jim Wych reached the world quarter-finals at his first attempt in 1980

It was there that Higgins became the first player in the history of the championship to run 15 reds and 15 blacks. The maximum and the £10,000 jackpot was clearly on, but Higgins ran slightly out of position in taking his 15th black and had to play the yellow with an enormous amount of check-side in order to gain position on the green, which was lying only a few inches from the baulk cushion. He potted the yellow but did not spin the cue-ball sharply enough off the side cushion.

This 122 break enabled him to split his first session with Steve Davis 4-4. He won

**Cliff Thorburn
became in 1980 the
first Canadian to
win the world title**

the last two frames of the middle session to lead 9-7, and with Davis starting to miss just a few of the long- and middle-distance pots he had earlier been sweeping in with almost uninterrupted success, the Irishman secured his semi-final place at 13-9.

Stevens, sailing in with all guns firing, potted brilliantly at distance and was fast and fluent in the balls as he recorded a 13-7 victory over Charlton, who had no previous record of losing to young players with all-out attacking styles. Thorburn's status in Canadian snooker was such that his younger countryman had a psychological barrier to overcome as well as his skill. He beat Wych comfortably 13-6.

The surprise of the quarter-finals was David Taylor's 13-11 win over Reardon. At 7-3, Reardon was well in command, until his own loss of concentration and Taylor's gathering confidence produced a 9-7 lead for Taylor, going into the final session.

From 7-10 Reardon levelled at 10-10 and again at 11-11 with an 87 break but it was, curiously, the easy shots he missed, rather than difficult ones under pressure, which cost him the match. Taylor buckled down, kept his nerve better than his previous record suggested that he might, and took advantage of Reardon's errors to win the next two frames to secure the best win of his career.

In the semi-finals, though, the Canadian's deliberate and for long periods error-free style gradually destroyed Taylor's touch and continuity. From 2-3, Thorburn won the next eight frames and ran out a 16-7 winner.

Stevens led Higgins 5-2 after one session of their semi-final and was level at 7-7 after two. However, his mistakes began to proliferate in the third so that Higgins accumulated a 13-9 overnight lead, which he converted next day to a 16-13 victory.

Had Higgins been content simply to win, rather than to win in a grand manner, he might well have become champion for the second time, for he led 5-1, 6-2 and 9-5 before he cast aside the restraint which had carried him thus far to give Thorburn a chance to level at 9-9 overnight.

In the remaining two sessions, Thorburn had to fight not only his opponent but also the psychological block which had so often affected him on the very brink of important successes. His cue arm twice tightened when attempting a pink which would have put him two up instead of level going into the last session. The final black from its spot, the sort of shot he would normally miss scarcely once a month, made the difference between level and two up with five to play. Most agonisingly of all, he failed at an easy brown from its spot, which would have put him two up with three to play.

Higgins was thus able to level at 16-16 but it was a measure of Thorburn's character that he should respond with a 119 break. He had faced his ultimate fear not of losing but of having victory snatched away. The most important battle, with himself, had been won and a flawless clinching frame gave him the match 18-16 and the title.

1980 EMBASSY WORLD CHAMPIONSHIP

FIRST ROUND: S. Davis beat P. Fagan 10-6; A. Higgins beat T. Meo 10-9; D. Mountjoy beat C. Wilson 10-6; J. Wych beat J. Pulman 10-5; J. Virgo beat J. Meadowcroft 10-2; K. Stevens beat G. Miles 10-3; David Taylor beat R. Edmonds 10-3; B. Werbeniuk beat W. Thorne 10-9

SECOND ROUND: Davis beat T. Griffiths 13-10; Higgins beat P. Mans 13-6; Stevens beat J. Spencer 13-8; E. Charlton beat Virgo 13-12; C. Thorburn beat Mountjoy 13-10; Wych beat Dennis Taylor 13-10; R. Reardon beat Werbeniuk 13-6; David Taylor beat F. Davis 13-5

QUARTER-FINALS: David Taylor beat Reardon 13-11; Thorburn beat Wych 13-6; Stevens beat Charlton 13-7; Higgins beat Davis 13-9

SEMI-FINALS: Thorburn beat Taylor 16-7; Higgins beat Stevens 16-13

FINAL: Thorburn beat Higgins 18-16

For Cliff Thorburn the world title proved, as it had for Terry Griffiths, a poisoned chalice. Despite his defeat of Griffiths 17-10 in a Canadian Open final made farcical by primitive television lighting, his new status affected neither his private life nor his public standing to any perceptible degree, apart from an initial burst of curiosity from the Canadian media. The public recognition which he believed to be part of the prize was denied him.

Lacking astute managership, he had no offers of lucrative endorsement contracts and, also lacking a naturally entertaining style, he was not as heavily in demand for exhibition engagements as a world champion might expect.

Recognising that much of his life would revolve round the British circuit, he tried to settle in Walton-on-Thames, but was like a fish out of water. He missed his Canadian friends and felt almost anonymous in a land which seemed to acknowledge that he was world champion in terms only of some aberrational departure from British dominance. Indeed, his morale became so low that, two years after his world title win, he returned to live in Toronto, reckoning that he could certainly do no worse by commuting when necessary.

His first British tournament as champion was the ill-fated Champion of Champions, promoted by Ray Davies at the New London Theatre. Although both television and sponsor lost interest amid internal wrangling and personality clashes, Davies, instead of cutting his losses by cancelling the tournament, saw it through. So when Doug Mountjoy received the winner's envelope after beating John Virgo 10-8 in the final, it was regrettably empty. The sour taste of this fiasco was marginally alleviated by a more successful staging of the State Express World Cup at the same venue immediately afterwards, Wales beating Canada in the final.

Jimmy White, at 16 years 11 months the youngest English amateur champion in 1979, became the youngest ever world amateur champion in 1980 by beating Ron Atkins, who was playing in his home town of Launceston, Tasmania, 11-2.

White had two anxious moments. First, in September, he was withdrawn from the event because he had been manifestly as drunk as a lord in losing 3-0 to Steve Newbury in the key England v Wales match in the home international championship at Prestatyn. Both he and the other English competitor in Launceston, Joe O'Boye, were the subjects of official complaints by the organising committee over alleged misconduct in their hotel in Tasmania. On the table, though, White had no problem until the quarter-finals, in which Newbury was within a ball of beating him 5-2 before he came through 5-4. He returned home a professional, having been accepted on the strength of a postdated application.

Simultaneously, a new age was dawning for snooker as Steve Davis comprehensively drubbed Terry Griffiths 9-0 in the semi-final and Alex Higgins 16-6 in the final to win his first major title, the Coral UK. To this £6,000 first prize, he added £5,000 for winning the Wilson Classic at Blighty's, a Bolton nightclub, on Granada TV the following week.

As a living text book of style, Davis had been greatly admired from his early days; however, his temperament, his capacity to keep his nerve in all the situations which need to be encountered to win at the highest level had not yet been proved. Once they were, he looked almost unbeatable. His success coincided with another significant increase of coverage from three days to nine by BBC TV. With the World Cup having already commanded another nine only a few weeks earlier, there was no sign of any diminution of the public appetite for snooker.

Davis's new dominance was briefly interrupted. Perhaps overconfident, he lost 5-3 to Mans on his debut in the Benson and Hedges Masters, which was eventfully won by Higgins. Down 5-1 to Thorburn in their semi-final, he was in such poor shape that he actually dozed off for ten minutes during the mid-session interval. He attributed the fact that he had 'thrown up five or six times' on the morning of the match to having eaten 'some west country mustard' with a steak the previous evening.

At 5-3, 57-0, Thorburn missed a red which may have been more difficult than it looked and Higgins sprang to life with an 85 clearance. Three factors combined to produce an inspired charge by Higgins: a reprieve, a big crowd roaring him on and, in the deciding 11th frame, a fluke of the kind which often seemed to convince him that the gods were on his side. Here, it led to a match-winning break of 77.

Maintaining his impetus, Higgins beat Griffiths 9-6 for the £6,000 first prize after the Welshman, needing two snookers in the eighth frame to stay in the match, had beaten Spencer 6-5 in the other semi-final and set a new tournament record of 136 in the final.

ITV's first sustained venture into networked 'same day' coverage of snooker, on the lines which the BBC had proved were popular with audiences, was the Yamaha Organs Trophy at Derby, a refined version of the untelevised British Gold Cup of the previous year.

Davis defeated David Taylor 9-6 to win the £10,000 first prize and immediately beat Tony Meo 9-3 to win the inaugural John Courage English professional

Jimmy White became the youngest-ever world champion in Launceston, Tasmania, in 1980

championship at Haden Hill Leisure Centre, Sandwell. Ray Edmonds, beaten 9-0 by Davis in the semi-finals, expressed an increasingly common feeling: 'Everyone who plays Steve these days seems to play as if he's hypnotised.'

Davis did lose 4-2 to Reardon in the quarter-finals of the Benson and Hedges Irish Masters, one of the last occasions on which best of seven was deemed sufficient in the early rounds of the major tournament, but as spring approached he was a clear favourite for the world title.

Griffiths, one of his obvious rivals, added to Thorburn's frustrations in the semi-finals by making breaks of 93 and 91 in the last two frames to beat him 6-5, and defeated Reardon 9-7 in the final. Although encouraged by this, the Welshman was not overjoyed to have Davis, then ranked only 13, as his likely quarter-final opponent at Sheffield.

EMBASSY WORLD CHAMPIONSHIP

The BBC's musical item, 'Makin' Your Mind Up' by Bucks Fizz, encapsulated the *joie de vivre* snooker was feeling as the Crucible's fifth championship provided the first of six world titles for Steve Davis. Doug Mountjoy, beaten 18-12 in the final, remarked: 'Now that he's won the title he's going to be very hard to beat in anything. You've seen how he's played in a long match. He starts every session so well that he's going to be very hard to beat in a short match as well. The top players are all on a par but he is a black better.'

As it turned out, Davis's closest match was his first, a 10-8 defeat of Jimmy White who himself, on his championship debut, had needed to win the last two frames to beat Jim Meadowcroft 9-8 to qualify for the Crucible.

White's brilliant potting and breakbuilding were demonstrated at such speed that some attention was distracted from the fact that Davis was more consistent, a shade more precise and the shrewder judge, positive as he was, of when to bide his time.

From 4-8, White closed to 7-8 and from 7-9 to 8-9, but then rushed a good chance early in the following frame, lost position and had to watch Davis clinch his 10-8 win with a break of 71.

After his 6-2 lead over Higgins at the end of the first session had been reduced to 9-7 after two, he ran from 10-8 to victory at 13-8 without any great difficulty. The key to his 13-9 quarter-final win over Griffiths was the middle session, in which he progressed from 4-4 to 9-5. This was another match in which, strongly as the opposition resisted, Davis never really looked like being broken, although his semi-final against Thorburn did provide him with this experience. He eventually rose above

Bill Werbeniuk in characteristic pose, enjoying a glass of tax-deductible lager

it to win 16-10.

Thorburn's year as champion having yielded him little in fame, fortune or success, he came to Sheffield fiercely determined – and beat Graham Miles and David Taylor by wide margins, albeit unspectacularly.

Davis led 4-3 at the first interval of their semi-final, the seven frames having occupied three hours 34 minutes, which was about par for this gruelling contest. Down 4-6, Thorburn produced a deadly combination of Scrooge-like safety and meticulous breakbuilding to which there was no apparent answer. For an hour, Davis did not pot a ball and in three frames he potted only three. He sat in his corner closing his eyes for half a minute at a time as he tried to clear his mind and motivate himself anew.

So it seemed extraordinary that after an afternoon's rest Davis should front up so apparently bright and fresh to receive the customary full-throated reception from his supporters at the start of the evening session. He won three of the first four frames, the one he lost taking 60 minutes, to level at 9-9. Each frame continued to be a grim battle, with the session continuing until 12.58 a.m., at which point he led 12-10.

In the first frame the following morning, Davis potted the brown to guarantee a lead of 13-10. Had the cue-ball just dropped into the middle pocket instead of perching on its edge, Thorburn would surely not have failed to clear the remaining colours for 11-12, but 13-10 was a different proposition. By adding the next three frames Davis prevailed 16-10.

There were a couple of close finishes in the other half of the draw, Dennis Taylor winning the last four frames to beat Kirk Stevens 13-11 and Ray Reardon winning the last two frames to beat his old adversary, John Spencer, 13-11. Mountjoy put out both of them in turn, Taylor 13-8 and Reardon, who had beaten Bill Werbeniuk

Jimmy White (right) making his Crucible debut against Steve Davis, who went on to win the 1981 championship

A dream fulfilled: Steve Davis at the moment of winning his first world title

The first frame of any final is important, not only in terms of who wins it but in what it does to a player's feelings and confidence. If he seizes a chance, feels his game and nerve in good working order, he will approach subsequent frames confidently. On this occasion, Mountjoy scored first with 40 but missed anxiously and did not score again that frame. Davis, amazingly fresh and eager after the rigours he had endured, led 6-0.

That was to be the margin by which he won the title, although Mountjoy pursued him doggedly to trail only by two frames at 8-10. At 11-13 he missed a simple blue which, with pink to follow, would have brought him to only one behind; from a second chance he struck the blue plumb to a baulk pocket, only to go in-off.

This gave Davis a breathing space of three frames at 14-11. Although Mountjoy creditably won the last frame of the day, Davis, coming into the final session with a 14-12 lead, quickly won two frames with breaks of 84 and 119 and added two more to win 18-12.

Unable to contain himself, Barry Hearn came charging across the arena and lifted him in the air. The Age of Steve had begun.

13-10 in the quarter-finals, 16-10 in the semis.

Mountjoy had always been, in Reardon's phrase, 'one of the best "in" players' in the game. Reardon initially used to beat him by imposing a tactical pattern, instead of allowing a breakbuilding contest to develop, but Mountjoy's tactical game had improved immeasurably in the last couple of years and he was now by far the sharper breakbuilder. At 6-5, Mountjoy made a break of 145, which earned him £5,000 for a new championship record and £1,200 for the biggest break of the championship.

In too many frames, Reardon seemed to need more than one bite at the cherry and from 13-9 going into the final session Mountjoy beat him 16-10 to reach the final.

1981 EMBASSY WORLD CHAMPIONSHIP

FIRST ROUND: G. Miles beat T. Knowles 10-8; David Taylor beat C. Wilson 10-6; D. Mountjoy beat W. Thorne 10-6; K. Stevens beat J. Dunning 10-4; T. Meo beat J. Virgo 10-6; S. Davis beat J. White 10-8; B. Werbeniuk beat D. Martin 10-4; J. Spencer beat R. Edmonds 10-9

SECOND ROUND: C. Thorburn beat Miles 13-2; David Taylor beat F. Davis 13-3; T. Griffiths beat Meo 13-6; S. Davis beat A. Higgins 13-8; Mountjoy beat E. Charlton 13-7; Dennis Taylor beat Stevens 13-11; Werbeniuk beat P. Mans 13-5; R. Reardon beat Spencer 13-11

QUARTER-FINALS: Thorburn beat David Taylor 13-6; Davis beat Griffiths 13-9; Mountjoy beat Dennis Taylor 13-8; Reardon beat Werbeniuk 13-10

SEMI-FINALS: Davis beat Thorburn 16-10; Mountjoy beat Reardon 16-10

FINAL: Davis beat Mountjoy 18-12

The championship had attracted so much public interest that when the WPBSA voted to increase the 24-player final phase at the Crucible to 32, the BBC happily increased its television coverage to 17 days.

In contrast to previous champions, Davis had the management ready to exploit the world title as, off table, it had never been exploited before. He was still ready to battle a whole week for a £2,000 first prize in the Guinness Open on the Isle of Wight, the latest and as it proved most commercially disastrous of the holiday camp tournaments, but his manager, Barry Hearn, was soon booking him for exhibitions at £1,500 a night. A three-year contract with Leisure Industries guaranteed him £100,000 in three years from miniature home table sales, while an equipment contract with E. J. Riley, two books and exhibition and promotional contracts with the *Daily Star* and Coral Racing all brought the money rolling in.

Top snooker players were wanted for everything from gameshows to the God slot: Ray Reardon appeared with Arthur Negus, Terry Griffiths with the Reverend Roger Royle.

Davis's confidence, already strong, appeared armour plated after his world title win. So dominating was he in winning the Jameson International – a new £66,500 event promoted by Mike Watterson to open the 1981-82 season and give ITV another weapon in its fight with BBC – and in retaining the Coral UK title, that Jean Rafferty wrote in her vivid portrait of that season, *The Cruel Game*: 'It's as if snooker has got itself into a tape loop and this scene is just going to go on repeating itself. No-one else will ever win again. It will always be Steve Davis standing there holding the trophy, putting the lid on his head, winning and winning and winning . . .'

With chilling efficiency, he demolished Dennis Taylor 9-0 in the Jameson final, making breaks of 135 and 105 in consecutive frames and heavily exploiting almost every chance. White, 9-0, and Griffiths, 16-3, were not so much beaten as executed in the last two rounds of the Coral UK, and Davis also played the hero's role in England's capture of the State Express World Cup at an impressive new venue, the Hexagon, Reading. Yet fearsome as these performances appeared on television, there were hints in between of the human fallibilities which led to his spectacular defeat on his return to Sheffield in defence of his world title at the end of the season.

He played his Jameson semi-final against Higgins after a flying visit to Jersey for exhibitions, which meant a 6 a.m. start for the return trip. Dog tired, he trailed 7-8 but summoned a decisive final burst, taking the final frame with a break of 95, to win 9-8. Danger had stimulated the flow of adrenalin and was to do so again, although it was becoming clear that just as much commitment was needed to maintain his high plateau of form as to reach it. Even if the body could stand a punishing schedule of exhibitions, travelling and promotional appearances, the mind could not. Hearn was to learn one of management's most underestimated arts – that of refusing lucrative engagements to maintain tournament success as his client's unyielding priority.

So intoxicating were Davis's triumphs on network television that without this stimulus he lost twice to White between his Jameson and Coral runaways, going down 6-5 in the semi-finals of the new Langs Scottish Masters, which was shown only on BBC Scotland, and 11-9 in the final of the untelevised Northern Ireland Classic.

White became, at 18, the youngest winner of a professional tournament, when he beat Thorburn 9-4 in the Langs final and also, under the new management of Sportsworld, an offshoot of Kennedy Street

Enterprises, the Manchester music entrepreneurs, acquired a new hairstyle and an elaborate re-shaping of his teeth. His new management also put his name to some ill-judged boasting and prediction of personal success before the Coral UK semi-final he was to lose 9-0 to Davis, not appearing to realise that publicity of this nature would put him rather than Davis under pressure.

Sadly, snooker's new status as a high-profile television entertainment was already stimulating raucous features as the tabloids sought to outdo each other. One early battleground was the signing up of players on exclusive contracts for ghosted columns – not a practice which encourages dispassionate or even unbiased coverage. Soon these newspapers began belabouring the public with inside stories about the private lives of the players. The game's new money also acted as a magnet for a new breed of manager, with no previous commitment to snooker, whose credentials were often accepted all too

Steve Davis made the first televised 147 maximum against John Spencer in the Lada Classic

easily by players ill equipped to make serious career decisions. Snooker's merry-go-round, with more passengers aboard, began to whirl ever faster, unseating riders from time to time, but allowing some to climb back on in the few and short remissions from its manic activity.

Davis, who was to be among the casualties in 1982, began that year by making the first televised 147 maximum in the Lada Classic at Oldham Civic Centre. His achievement was all the more remarkable, as he had just returned jetlagged from a round the world trip with Hearn. Lada were last-minute replacement sponsors for Wilsons, the Lancashire brewers, who felt that the increased asking price of £15,000 and the offer of coverage not only within Granada's area but outside it, where they did not sell their beer, made their support no longer worthwhile. For Lada, the Soviet car company, it turned into the sponsorship bargain of the year for Davis's 147, made in his 5-2 quarter-final win over Spencer, was shown not only as a network special but immortalised as a video. As the first tournament maximum to be made on a table whose pockets and other specifications were passed for record purposes, the break generated enormous publicity.

Midweek Sports Special asked for the final

Steve Davis and his manager Barry Hearn, as close as brothers, enjoy themselves on one of their exotic foreign trips

for the ITV network and were given an amazing finish in which Davis, still so jetlagged that he even fell asleep in the press room, made good his 3-8 deficit against Griffiths to level at 8-8. He had the first chance, a difficult one, at the black in the decider but Griffiths potted it to win 9-8.

'I should have won 9-3, and against most players I would have done, but against Steve you try that bit too hard. You get to think that he can't be beaten. You have a mental barrier against him,' said Griffiths.

This was the second of five consecutive Davis v Griffiths finals on the circuit, Davis winning the Benson and Hedges Masters 9-5 and the Yahama Organs trophy 9-7 – clinching victory with a 135 total clearance – and Griffiths the Benson and Hedges Irish Masters, 9-5, to complete his hat-trick of titles in that event.

So clearly did they appear to be currently the circuit's two best players that they were confidently expected to meet in the world final. But it did not work out like that.

EMBASSY WORLD CHAMPIONSHIP

Although it is only 100 miles from Birmingham to Sheffield, it seems more like a million from Selly Park British Legion – scene of Alex Higgins's capture of the untelevised, unsponsored world championship at his first attempt in 1972 – and the Crucible Theatre, on whose brilliantly lit stage Higgins became champion for the second time ten years later.

For beating John Spencer in the 1972 final, Higgins received £480. Inflation made that equivalent to £1,800 in 1982, so the record first prize of £25,000 he earned from beating Ray Reardon 18-15 in the final still provided a striking contrast in the immediate financial worth of his two world titles.

One could compare, too, the tiered seating on beer crates at Selly Park with the plush tip-ups at the Crucible; the one public phone in an unlit call box in 1972 with the dial-out phones and television monitors of the Embassy press room. Most remarkable, though, was the difference between the 1972 champion, a snooker star, and the 1982 champion, the kind of superstar which only television could create.

Julian Barnes, then the *Observer*'s television critic, mused: 'The canonisation of Alex Higgins as the People's Champion had a double-edged meaning: perhaps his fans should think twice about this sobriquet after what happened to Freddie Laker and the People's Airline.'

Barnes suspected that: 'Higgins's enormous popularity springs less from the authenticity of his origins than from his embodiment of an important and consoling myth: that of the Hero as Mess. Shambling and twitching, his pockets distended by duck mascots, rabbits' feet and four-leafed clovers, Higgins lurches appealingly around the table like a doomed lowlifer.'

This is one way someone with no specific commitment to snooker might look at it. Others more emotionally involved with the game might value more highly Higgins's grit, nerve and courage to risk all.

Prior to the championship, he was not thought to have a realistic chance of regaining the title. His tournament record for the season had been the poorest of his career and his frustration had surfaced explosively in an altercation with the crowd in his Benson and Hedges Irish Masters semi-final, an episode which resulted in his being fined £1,000 by the WPBSA the day following the championship.

Unforeseeably, Steve Davis and Terry Griffiths, who had dominated the season, both lost in the first round at Sheffield and

Higgins realised that, even below his best, he had at least an even chance against anyone else.

Davis went out ignominiously 10-1 to Tony Knowles, a full-time player since leaving art college in Bolton but only two years a professional, owing to the rejection a year earlier of his first application for WPBSA membership. Keeping his head when it was clear that Davis was but a husk of his normal self, not missing anything easy and exploiting his opponent's numerous mistakes, he accepted the chance for media glory presented to him by a champion mentally exhausted by the pressures he had allowed to accumulate.

Without noticing it, Davis had come to rely less on the game for his enjoyment and more on the by-products of success for which his skill had been responsible, through exposure to a variety of new experiences. As a result, he gave himself insufficient time to think, or even to remain aware of who he was or what he was becoming. In retrospect, the writing was on the wall in his 6-0 semi-final defeat by Reardon in the otherwise unimportant Highland Masters in Inverness the previous week.

On the very day of his championship defence, he was promoting his new instructional book. Both Davis and Hearn were to be warier of such a draining preparation in the future.

Dennis Taylor, another reasonably fancied contender, fell 10-7 to Silvino Francisco, a South African who was to reach the quarter-finals on his championship debut; Patsy Fagan, in temporary remission from his mental block against being able to hit the cue-ball when using the rest, beat David Taylor 10-9; Perrie Mans contrived as fine a clearance as he had ever produced in tournament play – 62 to the pink – to complete a 10-8 win over Tony Meo; Jimmy White buried Thorburn, who had not won a match since September, 10-4.

The pick of the second-round matches was the 13-12 win for Higgins over Mountjoy, who led 37-0 in the decider, only to see Higgins pot a red out of a snooker when one further mistake from him would have brought about his exit. The moment of truth arrived when Mountjoy committed a foul and Higgins had the choice of laying a snooker or taking a free-ball brown. 'I was in no mood for snookers. I was prepared to go out if I missed,' Higgins said later. But the free ball went in and a break of 35 was the result. Although it did not take him quite to the finishing line, a difficult green to the middle pocket soon did.

The quarter-finals brought Higgins a 13-10 win over Willie Thorne, who made a break of 143, the second-highest in the history of the championship. Twice in the final session he was only a frame behind, but did not have quite the competitive edge to close the gap.

White, with a 13-9 victory, dispossessed Kirk Stevens of his

Ray Reardon, beaten by Alex Higgins in the 1982 world final

Steve Davis prepares to enter the arena in 1982 for the defence of his world title but is to finish this match a 1-10 loser to Tony Knowles. The match referee, John Smyth, is between the two players

two-year-old distinction of having been the youngest semi-finalist in the event; Eddie Charlton, trailing Tony Knowles 6-11, revealed not for the first time his best qualities in adversity as he steadily won seven frames in succession to go through 13-11; Reardon was held to 10-8 by Francisco, before winning comfortably enough 13-8.

Reardon had always beaten Charlton when it mattered most and did so again 16-11 in their semi-final; from 11-11 after three sessions, he took the first five frames of the fourth to go through without further loss.

Having adjusted his sights from the exits of Davis and Griffiths and having prevailed so narrowly over Mountjoy, Higgins was now fired up to the full. Personal ambition alone might have unbalanced him, for so often winning had not been enough: he had felt compelled to try to win in the grand manner. This time, he was anchored in reality by his wife and 18-month-old daughter. 'Winning this will set Lynn and Lauren up for life,' he said, discounting the turbulence of his marriage and, of course, unaware that it would end three years later.

1982 EMBASSY WORLD CHAMPIONSHIP

FIRST ROUND: T. Knowles beat S. Davis 10-1; G. Miles beat D. Martin 10-5; B. Werbeniuk beat John Bear 10-7; E. Charlton beat C. Wilson 10-5; S. Francisco beat Dennis Taylor 10-7; D. Reynolds beat F. Davis 10-7; J. Virgo beat M. Hallett 10-4; R. Reardon beat J. Donnelly 10-5; A. Higgins beat J. Meadowcroft 10-5; D. Mountjoy beat R. Williams 10-3; P. Fagan beat David Taylor 10-9; K. Stevens beat J. Fitzmaurice 10-4; P. Mans beat T. Meo 10-8; J. White beat C. Thorburn 10-4

SECOND ROUND: Knowles beat Miles 13-7; Charlton beat Werbeniuk 13-5; Francisco beat Reynolds 13-8; Reardon beat Virgo 13-8; Thorne beat Spencer 13-5; Higgins beat Mountjoy 13-12; Stevens beat Fagan 13-7; White beat Mans 13-6

QUARTER-FINALS: Charlton beat Knowles 13-11; Reardon beat Francisco 13-8; Higgins beat Thorne 13-10; White beat Stevens 13-9

SEMI-FINALS: Reardon beat Charlton 16-11; Higgins beat White 16-15

FINAL: Higgins beat Reardon 18-15

Trailing White 7-8 overnight in their semi-final, he was in the theatre at six o'clock the next morning to practise until their 11 a.m. resumption. White was 11-8 ahead, but Higgins won the three remaining frames of the penultimate session, then at 13-12 recaptured the lead for the first time since his 4-1 advantage had been swallowed up. White won three consecutive frames to go two up with three to play, and although a break of 72 brought Higgins to only one behind, he hovered on the very precipice of defeat in the following frame. White, first in with 41, missed a black from its spot. He was second in too, but added only 18 and Higgins cleared the table with an effort of 69 which, as the BBC's frequent reprises of the footage confirm, was probably the finest match-saving clearance ever made.

Once Higgins had reached 15-15 only one result seemed possible. A 59 break took him almost to the line; White could not reply and Higgins, with 37, was in the final.

Not surprisingly Higgins showed some reaction from his great victory over White and trailed Reardon 5-3 at the first interval of the final the following day. After two sessions, though, Higgins led 10-7 and after three, 13-12, an advantage he converted to 15-12.

With the title in sight, he now began to betray signs of excessive anxiety, and when Reardon levelled at 15-15 after needing a snooker in the 30th frame, the pundits prepared to identify this as a turning point. However, the loss of his lead and the proximity of the finishing line seemed to concentrate Higgins's mind wonderfully, so that he made no further significant mistakes. Reardon crucially made one in each of the next two frames, first missing an initial red which was only a few inches from the top pocket and then failing at a black along the top cushion. Having won these two frames 79-0 and 112-9, Higgins needed only one more

Alex Higgins with
his wife and
daughter in the
emotional aftermath
of his recapture of
the world title in
1982

opportunity. Just able to get through to an
initial red from distance, he brought the
championship to a close with a 135 total
clearance.

His urge to live on life's dangerous edge
– stronger than any mere desire to win –
had been satisfied by three dramatic
victories in the last three rounds. He had

proved his nerve in the death or glory
situation for which he hungers. He
received the trophy amidst scenes of raw
emotion, tearfully calling for his wife and
baby to join him in the spotlight in his
moment of triumph. No scriptwriter
would have dared to invent such a
dramatic fade-out.

On his first day as champion, Higgins sent champagne with his compliments to the WPBSA board, who were sitting in disciplinary judgement on him following his altercation with the crowd during the Benson and Hedges Irish Masters. They fined him £1,000. The WPBSA also took steps to tighten its control of all televised snooker when, on the Saturday following the championship, Davis and Griffiths, who by now everyone had forgotten had been expected to be the world finalists, played a challenge match, under Barry Hearn's promotion, on ITV. Anglia TV's screening of the recorded Tolly Cobbold Classic – won by Davis – in direct opposition to BBC's championship coverage also upset them.

Now the WPBSA began to insist on holding all snooker's television contracts, although it did not attempt to enforce this policy in the Far East, where Hearn was building up a circuit during the British summers. One-man appearances on television, such as when Davis played celebrities, were also exempt. The overriding principle, in the game's best interests, was that of preventing television screens being flooded with cut-price events, which might diminish the public appetite for the authentic tournament circuit the WPBSA was trying to build up.

The WPBSA also changed the world ranking system to take account not just of the three preceding world championships, which had been the criterion since rankings were introduced in 1976, but of any other tournaments, open to all professionals, which it might designate. It stipulated that, from 1983, world championship ranking points should count double (i.e. ten for the winner, eight for the runner-up etc.), while the Jameson International and the new Professional Players Tournament would carry ordinary ranking points. A system of merit points was also devised to differentiate between players at the lower end of the rankings.

The unique inspiration of the PPT, for which the WPBSA supplied the £32,000 prize fund, was that the WPBSA was now accruing such substantial funds in television contracts – including £435,000 over three years from the BBC – that rather than pay much of it in tax, they preferred to distribute the money to members in the form of prizemoney. It was also intended to help overseas players by filling in the dates between the Jameson and the State Express World Cup. A circuit of tournaments occupying the entire British season was now only a couple of years away.

Davis beat Higgins 9-4 to win the Langs Scottish Masters but withdrew from the PPT. 'This year,' said Hearn, 'Steve will earn £350,000 before he takes his cue out of his case.' However, various long-term contracts ate away 120 days of his time, 40 being allotted to John Courage and another 40 to Leisure Industries.

His withdrawal from the PPT meant that he earned no ranking points from that source, a deprivation which no leading player subsequently felt willing to undergo. Surprisingly, he earned only two from the Jameson, where he fell 5-3 in the quarter-final to David Taylor. In the other half, Knowles, commendably solid, went on to take his first major title by beating Taylor 9-6. Sadly, it was not to be long before he was to underestimate the dedication to his game that was needed to maintain the high standard set by his Jameson success.

The PPT was played in the match arenas of two well-appointed Birmingham snooker clubs, but with no sponsor (by design) and negligible crowds (through lack of professional promotion), the event lacked atmosphere. It did, though, provide Reardon with his first title of any significance for five years when he beat White 10-5 in the final.

As the circuit expanded and the

television public became more accustomed
to seeing authentic tournament matches,
Pot Black grew to look more outdated. The
1983 series was recorded only after the
WPBSA withdrew a boycott threat, made
when the BBC's final offer of £18,000 plus
£9,000 for overseas rights was deemed
insufficient. The following year an increase
to £27,500 with a 50 per cent repeat fee
was negotiated, but the programme's days
were numbered and the 1986 series was
the last until it was revived in off-peak
slots in 1991.

As more money continued to flow into
the game, managers and agents
proliferated. Sportsworld had White,
Knowles, Thorne, David Taylor, Virgo,
Stevens and even Higgins under contract
at various times, but all were either wooed
or drifted away. No management camp
did anything to threaten Hearn's pre-
eminent position, which he had confirmed
by adding Meo and Griffiths to his stable.

In the mid-1980s he was to expand still
further by signing Dennis Taylor as world
champion in 1985, plus Thorne, Neal
Foulds, White and Thorburn.

In summer 1982, Foulds won the
British junior title by beating John Parrott
who, receiving 25, had beaten Reardon
7-4 for the £2,000 first prize in the
Pontins Open. They were soon to become
the circuit's most promising professional
recruits, a development made possible by
the experience they had rapidly been able
to gather from playing in a multitude of
amateur events carrying substantial
prizemoney. In this way, they were
effectively full-time professionals long
before attaining the official professional
status which came solely from
membership of the WPBSA. Parrott even
had a £5,000 cue contract with Peradon
and Fletcher, following his capture of the
junior *Pot Black* title on BBC2, while he
was still an amateur.

The core of the amateur game had shifted from social clubs, leagues and official national and local competitions to the new snooker centres and open tournaments. Aspiring young players were not only much better served than their elders had been, by having places where they could play, but were in many cases encouraged or even funded by a new generation of snooker centre owners. For anyone prepared to travel, there were first prizes of anything between £400 and £2,000 to be won almost every weekend.

There remained, of course, certain amateurs, particularly those bearing responsibilities of home and family, who preferred secure employment and played snooker only in their spare time. A classic case was Terry Parsons, a postman from Trealaw in the Rhondda Valley, who, after winning the fourth of his five Welsh amateur titles, won the 1982 world amateur championship in Calgary at the age of 47.

In contrast to the early championships, which had been largely confined to players from Britain and past and present Commonwealth countries, the event was steadily extending its geographical spread, with Thailand, Singapore, Hong Kong, Zimbabwe, Egypt and Sudan among the newcomers, even if the established countries still dominated.

Jim Bear looked like providing Canada with a home victory when he led 7-1 in the final but Parsons beat him 11-8. Pleased as he was, Parsons kept his sense of proportion about turning professional: 'It's too tough now. I'm a little old for it.'

Such an attitude was unusual, for the prevailing trend was to regard the amateur game merely as a ticket to the professional bandwagon. As snooker's cake was made bigger, it fed more mouths, although the biggest slices tended to disappear down the same few throats.

It was not Davis, however, but Griffiths who won the £11,000 first prize in the Coral UK. He brought down Davis 9-6 in the quarter-finals, beat Meo 9-7, and against Higgins swept from two down with three to play to take the title 16-15.

Davis and Meo, stablemates in the Hearn camp, collected the first of the four Hofmeister World Doubles titles they were to win in the next six years, but the cold, cavernous emptiness of the National Sports Centre, Crystal Palace, provided a wildly inappropriate setting. ITV had guaranteed four days' coverage in the week before Christmas, though, and this was increased to nine days the following year, with a change to a more suitable venue at the Derngate Centre, Northampton.

ITV also took nine days' coverage from a fine arena new to snooker, the Spectrum, Warrington, which was the setting for the Lada Classic, a 16-man event in 1983, which was opened the following year to full ranking status.

It was marked by a career-best performance by Bill Werbeniuk, whose gargantuan build and rolling gait made him an inspiration to all who aspired to be sporting heroes while lacking the figure for it. Most remarkably of all, he suffered from a hereditary nervous disorder which made his cue arm shake so much that he could not hold even a cup of coffee still. His discovery that the best way of controlling this tremor was to imbibe vast, if calculated, quantities of lager – roughly a pint per frame and up to 40 pints a day – caused him to balloon to 20 stone and persuaded the Inland Revenue to allow his lager expenditure to be tax deductible, a concession later withdrawn.

All this provided excellent copy as he defeated Higgins, Mountjoy and Stevens

Bill Werbeniuk gets hot under the collar

to reach what proved to be the only British final of his colourful career. He held Davis to 5-5 before missing one vital ball in each of the next two frames as he was beaten 9-5.

Having lost his world and UK titles, Davis needed this restorative to his confidence, although he slipped back again in the Benson and Hedges Masters quarter-final, losing 5-4 to Mountjoy after leading 4-1. The Masters did, though, signal Thorburn's return to the élite as he beat Charlton 6-5 from three down with four to play in the semi-finals, before beating Reardon 9-7 for a title he said that he regarded as 'the Big Daddy after the world championship'.

Reardon burnished his world title credentials by overwhelming Mountjoy 9-1 for the Welsh title and beating White 9-6 in the final of the Yamaha International Masters. Even the death of his father did not prevent him from beating Meo and Higgins in the Benson and Hedges Irish Masters, but against Davis in the final the delayed emotional impact of his bereavement descended with full force as he lost 9-2.

Promotionally, the Mike Watterson era was coming to an end. The WPBSA recruited his No. 2, Paul Hatherell, and set up its own promotions company which, as Watterson's contracts with existing sponsors ran out, came to promote most of the circuit's events. There had been unedifying personality clashes and endless rows about money. 'Any profits that may result from WPBSA Promotions Ltd will be ploughed back into the game and not end up in any individual's pocket,' said the WPBSA's secretary, Mike Green, pointedly.

The reality was rather different. While the WPBSA's inner circle allowed itself expenses with an ever more liberal hand, they also discovered that promoting events was not quite the licence to print money they had imagined Watterson to hold.

EMBASSY WORLD CHAMPIONSHIP

Although it was Steve Davis who departed the Crucible with his second world title, in every other sense it was Cliff Thorburn's championship, as the Canadian made the first 147 in the event's history and emerged the hero from a series of epic late-night finishes.

Davis was extended to 13-11 by Dennis Taylor in the second round, but won all his other matches by the proverbial street, beating both Higgins, the holder, and Thorburn in the last two rounds with a session to spare as he triumphantly re-established himself as snooker's No. 1.

The one-sidedness of the final, 18-6, was a result of the draining effect on Thorburn of three times in succession being taken the distance: 13-12 by Terry Griffiths, 13-12 by Kirk Stevens and 16-15 by Tony Knowles. His maximum, worth a £10,000 jackpot, came in the fourth frame of his match with Griffiths. In the 15 minutes 20 seconds from his first fluked red to the last black, his positional play was so accurate that only a couple of pots posed

A champagne moment for Cliff Thorburn – the first 147 break in world championship history

even marginal difficulty.

Most frames, though, ground along slowly, so that Thorburn's 8-6 lead after two sessions left a possible 11 for the final evening. Worse still, Charlton found it so difficult to nail Spencer from five up with six to play in the preceding session that he eventually won only 13-11, thus delaying the start of the Thorburn v Griffiths final session until 8.55 p.m.

At 2.18 a.m. Thorburn twice attempted the black which would have given him victory at 13-9, and at 2.56 another black which would have seen him home 13-10. At 3.26 Griffiths completed a 97 clearance

to level at 12-12, but Thorburn's nerve held steady as he took the decider with a break of 75. The final session, which lasted a record six hours 25 minutes, finally ended at 3.51, nearly two hours after the BBC had ceased recording at the end of agreed overtime. It was the first time they had missed a single ball of the action since they first came to the Crucible.

Although some 200 souls remained in the Crucible to the bitter end, with the television camera idle there was the eerily intimate atmosphere of a match behind closed doors.

Stevens had been only 12 years old when

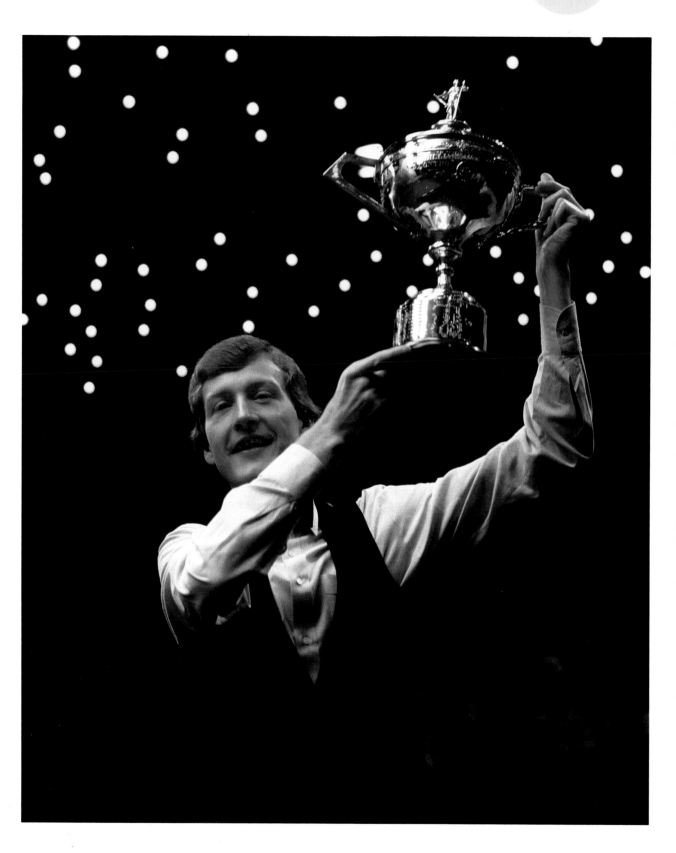

he painstakingly accrued $4 with which to challenge Thorburn, then a superstar only in the unreported subculture from which Canadian snooker had not yet even begun to emerge. Having conceded him 50 points per frame, Thorburn refused the $4, which Stevens nevertheless thrust upon him. An elder-younger brother relationship developed which, despite its many vicissitudes, survived the feelings of rivalry that loomed when the younger man closed the ability gap. As it happened, there was more than an ordinarily strong rivalry in their quarter-final as Stevens led 12-10, before Thorburn won frames of 32, 53 and 61 minutes' duration to win 13-12. Thorburn produced a priceless break of 45 in the decider, negotiating all sorts of difficulties until, sinking the last red with the aid of the half-butt spider, he needed to pot only a simple black to leave his opponent pursuing two snookers.

The final session lasted six hours 11 minutes and finished at 2.12 a.m., but after this late night Thorburn was immediately back in action against Knowles. The latter had made a 66 break

Friends since they were schoolmates, Tony Meo (left) and Jimmy White meet at the Crucible

in the decider to beat Reardon 13-12 before completing a 13-9 win over Meo, who was appearing in his first world quarter-final, by virtue of victories over White, 10-8, and Mountjoy, 13-11.

Thorburn led 12-10 going into the final session but was clearly flagging as Knowles went two up with three to play. Within two pots of clinching the match in the following frame, Knowles faltered on the pink as his lead was cut to 15-14. Two more clear-cut match-winning chances came his way in the 30th frame, but he could not take advantage of those either, and at 15-15 Thorburn played a typically tight deciding frame of 43 minutes to walk out of the arena the winner, after a session of four hours 45 minutes.

His prodigious triumphs of the mind and will brought him to the final 14 table-hours more tired than Davis, and even Thorburn's well of concentration proved not to be bottomless. He had nothing left. All he could do was bear up from a very early stage of the final to inevitable and excruciatingly long drawn-out defeat.

It was not simply luck, of course, which matched him with an opponent fresh and rested: Davis had earned his day off before the final by disposing of Higgins 16-5. Higgins, for once, was more sinned against than sinning. An exasperated wave of his hand in the course of his 13-11 quarter-final win over Bill Werbeniuk was wilfully construed as a V sign to the referee, and several of the tabloids went out of their way to stir up ill feeling between players by using emotively aggressive language. Werbeniuk was so offended by the treatment Higgins received that he declined to co-operate in the customary press conference. 'If he sneezed, they'd say he spat on the floor,' he remarked contemptuously.

1983 EMBASSY WORLD CHAMPIONSHIP

FIRST ROUND: A. Higgins beat D. Reynolds 10-4; W. Thorne beat J. Virgo 10-3; B. Werbeniuk beat D. Martin 10-4; David Taylor beat J. Meadowcroft 10-2; E. Charlton beat L. Dodd 10-7; J. Spencer beat M. Hallett 10-7; Dennis Taylor beat S. Francisco 10-9; S. Davis beat R. Williams 10-4; C. Thorburn beat J. Campbell 10-5; T. Griffiths beat M. Wildman 10-8; P. Mans beat I. Black 10-3; K. Stevens beat M. Fisher 10-2; D. Mountjoy beat C. Wilson 10-2; T. Meo beat J. White 10-8; A. Knowles beat G. Miles 10-3; R. Reardon beat E. Hughes 10-7

SECOND ROUND: Higgins beat Thorne 13-8; Werbeniuk beat David Taylor 13-10; Charlton beat Spencer 13-11; Davis beat Dennis Taylor 13-11; Thorburn beat Griffiths 13-12; Meo beat Mountjoy 13-11; Knowles beat Reardon 13-12; Stevens beat Mans 13-3

QUARTER-FINALS: Higgins beat Werbeniuk 13-11; Davis beat Charlton 13-5; Thorburn beat Stevens 13-12; Knowles beat Meo 13-9

SEMI-FINALS: Thorburn beat Knowles 16-15; Davis beat Higgins 16-5

FINAL: Davis beat Thorburn 18-6

nooker had become such a high profile television attraction in Britain that attempts were made, albeit unco-ordinated, to reproduce this success overseas. Winfield, the tobacco company, lengthened its matches in the Winfield Australian Masters from a *Pot Black* formula to a credible number of frames, even though Channel 10's studio B felt artificial in comparison with a public venue. Cliff Thorburn beat Bill Werbeniuk 7-3 in the final and Werbeniuk, despite having to set off for the venue two hours before everyone else to drink himself into readiness for action, won the Winfield New Zealand Masters, which remained only a sprint-style event.

Barry Hearn continued to develop the Far East circuit, moving on from a two-man exhibition tour by Davis and Meo the previous year to six-man tournaments, featuring those players plus Griffiths, Mountjoy and the best amateurs from the various host countries. Within two years, various Hearn touring parties had visited not only Singapore, Malaysia, Dubai and Bahrain but, in 1985, China. The trips were highly geared to selling products then endorsed by the Hearn camp – not least Riley tables – the deal being that any club buying a table was given a free exhibition.

Commercial aggrandisement, a fondness for the game and the personal satisfaction of bringing new projects to fruition all fitted into Hearn's scheme of things but, as new markets developed and playing standards rose, the benefits percolated into many corners of the snooker world. The only disappointment (and even this had its moments) was a combined snooker/pool challenge, in a Dallas shopping plaza, involving Davis, Griffiths and two leading American pool players, Jim Rempe and Mike Sigel.

The start of the new British season found Higgins at a low ebb, with divorce proceedings pending and the custody of his two children in question. In a state of great depression, he fell at the first fences posed by Dave Martin in the Jameson International and Mike Watterson, chiefly a promoter but also a talented player, in the second PPT.

Davis had no such problems, retaining the Langs Scottish Masters and regaining the Jameson International at a new venue, Eldon Square Leisure Centre, Newcastle. He beat Knowles 9-6 for the Langs and won the Jameson final over Thorburn, 9-4, the Canadian having beaten Griffiths from three down with four to play in the semi-finals.

The PPT, much more professionally staged this time at the Redwood Lodge Country Club, Bristol, provided so many dramatic matches that, ironically, it became clear that this was too important an event not to be televised. Having originated as a vehicle to distribute some of the WPBSA's excess income amongst its members, it became a means of making more money as Rothmans hovered in the wings to take over the event in 1984, with nine days' television coverage and a prize fund of £225,000.

Joe Johnson, who had made little impact in his six years as a professional since finishing runner-up in the 1978 English and world amateur championships, beat White, Charlton, Thorburn and Meo to reach the final. There Knowles led him 6-1, but eventually struggled home only 9-8 to win his second world ranking title. Davis, having been involved in a motor accident on the way to his second-round match, was eliminated 5-2 by Mike Hallett, whose first significant showing this was.

It seemed to be business as usual, though, at the Coral UK, where 9-4 was the best score against Davis on his way to the final. There he led Higgins 7-0 before an amazing reversal gave Higgins victory 16-15.

Trailing the Scottish champion, Murdo

Alex Higgins,
forever riding the
waves of success
and disappointment

Macleod, 0-4 in his first match, Higgins was still the forlorn figure of earlier in the season, until moves towards reconciliation with his wife took a hopeful turn as she arrived at Preston for an evening session, in which he completed victory at 9-6. This patching up, temporarily as it proved, of the cracks in his marriage lifted his spirits and helped carry him to the final in which, with immense grit and safety play of the highest order, he won seven frames out of eight in the second session to turn the match. Fired by the prospect of triumph and with Davis inhibited by the potential enormity of snatching defeat from the jaws of victory, Higgins ended a fluctuating final session by taking the last two frames to beat Davis for the first time in four and a half years.

The circumstances of this defeat fractured Davis's inner sense of certainty – a factor in his 1985 world final defeat by Dennis Taylor – but in the short term he appeared unaffected, retaining the Hofmeister World Doubles with Meo and winning the Lada Classic, now open to all professionals and thus for the first time carrying ranking points.

He was lucky in the deciding frame of the final when Meo, needing only a straightforward yellow-to-pink clearance for victory, was distracted by a spectator's untimely shout of 'Come on Tony'.

Earlier in the tournament, John Parrott had made his name to an extent possible only from television exposure by beating Mountjoy, Higgins and Knowles before extending Davis to 5-4 in the semi-finals. Rex Williams made a break of 143, a tournament record, in losing to Meo.

Prizemoney in amateur tournaments was increasing rapidly. Steve Newbury won three £2,000 first prizes around this time at Ealing, Basingstoke and Glasgow, and with a year's earnings of more than £8,000 from the amateur circuit was better off than any professional in the lower half of the ranking list. At the top of the

professional game, it was a different story, with Davis pocketing £159,511 in prizemoney by the end of the season.

Only £6,000 came from his bogey tournament, the Benson and Hedges Masters, in which Stevens beat him 5-3 in the quarter-finals, going on to make a 147 maximum against White in the semi-finals. Unperturbed, White ran 119 in the next frame to clinch his 6-4 victory and next day beat Griffiths 9-5 for the £35,000 first prize. The quality of his performance suggested that he might indeed supersede Higgins as the youngest world champion – even though Davis was competence personified in winning the last Yamaha International Masters, the Tolly Cobbold Classic and the Benson and Hedges Irish Masters.

On the lighter side – though not to those financially involved – a 12-man professional league, untelevised and unsponsored, lurched from one disaster to another so spectacularly that no prizemoney could be paid. All the participants were left to draw what consolation they could from the match practice the event had afforded them on the road to the Crucible, with John Virgo and Dennis Taylor finishing first and second respectively.

EMBASSY WORLD CHAMPIONSHIP

Steve Davis won the Embassy World Championship for the third time in four years, thus becoming the first champion to make a successful title defence at the Crucible. He also extended his lead at the top of the world rankings to a mammoth 11 points – one point per round in ordinary ranking tournaments and two in the world championship – as he made it clear that he bestrode the snooker world like a colossus.

Yet for all his technique, the world final came down to a test of nerve. He did crack in the final stages of his 18-16 defeat of Jimmy White, whom he had led 12-4

Kirk Stevens, loser of a gripping semi-final

overnight, but White himself eventually cracked just enough for Davis to get home.

The dramatic final, and a no less gripping semi-final in which White defeated Kirk Stevens 16-14, redeemed what was in some respects a disappointing championship. An exceptionally fine 17 days of spring weather possibly affected the atmosphere, and certainly affected television viewing figures, though snooker was the factor which enabled the BBC to claim a rare bigger audience share than ITV over the spread of the event, recording 52 per cent, 56 per cent and 52 per cent over each of the three weeks.

Even in the first week the figures were never lower than one million in the mornings and around two million in the afternoons, before swelling to 5.5 million in the evenings. In the second week the figures varied from two million to 6.1

million and those for the final were extraordinarily high. Once its final session was under way, the lowest audience was 6.3 million (opposite *Coronation Street* on ITV) and the highest 12.8 million and 13.1 million in the last two 15-minute segments of the match.

Only three first-round matches were of more than ordinary interest. Neal Foulds, 20 years of age and rising, won the last two frames to beat Alex Higgins 10-9 and Willie Thorne also won the last two frames for his 10-9 win over John Virgo.

Tony Knowles, who in the *Sun* had dismissively assessed all title contenders except for Davis, Higgins, White and himself, was a 10-7 first-round loser to John Parrott, who had beaten Knowles 5-1 in the quarter-finals of the Lada Classic without, it seems, arousing his suspicion that he might beat him again.

The tabloids waged their circulation wars with the familiar weapons of tatty exclusives and ghosted columns. The *Sun* ran a three-part farrago of sexual boating by Knowles, publication of which brought him a WPBSA fine of £5,000 for bringing the game into disrepute; the *Daily Star* set up John Parrott in opposition as their own clean-cut, clean-living young hero.

Parrott was involved in the best second-round match, in which he eventually conceded defeat to Dennis Taylor 13-11. From five down with six to play, Parrott closed to 11-12 before Taylor produced his highest break of the match, 73, to go through to the quarter-finals.

The closest quarter-final was that in which Davis beat Griffiths – as he always has at the Crucible – 13-10, Griffiths having led 6-3 and, early in the final session, 9-8. Ray Reardon, the subject of a BBC profile on the eve of the championship in which he admitted that

he was at the beginning of the end of a great career, was overwhelmed 13-2 by Stevens.

Convincingly, if lacking in spontaneous ease, Davis beat Dennis Taylor 16-9 in one semi-final while White, 10-12 down going into the final session, beat Stevens 16-14 in the other.

The first frame of the final session in that match was crucial. Having sat out his opponent's solid opening break of 53, White staked all on his difficult opening pot, which dislodged all the awkwardly placed balls into pottable positions. He replied with 33 before snookering himself on the last red. Stevens potted this but did not drop on a colour, and White swept up in a flash to win on the black. This started the five-frame winning streak, which took him three up with four to play at 15-12.

'The Kirk Stevens match took it all out of me,' said White, in explanation of his low-key performance on the first day of

Tony Knowles, signed up by the *Sun*, and John Parrott, signed up for the duration by the *Daily Star*, sit out between frames of their Crucible match

the final, which ended with Davis 12-4 ahead. Only much later did it emerge that he also had serious problems with his tip, which Jim Meadowcroft, then a BBC commentator, changed for him at close of play.

The second day's play provided a completely different story as White

immediately hit his stride with a break of 119 and won seven frames out of eight in the third session. Davis won the first two frames of the evening to regain a four-frame lead at 15-11 and was still four in front at 16-12 when another furious charge from White reduced the gap to 15-16.

Mounting pressure exerted its toll in Davis's frightful miss at the penultimate red in the next frame. However, White's failure at the yellow from distance gave him a second bite of the cherry and, recovering his composure admirably, he cleared the colours to win on the black and go two up with three to play.

Inviting comparison with the 69 clearance with which Higgins had denied White in the semi-finals two years earlier, White produced an equally sublime clearance of 65 to win the next frame on the black but, in what proved to be the last frame, White also began to show unmistakable signs of strain. A scrappy frame was resolved when he sent a long green well wide of the corner pocket to give Davis an easy chance to clinch the title.

Jimmy White in play against Steve Davis in their dramatic 1984 final

1984 EMBASSY WORLD CHAMPIONSHIP

FIRST ROUND: S. Davis beat W. King 10-3; J. Spencer beat G. Miles 10-3; T. Griffiths beat P. Mifsud 10-2; B. Werbeniuk beat F. Davis 10-4; N. Foulds beat A. Higgins 10-9; D. Mountjoy beat M. Hallett 10-4; Dennis Taylor beat J. Johnson 10-1; J. Parrott beat A. Knowles 10-7; C. Thorburn beat M. Morra 10-3; W. Thorne beat J. Virgo 10-9; J. White beat R. Williams 10-6; E. Charlton beat R. Andrewartha 10-4; K. Stevens beat E. Sinclair 10-1; David Taylor beat M. Gauvreau 10-5; S. Francisco beat T. Meo 10-5; R. Reardon beat J. Wych 10-7

SECOND ROUND: Davis beat Spencer 13-5; Griffiths beat Werbeniuk 13-5; Mountjoy beat Foulds 13-6; Dennis Taylor beat Parrott 13-11; Thorburn beat Thorne 13-11; White beat Charlton 13-7; Stevens beat David Taylor 13-10; Reardon beat Francisco 13-8

QUARTER-FINALS: Davis beat Griffiths 13-10; Dennis Taylor beat Mountjoy 13-8; White beat Thorburn 13-8; Stevens beat Reardon 13-2

SEMI-FINALS: Davis beat Dennis Taylor 16-9; White beat Stevens 16-14

FINAL: Davis beat White 18-16

uring the 1984 British summer Tony Knowles began his rehabilitation as a player by winning the Winfield Masters in Sydney; Dennis Taylor won the Costa Del Sol Classic, the first professional event held in Spain; and the Far East tour, promoted by Hearn, continued to grow with small tournaments in Singapore, Kuala Lumpur, Bangkok and Hong Kong; in the Dublin studios of Radio Telefis Eireann, the new four-man Carlsberg Challenge, a lucrative pipe-opener to the main British circuit, was won by White.

In the autumn, Davis not only completed a hat-trick of Langs Scottish Masters titles but won the Jameson International for the third time in four years, dropping only eight frames in five matches, but he was beaten 9-7 by Thorburn in the semi-finals of the Rothmans Grand Prix, a sponsored version of the PPT staged at the Hexagon, Reading, with the nine days' BBC

coverage formerly allocated to the State Express World Cup.

'I'm a better player now because Steve has set such a high standard,' claimed Thorburn. 'I've got a great attitude now. I'm a rejuvenated man. It's good that after playing for 20 years I can still improve.' Undoubtedly his mental stamina was depleted as he lost 10-2 to Dennis Taylor in the final the following day, but this was an occasion on which Taylor was in any case playing like a man possessed.

Three weeks earlier, Taylor's mother had died suddenly and he had therefore scratched from the Jameson quarter-finals next day. Initially, he had little appetite for the Rothmans, but once he became involved in the fray, his concentration and mental approach were never more positive. His bereavement put snooker in perspective: winning offered a means of uniting his large and loving family in joy as they had been in sorrow.

An overall improvement in his game

Dennis Taylor played through bereavement to take his first major title, the 1984 Rothmans Grand Prix

had also arisen through adopting a specially made type of snooker spectacles which became his trademark. They were worn so high on the face that he could look down the cue through the optical centre of the lens, rather than downwards through slight distortion, which was often the case even with conventional swivel lenses. The larger lens area also gave him better peripheral vision for pots which were not so straight.

'It looks a different game now,' he observed.

On the amateur front, playing and political history was made at the Grand Hotel, Dublin, when Omprakesh Agrawal became the first Indian – indeed non-British – player to win the world amateur title. Off table, the International Billiards and Snooker Federation, responsible for world amateur championships since 1972, effectively superseded the Billiards and Snooker Control Council as the accepted world amateur governing body, even though a few formalities remained to complete the transfer of power.

As the scope of the world amateur field widened to include such nations as Sweden, Iceland, Belgium and Mauritius in its total of 22, the professional ranks swelled to a point where the WPBSA felt it necessary to fix a limit of 128 members with full tournament playing rights. It also instituted a series of professional ticket events, as an improvement on the system of aspiring amateurs having their applications for professional status considered – all too often illogically and haphazardly – by a WPBSA sub-committee. The sentiment was admirable but, in practice, playing these events in holiday camps without any atmosphere, whether in high summer or out of season, was less than ideal. It also gave too great an advantage to British aspirants over overseas amateurs, whose only realistic route into professional ranks now lay through winning the world amateur championship.

The WPBSA also recognised that its trump card in stamping its authority on the game and co-ordinating the circuit lay in the ranking points system. This winter, two more events, the Coral UK, having previously been restricted to UK nationals and permanent residents, and the new Dulux British Open, superseding the sprint-style Yamaha International Masters, were given this status.

Although Coral were themselves not keen to change, their long-term contract with the WPBSA provided for a scale of prizemoney which suffered in comparison with the newer events. Hearn said categorically that Davis would not play unless ranking points, and by implication more money, were at stake. The WPBSA felt that with nine days' BBC coverage the event should offer the public all the game's leading players.

Despite this change, the 1984 final was a repeat of the previous year's, except that Davis this time defeated Higgins 16-8. He led 6-1, just held off Higgins at 9-8 when the Irishman looked like levelling, and avoided panic to reel off seven frames to win the title for the third time in five years.

Neither had he panicked in the second round when Meo, leading him 7-4 and by 25 in the 12th frame, refused a reasonable chance at the last red. If he had potted it, it would have been simple to go four up with five to play. Davis won that frame on the black and aggregated 474-30 in winning the next four frames for the match.

There was another remarkable recovery in the quarter-finals, in which Thorburn beat Reardon from four down with five to play. The Canadian's semi-final against Higgins was turned by an incident when he was leading 6-5. Having snookered himself, Thorburn nominated green but the referee, John Smyth, did not hear him and called a foul. Thorburn appealed to

Higgins for support but Higgins said he had not heard him either.

Higgins, partnering White, was the hero of a 9-6 semi-final victory over Davis and Meo in the Hofmeister World Doubles. This new partnership went on to beat Thorburn and Thorne 10-2 in the final but the losers, a couple of weeks later, met in the final of the Mercantile Classic, which took over the Lada Classic's slot at the Spectrum Arena, Warrington.

Thorne's capture of the £40,000 first prize was the breakthrough his natural ability had long promised. He had become notorious for following good wins with bad losses, for losing close finishes and for his difficulty in clinching winning positions on big occasions, but had nevertheless risen to 12th in the world rankings and had been knocking on the door long enough for it eventually to open. After a 9-8 defeat of Davis in the semi-finals, the middle session of his 13-8 victory over Thorburn was one of the very best ever seen on the circuit, producing three centuries, several other fine breaks and three close finishes in its eight frames. In contrast, the final session was of disappointing quality, with Thorburn fading uncharacteristically as Thorne took the last five frames in a row. Thorburn won the Benson and Hedges Masters for the second time in three years, although the match of the tournament was the 5-4 first-round win for Higgins over Davis. An unruly element became manifest at a major tournament for the first time and ugly boos were heard at the entrance of Davis, whose most odious crime appeared to have been to excite envy at his success and status.

However imperfectly some of the

followers of Higgins may have behaved, his own fine of £1,500 was absurdly harsh for one adverbial expletive, not intended for television consumption and uttered only to his own supporters in the first exultant seconds of victory.

More constructively, the WPBSA voted a subsidy of £1,000 per entrant to the prize funds for national professional championships, simultaneously boosting interest in the competitions as well as the prizemoney. Davis won the Tolly Cobbold English Championship, covered by Anglia TV from the Corn Exchange, Ipswich; Murdo Macleod became Scottish champion for the second time; Dennis Taylor retained the Strongbow Irish Championship; and Griffiths won the BCE Welsh.

The Dulux British Open produced from

Willie Thorne for once exploited his talent to the full in winning the 1985 Mercantile Classic

Higgins his highest break in competition, 142; a fine 9-7 semi-final victory for Stevens over Davis; and a surprise winner in Silvino Francisco, who beat White, Meo, Higgins and Stevens to take the then record £50,000 first prize.

It was the first major final to be contested by two non-British players. As a South African, Francisco had been frustrated by his exclusion from world amateur championships owing to the apartheid issue, and had turned professional to gain more fulfilment as a player. Realising that he needed to play the British circuit full time, he moved to Chesterfield and gradually worked his way up the rankings. Sadly, the title which should have been his springboard to further glories plunged him indirectly into all manner of difficulties.

Throughout the final at Derby, throughout the World Cup (which had a new sponsor, Guinness, a new venue, the Bournemouth International Centre, a new four-day BBC television slot and new winners, Ireland) and throughout the Benson and Hedges Irish Masters (won by White), an undercurrent was gathering force before exploding in a tidal wave of publicity at the Embassy World Championship.

During the Dulux final, Francisco had been convinced that Stevens was under the influence of drugs. He may have been especially alert to this possibility through having lived in a flat adjacent to the young Canadian's in Chesterfield. He was certainly angry at the prospect, as he saw it, of having his first major title snatched away by an opponent playing with the aid of an illegal stimulant. He protested verbally on the first evening of the final to the tournament director but, in the absence of any action, followed Stevens to the toilets between frames the following afternoon and confronted him angrily. The situation was resolved between the players themselves and the match proceeded to its conclusion, a 12-9 win for Francisco, but his sentiments, privately expressed, came to the attention of the *Daily Star*'s chief news reporter, Neil Wallis. While the WPBSA, anxious to avoid a scandal, announced that drug tests would be instituted in time for the Embassy World Championship, the *Daily Star* was preparing an exclusive which was to rock the snooker world.

EMBASSY WORLD CHAMPIONSHIP

Only being there could do justice to the drama and emotion of the climax of the 1985 Embassy World Championship, Dennis Taylor's 18-17 victory on the final black over Steve Davis.

The bewildering kaleidoscope of skill, fortitude, heart, nerve, fear, will and

Silvino Francisco holds the Dulux British Open trophy after beating Kirk Stevens in the 1985 final, a match which was to focus media attention on the drugs issue in snooker

courage finally settled to reveal a popular and engaging new champion and an unprecedented television success story. There were three new records set by the 18.5 million who watched the final from midnight onwards: the largest British television audience for a sporting event; the largest BBC2 audience ever recorded; and the largest British after-midnight audience.

The finalists had begun their challenge for the title in contrasting fashion. In the first round, Neal Foulds missed a black from distance which would have put him 9-8 up and Davis was relieved to win 10-8.

Taylor, his confidence high after beating Higgins for the Irish title, had no trouble whatsoever in beating Silvino Francisco 10-2. The South African was distracted by the *Daily Star*'s exclusive story that morning, which had featured his off-the-record remarks that had in fact been tape recorded and quoted.

Francisco's most damaging allegation was that Kirk Stevens was 'as high as a kite, out of his mind on dope' during the Dulux final. Immediately after his opening session against Taylor, he was hustled into a meeting with WPBSA notables and took the ill advised decision to repudiate the *Daily Star*'s story at a hastily convened press conference. Shortly afterwards, the WPBSA instituted disciplinary proceedings against him, alleging that he had brought the game into disrepute by giving an unauthorised interview, by delaying play during the Dulux final and by physical and mental abuse of Stevens. As no such allegations had been made prior to the appearance of the *Daily Star* article, it was widely inferred that the WPBSA wished to punish him for rocking the boat.

The furore did not do Stevens much good at the Crucible, either. He scraped past Ray Edmonds at 10-8 but subsided tamely 13-6 to John Parrott.

The pick of the first-round matches was a characteristic recovery by Cliff Thorburn, who trailed Mike Hallett 6-1 before getting through 10-8. Having been 52-1 ahead at 7-4 and 43-0 at 8-7, Hallett let both these crucial frames slip away as his own inexperience and the determined quality of Thorburn's resistance swung the match round.

The closest second-round match provided a 13-11 win for Jimmy White over his lifelong friend Tony Meo, while an interesting contest at the same stage produced a 13-9 win for Ray Reardon over Patsy Fagan.

Having played two tournaments in spectacles and one wearing a green eye shade, the veteran former champion chose to rely again on unassisted vision, which was just good enough, as it turned out, to beat Eugene Hughes 10-9 in the opening round. Fagan had slithered down the rankings to 37th, hampered since the late 1970s by the psychological block which affected him when using the rest and was at times so acute that he could not even strike the cue-ball. He had experienced sporadic remission from his problem, and coming to the Crucible this time he felt that he had conquered it for good. There was reason to hope that the spectre of rest shots past had been finally dispelled by the blue for pink which crucially gave him 9-6 in his 10-6 first-round win over Willie Thorne.

He played quite well against Reardon but not quite well enough. When Reardon's tip came off in what proved to be the clinching frame, Fagan generously offered his own cue to finish off the match. Sadly, Fagan's psychological block returned soon afterwards and this time his slide down the rankings was so irretrievable as to take him out of the game and into working as a security guard and, later, a milkman.

Reardon, meanwhile, went on to beat Parrott 13-12 in the quarter-finals in an

DENNIS TAYLOR'S DESERT ISLAND FRAME

It was a time for bravery; it was a time for caution; it was a time for hope; it was a time for fear. After 34 frames and 15 hours battling, the Embassy World Championship final depended on the last four colours of the 35th and final frame. Davis needed to pot only one to leave Taylor needing a snooker; Taylor needed all four. The illustrations opposite analyse the last ten shots of what the new world champion will always store in his memory as Dennis Taylor's Desert Island Frame

archetypal confrontation of Experience v Youth to reach his first semi-final of the season. Parrott led 4-0, 7-3 and 9-5 before Reardon steadily hauled back the deficit, so that from 7-9 going into the final session he won the first five frames of the evening to lead 12-9. A run of three frames for Parrott levelled the match at 12-12, whereupon Reardon laid a masterly snooker on the last red in the decider, extracted a free ball from it and did not allow his opponent another shot.

In the other quarter-finals, Davis overturned a 0-4 deficit to beat Griffiths 13-6; Knowles, more assured under pressure, beat White 13-10; and Taylor ground out a 13-5 win over Thorburn, the middle session of which did not finish until 1.21 a.m.

Reardon's immense experience got him nowhere against Davis, who beat him 16-5 with a session to spare. The same fate befell Knowles at the hands of Dennis Taylor in the other semi-final.

Davis was massively impressive in winning the first eight frames of the final, his safety shots settling magnetically on the baulk cushion, his potting sure, and the infrequency of his mistakes offering his opponent minimal encouragement. Taylor's head sank deeper into his collar, his face an ever deepening shade of red, not through anger but through the kind of frustration which is bottled up anger.

Two long frames in the next three went to Taylor, who then found himself cueing freely. Davis had started so well that he could only deteriorate, while Taylor had been so overwhelmed that any positive return seemed a bonus. Taylor won the five remaining frames of the day to trail only 7-9. The following afternoon, Davis was caught at 11-11 before two black-ball wins gave him a 13-11 lead after three sessions.

No summary could possibly convey a tithe of the excitement and emotion of the last evening's play. Taylor was judiciously

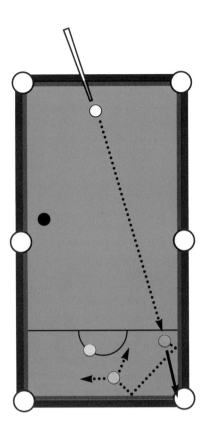

2 (Taylor)
Taylor was forced into playing the brown because it was so difficult to play safe; better to go for the pot with a 50-50 chance the brown might go safe than lose the match on a safety shot. The brown flew in and the cue-ball kissed the blue slightly towards the other baulk pocket.

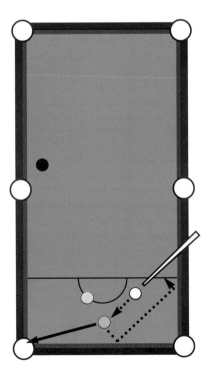

2 (Taylor)
The obvious percentage shot was to stun the blue round the table leaving the cue-ball on the baulk cushion, perhaps even behind the pink. Despite knowing that the match was over if he missed it, Taylor potted the blue with a slow cut.

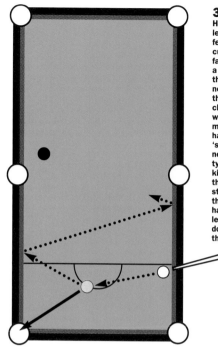

3 (Taylor)
Having intended to leave the cue-ball a few inches off the cushion, Taylor in fact left it less than a ball's width from the rail. There was no safety shot, only the slightest chance the pink would run safe if he missed it. Taylor had been a 'snatcher' of some notoriety on this type of shot in this kind of situation but this time not only struck bravely through the ball but had it in his mind to leave position to double the black for the championship.

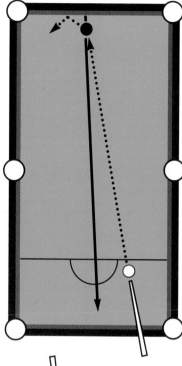

5 (Davis)
Davis played a superb safety in the circumstances. Playing across the black as he was, the double kiss and thus the fatal error was a distinct possibility. Too thin a contact would almost certainly have been disastrous too.

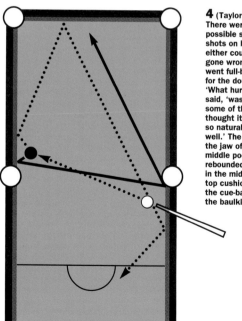

4 (Taylor)
There were two possible safety shots on but, as either could have gone wrong, Taylor went full-bloodedly for the double. 'What hurt,' he said, 'was that some of the crowd thought it was in, so naturally I did as well.' The black hit the jaw of the middle pocket and rebounded to safety in the middle of the top cushion with the cue-ball near the baulkline.

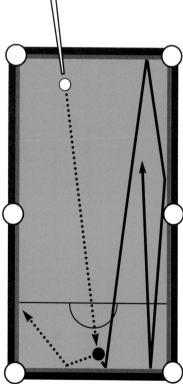

6 (Taylor)
Taylor was left with virtually the same shot but with the added difficulty of having to play against the nap. He knew there was an outside chance of doubling the black into the top pocket but concentrated mostly on keeping the cue-ball as near as he could to the baulk and side cushion in the 'green' pocket area. He hoped also to put distance between cue-ball and black for Davis.

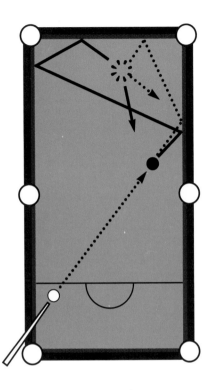

7 (Davis)
The black having just crept past the middle pocket, Davis faced a tricky safety shot. His intention was to double the black to safety off side, top and side cushions but too full a contact on the black – perhaps because he was also trying to get the cue-ball tight to the cushion behind the black spot – led to the black striking both side cushions before it struck the top. A kiss ensued.

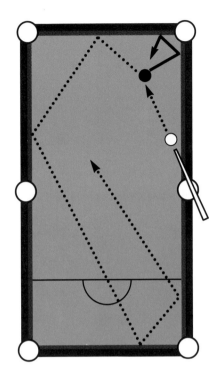

9 (Davis)
Davis would probably have potted the black four times out of five but two elements of technical difficulty contributed to his match-losing mistake. With the cue-ball close to the side cushion, he had to strike across the rail slightly downwards, thus exaggerating the effect of any minuscule off-centre cueing. Worse, cutting at a quarter-ball, the pocket was out of vision as he aimed through the cue-ball to the point of the black he wanted it to strike. The pressure of having to 'remember' where the pocket was, instead of having it in his line of sight, stimulated the anxiety and thus the overcut.

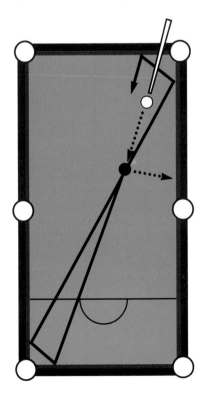

8 (Taylor)
Attempting the championship-ball black, Taylor had a threequarter ball angle and not much distance between cue-ball and object-ball. In retrospect, it was probably a slightly easier chance than the one he was to leave Davis. When he saw the black had missed the baulk pocket and was returning towards the top, he did not even stop to see where it was going to finish. He assumed he had lost and it was only when he was back in his chair that he realised that the black was not quite a formality.

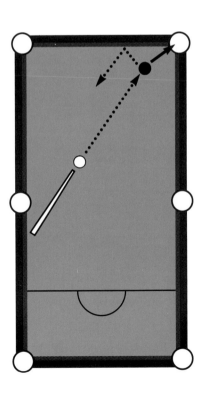

10 (Taylor)
Davis having made too thin a contact on the black, most of the speed of the shot remained on the cue-ball with so little of it transferred to the black that the black could not run very far from the pocket. Taylor could not have asked for a much easier championship-winning opportunity but, as he said with feeling: 'It was a good job the black was over the pocket.'

Dennis Taylor exultant, having potted the final black to beat Steve Davis 18-17 in their epic 1985 world final

brave, Davis instinctively apprehensive at the prospect of having victory, which had seemed assured at 8-0, snatched away. To make this worse, he carried the emotional scar tissue of having lost the 1983 UK final to Higgins 15-16 after leading 7-0.

Taylor levelled at 15-15 but again fell behind with three to play. At 17-17, Taylor needed the last four colours to win. He potted brown, blue and pink and twice attempted the black to Davis's once before sinking it for the title. The deciding frame, in which Davis should have pre-empted any possibility of a close finish by taking advantage of a close-range chance in mid-frame, took 68 minutes. Its climax will be forever counted among the great moments in sport.

1985 EMBASSY WORLD CHAMPIONSHIP

FIRST ROUND: S. Davis beat N. Foulds 10-8; David Taylor beat D. O'Kane 10-4; A. Higgins beat D. Reynolds 10-4; T. Griffiths beat R. Williams 10-3; R. Reardon beat E. Hughes 10-9; P. Fagan beat W. Thorne 10-6; J. Parrott beat J. Spencer 10-3; K. Stevens beat R. Edmonds 10-8; C. Thorburn beat M. Hallett 10-8; B. Werbeniuk beat J. Johnson 10-8; Dennis Taylor beat S. Francisco 10-2; E. Charlton beat J. Campbell 10-3; J. White beat W. Jones 10-4; T. Meo beat J. Virgo 10-6; D. Mountjoy beat M. Macleod 10-5; A. Knowles beat T. Jones 10-8

SECOND ROUND: Davis beat David Taylor 13-4; Griffiths beat Higgins 13-7; Reardon beat Fagan 13-9; Parrott beat Stevens 13-6; Thorburn beat Werbeniuk 13-3; Taylor beat Charlton 13-6; White beat Meo 13-11; Knowles beat Mountjoy 13-6

QUARTER-FINALS: Davis beat Griffiths 13-6; Reardon beat Parrott 13-12; Taylor beat Thorburn 13-5; Knowles beat White 13-10

SEMI-FINALS: Davis beat Reardon 16-5; Taylor beat Knowles 16-5

FINAL: Taylor beat Davis 18-17

Dennis Taylor, the new world champion, immediately perceived that he could not continue to run his affairs like a cottage industry. He signed with Hearn, thus enrolling himself for the Far East summer circuit and a first trip to China. He also became involved in corporate efforts as various as royalty-based contracts with Goya's range of men's toiletries and a Chas 'n' Dave single, 'Snooker Loopy', which, with all Hearn's Matchroom players as the backing group, reached fifth place in the charts.

Davis, having again topped the money list with £182,501, broke new ground in Brazil. Before a television audience of 40 million, he played their national champion, Rui Chapeu, at the Brazilian variant of the game, using only one red and the colours on an eight-foot table. Trips to Dubai, Muscat, Oman and the continent of Europe, primarily or incidentally promoting Riley tables, were other passing shows in the rich pageant of Hearn's expanding empire.

Meo, the least well known of his players, won the Winfield Australian Masters by beating John Campbell, who a few weeks later deprived Eddie Charlton of the Australian championship he had held every year except one since 1964. Reardon was awarded the MBE, which proved to be a prelude to a dire season, in which his game disintegrated so badly that he won only two matches in the entire campaign.

The WPBSA's disciplinary structure, in reality little more than a kangaroo court, was exposed as the most precarious of edifices. A few weeks after the championship, the WPBSA fined Francisco £6,000 for his reported remarks about Stevens and deducted two of his world ranking points, a savage and unprecedented punishment which left him no alternative but to seek legal redress. It quickly became clear that the accepted principle of natural justice had not been observed. The WPBSA gave ground more grudgingly than might be considered fitting in dealing with one of its own members, eventually quashing its own decision, only to insist that the case be considered anew by an independent tribunal.

The WPBSA engaged Gavin Lightman, QC, to act in this capacity. Long before this point was reached, it emerged that, at the time in question, Stevens had been, as he put it in a signed *Daily Star* exclusive in June 1985, 'helplessly addicted to cocaine'. The *Daily Star* arranged and paid for his treatment in a Toronto drug clinic, without which he would have been unable to continue his snooker career.

Several newspapers formed the opinion that the WPBSA had not dealt with the matter in the most evenhanded and open manner possible. Inevitably, the WPBSA was exposed to a degree of critical scrutiny it had never previously experienced. Its relationship with all but the most malleable elements of the press deteriorated. Criticism of their handling of the matter did not subside, even after Lightman delivered judgement, in March 1986, that Francisco be fined £2,000 with £1,500 costs. In the year prior to this, Francisco hardly won a match of any significance.

The domestic season began with Davis making no defence of his Langs Scottish Masters title. With 40 days a year committed to his Courage contract and other segments of his time apportioned elsewhere, he decided to pick and choose to avoid burning himself out by an overcrowded schedule. He did not play in the Benson and Hedges Irish Masters either.

In his absence, Thorburn won the Scottish Masters, making total clearances of 133 and 142 in beating Francisco 6-0 in the semi-finals, before defeating Thorne 9-7 in the final. Thorburn also won the first ranking tournament of the season, in

Cliff Thorburn (to play) and Jimmy White pictured during the Goya International final in which Thorburn recovered from the loss of the first seven frames to win 12-10

and won 12-10.

The Rothmans Grand Prix final seemed unlikely to run the full distance when the interval arrived with Davis leading Taylor 6-1. However, as some negativity entered Davis's approach, Taylor grew heartened, so it was not until 2.14 a.m., the latest finish to a major final, that Davis secured the 10-9 victory which was worth £50,000 and an immeasurable amount in restored confidence.

Less than five hours later, the snooker circus was on the road to the inaugural BCE Canadian Masters, staged in the Canadian Broadcasting Corporation's biggest studio in Toronto. It was CBC's first attempt at self-originated extended coverage and the quality of play, particularly in the final, could not have been a better advertisement for the game. Davis led 3-1 but Taylor went ahead 4-3 at the interval, having made three centuries in four frames, the first such sequence since John Spencer's in the 1970 world final in Australia. There was a century on either side in the evening session before Taylor completed his 9-5 victory.

The Coral UK final seemed to be developing into another disappointment for Davis. Thorne, who had set a new tournament break record of 140 in his first match, disposed of Virgo 9-8 in a match in which the loser made three of the five centuries, before beating Thorburn 9-7, Griffiths 9-7 and Taylor 9-7. He maintained the same deadly consistency of breakbuilding to lead Davis 13-8 going into the final session. A tiddler of a blue, all he needed to go 14-8, eluded him in the first frame of the evening, whereupon Davis responded with all the new energy

which Jameson yielded its sponsorship to Goya at a new venue, Trentham Gardens, Stoke.

The first session of the final was, according to Thorburn, 'the finest exhibition of snooker I've ever seen'. The opening frame of the middle session turned the match. When it began White, who had beaten Davis in the quarter-finals, was 7-0 ahead. He led 74-0 with four reds remaining but three fouls, two of them leaving free balls, led to Thorburn clearing with 42 to win on the black. No frame in professional snooker had been won from such a deficit. White's feeling of omnipotence was shaken and Thorburn's self-esteem restored, to the extent that having closed to 6-8 overnight, Thorburn took five frames in succession from 6-9

of a reprieved man and, as Thorne faded, won 16-14.

Davis and Meo won the Hofmeister World Doubles for the third time in four years, albeit with ITV's coverage blacked out by industrial action. ITV were also unlucky that neither Thorne, the defending champion, nor Taylor, the world champion, survived to the televised phases of two of their other tournaments, the Mercantile Classic and the Dulux British Open.

The Mercantile Classic paralleled the Goya Trophy, not only in bringing a quarter-final defeat of Davis by White but in producing a White v Thorburn final. Having led 11-9 and 12-11, White

appeared to have missed the boat at 12-12, but with only pink and black remaining he obtained the snooker he needed and potted the two colours to win 13-12.

Off stage, Higgins's turbulent marriage came irrevocably apart, every detail meticulously researched by the tabloids. He beat Taylor in the Mercantile whilst sporting a black eye from a fist fight with one of his regular practice opponents, although he claimed in a television interview at the time that it had been sustained through a kick from a horse called Dreadnought. He later admitted the truth but was beaten by Williams, the WPBSA chairman, in a quarter-final which reminded the press room wags of an

Steve Davis (left) and Tony Meo, four times world doubles champions, both watch intently for the outcome of an opponent's shot

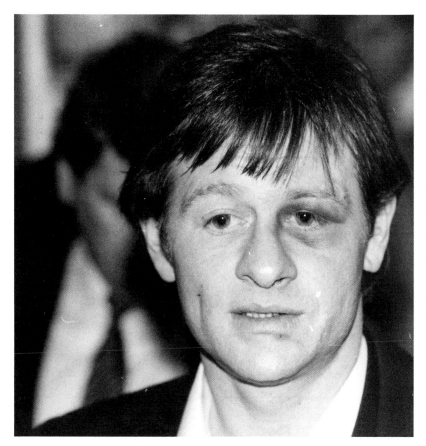

Alex Higgins (left), sporting a black eye which was not caused by a horse called Dreadnought, and Rex Williams, often a headmaster figure as WPBSA chairman

encounter between naughty pupil and headmaster. His frustrations, for neither the first nor last time, boiled over in defeat and his backstage conduct led to an appearance before a WPBSA disciplinary tribunal.

New ground was broken in Europe with the promotion of the BCE Belgian Classic, in which Griffiths beat Davis, Knowles and Stevens to win the £12,000 first prize, but *Pot Black* was discontinued after the 1986 series. Its one-frame, unsponsored studio-recorded format was generally perceived as outdated. With the WPBSA and the BBC both wishing to guard against overexposure, it was the game's most obvious candidate for redundancy.

Improving standards in the newer snooker nations were also evident in the 1985 world amateur championship, which attracted entrants from 25 countries to the

Tower Ballroom, Blackpool to celebrate the centenary of the B&SCC. Paul Mifsud, a Maltese who had renounced his briefly held professional status, won the title by beating a former Cardiff City goalkeeper, Dilwyn John, 11-6 in the final.

The Benson and Hedges Masters produced the third Thorburn-White final of the season, following White's semi-final victory over Davis, which was also his third of the campaign. Thorburn's 9-5 victory gave him the title for the third time in four years.

Meo, having lost all ten of his previous meetings with Davis, beat him 9-7 in the semi-finals of the Tolly Cobbold English championship and took the title by beating Foulds 9-7. Griffiths retained the Welsh championship under the new sponsorship of Zetters, and Stephen Hendry, having won the first of his two consecutive Scottish amateur titles at the age of 15, won the corresponding professional title at the age of 17.

Such was Davis's stature that if he went a couple of months without winning a tournament, it was invariably suggested that he was in some kind of irreversible decline. He belied this by crushing all and sundry at the Dulux British Open – including Thorne 12-7 in the final – then, having opted out of the Irish Masters, which was retained by White, he needed to maintain his peak for the Embassy World Championship seven weeks ahead.

EMBASSY WORLD CHAMPIONSHIP

For all Joe Johnson's steady progression in the world rankings, season by season: 52, 31, 22, 19 and 16, Coral could quote him at 150-1 for the title without evincing much interest from the betting fraternity. Despite having reached the final of the untelevised 1983 PPT, he had appeared in only one major semi-final on television. He had never won a match at the Crucible, and there was nothing remarkable in his early-round matches.

Bubbling beneath the surface, though, were a couple of positive factors, beyond the normal desire to do well, which helped account for his extraordinary capture of the title. Cheerfully admitting that he was 'besotted' with his second wife Terryll, he exuded happiness in his personal life. The championship also coincided with the anniversary of the Bradford Football Club fire disaster, and in his off-duty moments he wore a 'Bradford's Bouncing Back' T-shirt.

Wally Springett, then his manager, commented: 'I wouldn't say Joe lost a really close pal but he knows most of the Bradford families. You see, the sporting public round here come from the working men's clubs, which is Joe's world. We were saying, "Wouldn't it be great if we got a result and in a way reversed the situation".'

Stephen Hendry in his debut year at the Crucible

His path was smoothed at the beginning by an opening-day defeat, 10-6 by Mike Hallett, for Dennis Taylor who, like John Spencer in 1978, Terry Griffiths in 1980 and Steve Davis in 1982, thus failed to survive his first match on his return to the Crucible as champion.

A player who wins the title for the first time is under considerable pressure to capitalise on what may be a unique opportunity to lay a firm foundation of financial security for life. Accepting many lucrative offers to go here, there and everywhere and to do this, that and the other, he inevitably has less time to practise. Over a period, too, increasing tiredness limits the value of what practice he does still manage.

'I felt fine until I went into the arena. Then it hit me,' said Taylor, who lost the first seven frames. From 1-8, he did make a fight of it in the evening but had to concede defeat at 10-6.

Tony Knowles beat Neal Foulds 10-9, the first time in nine matches as a professional in which Foulds had lost by the odd frame; the tall Australian John Campbell, trailing 3-6 at the interval, recovered to record a 10-8 victory over Ray Reardon, a fast-fading force; Willie Thorne only just held off Crucible debutant Stephen Hendry, 10-8.

Johnson progressed quietly to the quarter-finals by beating Dave Martin 10-3 and Hallett, who appeared mentally drained from the effort of ousting Taylor,

13-6. He nevertheless remained the outsider to reach the final from the top half of the draw, in which the other quarter-finalists were Griffiths, a 13-12 winner over Higgins, Stevens, who beat Eddie Charlton from two down with three to play, and Knowles, who from 8-9 beat Silvino Francisco 13-10. In the bottom half, there were straightforward wins for Thorburn, Thorne, White and Davis.

Johnson's 13-12 quarter-final win over Griffiths convinced him for the first time of his title-winning potential: 'That's when I knew I was a good player.' From 7-9, Griffiths went three up with four to play, but early in the next frame, screwing back from green for a choice of easy reds, he uncharacteristically rushed his shot.

The enormity of his mistake soon became apparent as Johnson ran off a break of 102 to regain all his lost confidence. He added two more frame-winning breaks, 44

Joe Johnson played inspired snooker to beat Terry Griffiths from three down with four to play in their 1986 world quarter-final

Joe Johnson celebrates with his wife, Terryll, his unexpected capture of the 1986 world title

12-12 before a hard half-hour frame went to Davis, as did, crucially, one of 62 minutes which broke Thorburn's resistance.

Even though Johnson beat Knowles by the handy margin of 16-8 in the other semi-final, he began the final as the classic underdog, an impression which was strengthened by Davis making consecutive breaks of 108 and 107 to lead 3-1. Yet abruptly he went curiously flat, so that when Johnson ended the first session 4-3 ahead a few observers started to think the unthinkable.

Level at 8-8 overnight, Johnson led 13-11 after the third session, completed as it was by a 100 break from Davis in its last frame, and split the first two frames of the final session to lead 14-12. Once Davis had beaten White and Thorburn, the title had loomed like an open goal – except that suddenly the ball was no longer at his feet. The surge of inspiration he needed was not forthcoming, whereas Johnson was playing and feeling like a winner as the next four frames gave him the title. The final session was watched by an average of 11.3 million viewers, with a peak of 15.6 million.

and 110, and scored first in the decider with 54. Griffiths caught a tricky safety wrongly and Johnson, with 33, completed the amazing 52-minute four-frame burst which carried him to the semi-finals.

From 8-8, Knowles beat Stevens 13-9, and Thorburn, from 6-1, beat Thorne 13-6. Davis won by a much wider margin than expected, recording a 13-5 victory over White. Davis's 16-12 semi-final win over Thorburn, though, was closer than the score suggested, and certainly more exhausting, with frame upon frame producing long drawn-out safety duels of the highest quality, usually resolved by one decisive break. The match was level at

1986 EMBASSY WORLD CHAMPIONSHIP

FIRST ROUND: M. Hallett beat Dennis Taylor 10-6; J. Johnson beat D. Martin 10-3; A. Higgins beat J. Spencer 10-7; T. Griffiths beat D. Fowler 10-2; K. Stevens beat D. Reynolds 10-6; E. Charlton beat C. Wilson 10-6; S. Francisco beat R. Williams 10-4; A. Knowles beat N. Foulds 10-9; C. Thorburn beat B. Werbeniuk 10-5; E. Hughes beat David Taylor 10-7; W. Thorne beat S. Hendry 10-8; J. Campbell beat R. Reardon 10-8; J. White beat J. Virgo 10-7; J. Parrott beat T. Meo 10-4; D. Mountjoy beat P. Mans 10-3; S. Davis beat R. Edmonds 10-4

SECOND ROUND: Johnson beat Hallett 13-6; Griffiths beat Higgins 13-12; Stevens beat Charlton 13-12; Knowles beat Francisco 13-10; Thorburn beat Hughes 13-6; Thorne beat Campbell 13-9; White beat Parrott 13-8; Davis beat Mountjoy 13-5

QUARTER-FINALS: Johnson beat Griffiths 13-12; Knowles beat Stevens 13-9; Thorburn beat Thorne 13-6; Davis beat White 13-5

SEMI-FINALS: Johnson beat Knowles 16-8; Davis beat Thorburn 16-12

FINAL: Johnson beat Davis 18-12

Steve Davis's defeat by Joe Johnson in the world final affected his top place in neither the world rankings nor the money list, in which his £244,333 overshadowed even the three other totals exceeding £100,000.

Barry Hearn strengthened Matchroom's managerial and entrepreneurial hand by signing Jimmy White, thus giving him seven of the top 13 players, and negotiated sponsorship from Rothmans to start a January-to-May league comprising 28 matches in 14 British venues. There were critical murmurs that Hearn, while sitting on the WPBSA board, had approached a WPBSA sponsor to support his own event. Such criticism was deflected by Rothmans continuing their Grand Prix sponsorship until they withdrew from major sponsorship altogether in 1992.

During the summer, Davis visited Brazil for the second time and the Hearn troupe again went to the Far East, where James Wattana made his first notable impact by beating Taylor, Davis and Griffiths to win the Camus Thailand Masters. These matches were only of the best of three frames, but for a 17-year-old such a trio of victories was still no mean feat.

At home, Thorne beat Taylor and Davis to win the Matchroom Trophy, an event held at Southend solely for Hearn's players and run in date conflict with the established Langs Scottish Masters, which was won by Thorburn.

There was a whiff in the air of Hearn versus the WPBSA, which grew stronger with a squabble over a clash between the WPBSA's BCE Belgian Classic and two Hearn promotions, the Rothmans Matchroom League and an eight-man trip to Peking. Hearn obtained sponsorship of £100,000 from British American Tobacco for Peking and the Belgian Classic was cancelled, a turn of events which confirmed Hearn's position as the most potent force in snooker's overseas

development. Starting from scratch, he had taken his players to play tournaments in Hong Kong, Thailand, Singapore, Malaysia, China, Brazil and Japan. However, he appeared to want the best of both worlds: his manager's cut of the prizemoney his players could earn from WPBSA tournaments, as well as total freedom to organise his own events.

Off stage, Kirk Stevens almost died in a cocaine coma in early June; Silvino Francisco instituted libel actions against Rex Williams and John Virgo, respectively chairman and vice-chairman of the WPBSA, for remarks made in the aftermath of the Lightman hearing which resolved disciplinary charges against him. (These actions were ultimately settled in Francisco's favour.)

White, defending the Goya International, which had become the BCE International through a change of sponsorship, was a surprise 2-5 third-round loser to Ken Owers, who was playing in his first professional tournament. Eugene Hughes beat Steve Davis 5-4 in the quarter-finals but Neal Foulds, with some remarkably consistent long potting and a very positive attitude, founded on his belief that he was ready for major success, beat Hughes 9-8 in the semis and went on to win his first and so far only world ranking tournament title by beating Thorburn 12-9.

White won the Rothmans Grand Prix, but the star of the event was Rex Williams, who at the age of 53 not only beat Higgins 5-1, Davis 5-1 and Foulds 9-8, but led White 5-2 in the final before losing 6-10.

Davis won the second Canadian Masters in Toronto and beat Foulds 16-7 to win his third UK in succession and fifth in all at Preston, although this tended to be forgotten in the blaze of publicity attracted by an incident extraordinary even by the standards of Higgins.

A 9-8 winner over the 17-year-old

Stephen Hendry in a stirring third-round match, Higgins was asked to take a drugs test after he had beaten Mike Hallett 9-7 in the fifth to reach the quarter-finals. When he felt he was being hurried by the tournament director, Paul Hatherell, he head-butted him.

On borrowed time, Higgins beat Wayne Jones 9-5, but as he was losing 3-9 to Davis in the semis, it was already clear that he had a hefty punishment to look forward to. At Preston Magistrates Court, he was fined £200 for assault and £50 for criminal damage to a door. His trial over, the Lightman tribunal followed. He was fined £12,000, easily a record for snooker, and suspended from five tournaments.

Davis, who had overcome Tony Drago 9-8 in the quarter-finals only because the dashing Maltese had missed a simple yellow in the decider, beat Foulds 16-7 in the final. He was to go three months without defeat, retaining the Hofmeister World Doubles with Meo and beating White 13-12 to win the Mercantile Classic.

The first trace of a Davis v Hendry rivalry was becoming discernible. The young Scot's talent was obvious as he partnered Mike Hallett to the final of the Hofmeister World Doubles, in which they were beaten 12-3 by Davis and Meo, and in reaching the semi-finals of the Mercantile Classic, in which Davis, clearly feeling the need to assert himself against the Young Pretender, beat him 9-3.

There were some things Hendry could learn only by playing Davis more often. So his manager, Ian Doyle, arranged a series of matches in Scotland which Davis was to win 6-0, although the young Scot was the greater beneficiary in experience and first-hand appreciation of shot selection.

Davis lost at last, going down 2-5 to Doug Mountjoy in the first round of the Benson and Hedges Masters. Dennis Taylor, having won only one match in the Masters in ten attempts, took the title by beating Thorburn 6-5 on the final black and Higgins from three down with four to play in a final which ran until 1.09 a.m. Higgins, at 8-5 within a ball of winning his first major title since the 1983 UK, missed a difficult black from distance.

Off table, there was uproar when the WPBSA board proposed to change the World Cup format from national teams of three to eight trios selected arbitrarily

Alex Higgins faces the world after his notorious head-butt

from the top 24 in the rankings. Critics were quick to point out that television exposure and prizemoney was thereby guaranteed to three players on the ten-man board who would otherwise not have qualified. Another board member, Barry Hearn, was also a potential beneficiary as the manager of three players who would otherwise have been excluded. Such was the reaction that the board caved in.

Out of the blue, John Virgo beat Davis 5-4 in the last 32 of the Dulux British Open. Neal Foulds, making two total clearances of 144 and 140 in beating Tony Knowles 9-2 in the semi-finals, actually nosed ahead of Davis in ranking points earned that season, but lost the final 13-9 to White.

Perhaps the accumulated strain of playing so many pressure matches in one season finally got through to Foulds, for having led 8-7 overnight, he won only one frame on the last afternoon. He was also under stress from a disintegrating marriage and when, a couple of weeks later, his heart began to beat alarmingly rapidly as he lay in bed, he was prescribed Tenormin – and unwittingly sent the beta blocker issue in snooker sky high.

At the Benson and Hedges Irish Masters, indignant bookmakers alleged, with the minimum of evidence, that certain matches were being rigged by the players. A couple of bets of about £1,000 were frantically laid off all over Southern Ireland, thus giving credence to a scare that a coup was afoot. Malcolm Palmer of Coral, who in their long association with snooker never cast a single slur against the integrity of the players, explained: 'We used to have an Irishman who had an uncanny knack with frame scores. He said he had a system and promised to explain it to us one day. What sometimes happens is that a punter may fancy a sizeable bet and decides to spread it around. You only have to have a few bets on the same score, for instance, and it can look like a coup.'

The furore had died down by the time Davis won the tournament, dropping only five frames out of 25 and offering a foretaste of the formidable consistency he was to show at Sheffield.

EMBASSY WORLD CHAMPIONSHIP

'Winning this is better than 1981 because I've experienced getting beat in the final and it's horrible,' said Davis after winning his fourth title.

The fear of experiencing again the trauma of unexpected defeat on snooker's most special occasion, as he had in losing to Johnson in 1986, or worse, of feeling again the mounting panic of having an almost invulnerable lead whittled away, as had happened against Taylor in 1985, added a cruelly testing mental dimension to the technical challenges which the occasion, the game itself and the opposition invariably posed.

He came under unexpected pressure in his opening match against Warren King, who put together four fine frames to close to 7-8, Davis having led 7-2 and 8-3. The Australian also led 51-2 in the 16th as 8-8 loomed, before Davis snookered him and from the resultant leave cleared with 63 for the black-ball win which gave him 9-7. Another black-ball win completed his 10-7 victory.

Ray Reardon played his best half session against a top player for two seasons in leading Davis 3-1 in the second round but lost 13-4. 'It's a young man's game now,' said Reardon wistfully. 'You hang in there for five furlongs, then they pot you off the table. Let's hope they keep up the tradition of our game.'

After a tough 4-3 first session, Davis disposed of Griffiths for the fifth time at the Crucible, 13-5, prior to his 16-11 semi-final victory over White. 'If you don't stay with Steve, he gets stronger and stronger,' said White, identifying Davis's four-frame surge from 4-4 to 8-4 as key. Perhaps he preferred to forget potting the

Dene O'Kane, twice a world quarter-finalist

first ten reds with nine blacks at 6-9, only for Davis to win the frame after needing two snookers.

White had not reached the semi-finals the easy way. Down 7-8 to Dean Reynolds, he flew past the post at 10-8 with three frame-winning breaks, 70, 75 and 59, and was within a ball of being taken the full distance by John Parrott before a black-ball win made him a 13-11 winner.

His 13-6 quarter-final win over Dene O'Kane was based on an 8-0 opening-session whitewash, but the New Zealander had already covered himself in glory by beating Thorburn and Mountjoy. Thorburn, 5-1 ahead, had split his tip and neither that day, nor with a new tip the following afternoon, did he win another frame. It was a similar story in the next round as O'Kane took 13 of the last 15 frames to beat Mountjoy 13-5.

Johnson's year as champion had been an almost unmitigated disaster, with a semi-final and a last 16 as his two best finishes. The one factor in his favour was that he had suffered so many disappointments that the worst was out of his system by the time his title defence fell due.

He was thought to have every chance of losing in the first round, but managed a

10-9 win over Eugene Hughes. Murdo Macleod, a 10-5 winner over Rex Williams to become the first Scot to win a match at the Crucible, was Johnson's 13-7 second-round victim. Another Scot, Stephen Hendry, qualified to meet him in the quarter-finals by beating Thorne, to whom he had lost on his Crucible debut the previous year, and Steve Longworth.

Hendry, still inconsistent, dropped the first session of his quarter-final 7-1 to Johnson. At 9-3 and 12-8, Johnson was still in a commanding position, but from 0-47 in the next frame, Hendry cleared with 80 and reeled off three more frames for 12-12. Johnson kept cool, making a 46 in the decider and forcing the young Scot's resignation with two reds remaining, but he was warm in his appreciation of his performance.

Foulds, Johnson's semi-final opponent, had the misfortune of being trapped in the uproar over beta blockers, a group of perfectly respectable drugs which slow the heartbeat and tend to reduce tremor and anxiety symptoms. Because of this quality, they are widely held to be capable of enhancing performance in sports like archery, shooting and snooker.

The WPBSA never intended their use to be questioned, but the board, hearing rumours of Stevens's problems with narcotics two years earlier, was nervous of damaging publicity if this came to light. Naïvely, they thought that drug testing would be directed against drugs which were against the law, rather than those which informed medical opinion consid-ered might be potentially performance enhancing.

Not very far into its relationship with the Sports Council and its drug testing unit at King's College, Chelsea, the WPBSA found that the use of beta

blockers was taken very seriously and that
they were within a few months of being
banned by the Medical Commission of the
International Olympic Committee. In vain
did the WPBSA say that snooker was not
an Olympic sport. The Sports Council

attitude was that if the WPBSA wanted
the credibility which they and their drug
testing procedures represented, they would
have to toe the line.

The most embarrassing aspect of this
was that Rex Williams, the WPBSA

Steve Davis reverses his defeat by Joe Johnson in the 1986 world final to recapture the title in 1987

chairman, was revealed by the *Sunday Times* to be an unrepentant beta blocker taker and that several other players were also using them regularly. At various times the names of the gargantuan Canadian Bill Werbeniuk, two Scottish professionals, Murdo Macleod and Eddie Sinclair, Alex Higgins and John Dunning, a veteran Yorkshireman with a heart condition, came to light. Anecdotal evidence was that some forms of beta blocker may have been helpful to performance, others not. The Minister for Sport, Colin Moynihan, was unequivocal in his assessment that taking them was 'tantamount to cheating'.

Foulds had been prescribed Tenormin for sound medical reasons and was certainly not the type knowingly to try to assist himself with a performance enhancing drug. Trailing Johnson 4-3 after the first of the four sessions of their semi-final, he decided to take a chance medically and not swallow his prescribed tablet. He won the session 4-3 to level at 7-7. Feeling muzzy later on, he felt he needed a tablet. That evening, he lost the third session 7-1 and Johnson went on to win 16-9, elated to reach the final again.

This year, though, inspiration of his 1986 vintage was not forthcoming, and Davis was fresher. Johnson led 4-3 after

one session but trailed 7-9 after two and 10-14 after three.

The first three frames of the final session provided the most exciting phase of the match. All the ghosts of the previous two Crucible finals returned to haunt Davis, while Johnson raised visions of an astounding victory as he recovered to 13-14.

The pressure Davis was certainly feeling was reflected as he missed a couple of balls, but Johnson's first attempt at a long pot in the 28th frame scattered the pack and let Davis in for 64. With 40 for good measure, he had the reassurance of a two-frame lead of 15-13 at the intermission. Two more rock solid frames put him four up with five to play and victory arrived at 18-14.

Johnson, hard as he had tried, was in some ways relieved to be divested of the burdens of title and celebrity. His only thought on arrival at the Crucible had been to try to beat Eugene Hughes in the first round. Sadly the easygoing Yorkshireman was to suffer problems which ranged from eyesight to mismanagement to a heart attack, which could so easily have ended not merely his career but his life.

1987 EMBASSY WORLD CHAMPIONSHIP

FIRST ROUND: J. Johnson beat E. Hughes 10-9; M. Macleod beat R. Williams 10-5; J. Longworth beat K. Stevens 10-4; S. Hendry beat W. Thorne 10-7; M. Hallett beat A. Knowles 10-6; S. Francisco beat J. Campbell 10-3; N. Foulds beat J. Virgo 10-4; Dennis Taylor beat M. Bennett 10-4; D. O'Kane beat C. Thorburn 10-5; D. Mountjoy beat David Taylor 10-5; J. Parrott beat T. Meo 10-8; J. White beat D. Reynolds 10-8; A. Higgins beat J. Wright 10-6; T. Griffiths beat J. Wych 10-4; R. Reardon beat B. West 10-5; S. Davis beat W. King 10-7

SECOND ROUND: Johnson beat Macleod 13-7; Hendry beat Longworth 13-7; Hallett beat Francisco 13-9; Foulds beat Dennis Taylor 13-10; O'Kane beat Mountjoy 13-5; White beat Parrott 13-11; Griffiths beat Higgins 13-10; Davis beat Reardon 13-4

QUARTER-FINALS: Johnson beat Hendry 13-12; Foulds beat Hallett 13-9; White beat O'Kane 13-6; Davis beat Griffiths 13-5

SEMI-FINALS: Johnson beat Foulds 16-9; Davis beat White 16-11

FINAL: Davis beat Johnson 18-14

The money list for the 1986-87 season had been divided into Hearners and non-Hearners. The Hearn camp (Davis, White, Foulds, Thorne, Meo, Taylor and Griffiths) had won all six world ranking tournaments (Davis three, White two, Foulds one) and aggregated £1,076,680 in prizemoney.

Hearn, reigning over a wide off-table empire, offered the board – of which he was a member – £12.5 million for the television and promotional rights to the championship from 1991 to 2000. At the time, the WPBSA's contracts with the BBC, Embassy and the Crucible were due to run out with the 1990 championship. Hearn believed that snooker was 'on the verge of a global breakthrough, the like of which no sport has seen for a hundred years'. He had noted, though, that Davis's £80,000 prize for his fourth world title had been only about half Wimbledon's first prize, whereas in 1981 the prize for his first title had been about the same as John McEnroe had received for winning Wimbledon. The offer made no progress and, indeed, may never have been put in writing.

Hearn, on his side, was voicing criticism of the champagne lifestyle of the WPBSA's inner circle and was worried that the association was not commercially as healthy as it should have been. WPBSA Ltd seemed to have started a wholly owned subsidiary, WPBSA Promotions Ltd, for little reason other than to keep the financial details of tournaments under the kind of wraps that this arrangement permitted.

The key figure at the WPBSA's Bristol headquarters was Del Simmons, by now the WPBSA's £65,000 a year contracts negotiator, whose skill at interpersonal politics made him a formidable internal power broker. He was one of three board members due for re-election at the 1987 AGM. There were only three places available but it transpired, after legal consultation, that the voting members (at that stage the top 20 in the rankings for the last three years plus members of the board) could exercise a 'yes' or 'no' vote regardless. Phone lines hummed and proxies were organised until, with a proxy vote of 18-1 standing against him, Simmons resigned before the meeting.

This created a vacancy on the board which Hearn proposed be filled by Howard Kruger, who had met Tony Knowles on a beach in Marbella and decided to go into snooker management. Alex Higgins, Joe Johnson, Eugene Hughes, Mark Bennett and, on a more limited arrangement, John Parrott were already in his Framework stable, which was to mushroom, collapse and leave most players involved in it with severe financial bruising. The WPBSA badly needed men of vision who could assess its shortcomings, tackle the problems inherent in its constitutional and disciplinary systems, and work out long-term policies. Instead, it seemed steadfastly determined to keep power within an inner group and to react issue by issue on a contingency basis.

Neither was it above adopting a threatening tone to any player considered to be rocking the boat. When Dean Reynolds (who was to become another dissatisfied Kruger client) was critical of players using beta blockers, he was 'reprimanded' – a disciplinary action which was taken into account on a subsequent issue. The decision was taken by a disciplinary panel of three, chaired by one beta blocker user, Williams, and containing Hearn, who managed another, Foulds.

The bulk of Hearn's energies were, as ever, directed commercially. He did not agree terms for any of his players to compete in the Winfield Australian Masters in Sydney, which was won by Hendry, an achievement less widely recognised than it might have been, as the anti-tobacco lobby prevented the event being screened.

Hearn did make a cautious alliance with Mark McCormack's International Management Group, who were dipping their toe in snooker waters with a straight pool/snooker/nine ball triathlon featuring Davis and the American pool star, Steve Mizerak. IMG's television arm, Trans World International, promoted and recorded this at the Palace Hotel in St Moritz for showing on the American ESPN network and elsewhere. Indeed, had Hearn and TWI's head of European affairs, Bill Sinrich, been able to unite on the snooker front for their common benefit, the WPBSA could easily have been reduced to some kind of organisational shell. As it was, they soon fell out and Hearn declined to allow TWI a piece of World Series, eight linked events in Tokyo, Hong Kong, Toronto, Las Vegas and four other cities which were never, in fact, decided upon.

The WPBSA board had abandoned its hopes of building up an international circuit, by resolving in December 1986 to work with individual promoters, like Hearn, rather than to promote any more overseas events itself. This board also voted a £50,000 WPBSA subsidy for the Toronto leg of World Series.

Very properly, Hearn then resigned from the WPBSA board on the grounds that his private promotion of World Series was in conflict with his responsibility to the WPBSA's world championship contract with Embassy, which expressly precluded the WPBSA from sanctioning the use of the word 'world' in any other singles competition.

Hearn's resignation was immediately followed by the remaining directors passing a vote of no confidence in the chairmanship of Williams. While the beta blocker controversy had done him no good and some did not like his style, the chief complaint appeared to be that he had

allied himself too closely with Hearn, who had invited him to commentate on the Tokyo and Hong Kong legs. He had also joined Hearn's seven players on the visit to Peking the previous April, ostensibly on the grounds that the Chinese premier, Deng Xiao Ping, had a sentimental attachment to billiards because he had played it as a young man. Williams played a billiards exhibition with Davis but Deng did not attend.

While Williams remained for a while as chairman on a technicality, snooker threatened to split apart. Hearn considered setting up, as the boxing world long since had, an alternative governing body, perhaps with Williams as chairman, but was not convinced this was necessary and was certainly reluctant to forgo income from the prize funds of WPBSA tournaments.

In opposition, Hearn ran rings round the WPBSA. In managership, overseas promotion and high-profile publicity getting, snooker had never had anyone like him. He had chanced upon a commercially under-exploited sport at its point of maximum growth and had found it almost too easy to become king.

His frailties were his entrepreneurial restlessness and his wish to become a star himself. He moved into boxing to promote the Frank Bruno v Joe Bugner fight at White Hart Lane, and it was not long before his snooker players began to gripe that his interests had shifted. At the same time, another boxing figure, Frank Warren, took over Rex Williams's Leisure plc and began to express an interest in snooker.

Barry Hearn, snooker's foremost manager and entrepreneur in the 1980s

With Hearn gone from the board, Ian Doyle, whose managership of Stephen Hendry was the foundation of his Cuemasters group which grew to ten players, declined the opportunity to replace him. 'Ideally, I should not be on the board; but who is there in snooker who does not have a vested interest of one sort or another?' he asked. This was the WPBSA's chief problem in a nutshell.

It had become true of Hearn that the more significantly his players performed, the more influence he had. On this principle, Doyle's clout in the game's internal politics rose with Hendry.

The first world ranking tournament of the 1987-88 season, sponsored by Fidelity Unit Trusts, was won by Davis, who beat Thorburn 12-5 in the final, Hendry having lost 1-9 to Thorburn in the semi. Hendry's major breakthrough came unexpectedly swiftly. After beating Davis 5-2 in the last 16 of the Rothmans Grand Prix, he disposed of Tony Knowles 5-2, John Parrott 9-7 and Dennis Taylor 10-7 to win the title. No other 18-year-old had ever got near to winning a ranking event.

The following week Taylor won the BCE Canadian Masters by beating Jimmy White 9-7. That event was promoted, as it had previously been, as a self-contained tournament, rather than as the third leg of World Series, whose fundamental problem, it was becoming clear, was that Hearn had announced it without having all events securely in place.

His own Tournament of Champions at Southend for his seven players was won by Taylor, who beat Davis for the third time in four attempts in the semi-finals. Hearn, years ahead of the WPBSA in carving out niches in the burgeoning world of satellite television, had the event covered by Super Channel and syndicated its highlights.

IMG, rebuffed by Hearn when they wanted to be involved in World Series, concentrated on an alliance with the WPBSA who, fearful that this smooth,

well connected, octopus of an organisation might acquire too much influence in the sport, surprisingly rejected its first offer of £925,000 prizemoney for four overseas world ranking tournaments. In due course, no-one came to be more relieved about this than IMG.

At the Tennents UK Championship, Hendry fell to earth, losing 7-9 in the third round to Jim Wych. Dennis Taylor beat Les Dodd 9-8, having to take the last seven frames; Alex Higgins, back from suspension in his old head-butting haunt, lost 2-9 to Davis in the last 16; Willie Thorne made three centuries in the evening session in beating Cliff Thorburn 9-8 in the quarter-finals. In another quarter-final, Joe Johnson was trailing Mike Hallett 3-4 after their afternoon session, having developed chest pains and a shaking in his hands. When he was examined by a doctor during the interval, nothing amiss was found, but the doctor offered to prescribe him a beta blocker.

Stephen Hendry won the 1987 Rothmans Grand Prix to become, at the age of 18, the youngest-ever winner of a world ranking title

With a quip of 'No thanks. I'd rather die,' Johnson returned in the evening to win 9-7.

Johnson's semi-final against Jimmy White was psychologically decided by the third frame, in which he was within two pots of a 147 maximum and a £50,000 jackpot. He left the cue-ball the wrong side of the blue and missed the pink from middle distance. The disappointment, the expenditure of nervous energy and the anticlimax drained him. 'I couldn't play after that. I was lucky to win another frame,' he said after losing 4-9.

Davis beat Thorne 9-2 in the other semi and White 16-14 in a final which he regarded as 'the highest-standard match I've ever played in'. The first day's 14 frames produced 12 breaks over 50, including three centuries, as frame after frame was decided simply by some initial sparring and one knockout blow.

White led 12-11, but at 14-14, Davis's 110, his third century of the session and fifth of the match, put him one up with two to play. Then, trailing by 25, he forced White into a safety error and cleared to the pink with 42 to take the title.

What proved to be the last world doubles championship saw a 20 per cent decline in attendances, which posed the question whether doubles was a commercially attractive form of the game. Davis and Tony Meo, champions on four of the five occasions it had been contested, were beaten 5-1 in the third round by Martin Clark and Jim Chambers, with Hendry and Hallett taking the title.

The first post-Christmas tournament, the Mercantile Classic, was notable for John Parrott, who had improved his ranking each year he had been a professional, reaching his first major final via convincing wins over Dennis Taylor and Tony Knowles. Down 5-9 after two sessions to Davis, he started the last with a break of 103 and led 11-10.

However, by this stage of his career, Davis had won so much and so regularly that his fear of losing, except in world championships, was comparatively slight. Parrott, in contrast, was still at the stage where the imminent prospect of a first major title could disturb his concentration. Well in with 31, the heady vision of two up with three to play loomed, until an easy red eluded him and Davis, with three frame-winning breaks of 83, 68 and 99, prevailed 13-11.

Having come so close to snooker's runaway No. 1 in a major final, Parrott had a right to be confident, but a premature assumption of victory undid him in the semi-final of the Benson and Hedges Masters. Luck had appeared to be running his way when he fluked a crucial ball in the deciding ninth frames against both Neal Foulds and Cliff Thorburn but, from 43 in front with only the colours remaining, he contrived to lose 5-6 to Mike Hallett. Davis, mindful that he had won only one Masters, took his second by annihilating Hallett 9-0.

Behind the scenes, the first World Series crashed. Hearn released a story to the Press Association's wire service – timed for 4.30 on a Saturday afternoon, just before the football results, to ensure minimal impact – saying that World Series would not be completed in 1988 but might be relaunched in 1989. He cheerily stated that clashes with the Olympic Games and the World Cup, which he might have been expected to foresee, had made it too difficult to sell television packages.

The killing thrust, apparently, was that Howard Kruger, who had built up a management stable of his own, had undercut the Hearn promotion with the sponsors, British American Tobacco. Hearn rubbished the Kruger venture, not without justification as it turned out, and admitted that he was considering an alternative governing body, International Snooker Federation, with the aim of

ensuring 'that the very top players are properly represented'.

The WPBSA, of which John Virgo had become chairman in succession to Rex Williams, had a slightly different objective: as many tournaments as possible open to all members, and a somewhat wider spread of the prize funds than was envisaged by the limited-field invitation events which Hearn was trying to sell to sponsors.

The national professional championships, whose prize funds were subsidised to the tune of £1,000 per entrant from the WPBSA's own coffers, gave practical support for this policy. Dean Reynolds and Jack McLaughlin were surprise winners of the English and Irish titles respectively, while Terry Griffiths

won the Welsh for the third time, and Hendry won the Scottish so commandingly that his manager, Ian Doyle, tactlessly said it was not worth his time to compete against such poor opposition.

Hearn then struck at the WPBSA by allying himself with Frank Warren (who wanted quality events for the much delayed London Arena in Docklands) and Bill Sinrich of TWI (rebuffed by the WPBSA and still seeking an angle of entry to snooker) to announce – during the WPBSA's MIM Britannia British Open – a World Matchplay Championship and World Open Championships.

The latter was never staged and the former involved dislodging one of the four elements of the WPBSA's ITV contract,

The commercial triumvirate who challenged the WPBSA: Frank Warren, the boxing promoter (left), Barry Hearn (centre) and Bill Sinrich of Mark McCormack's International Management Group

that for the World Doubles, the weakest in viewing terms. Trevor East, a friend of Hearn and ITV's executive producer in charge of network snooker, liked the sound of an eight-man world matchplay. None of the WPBSA's other 120 professionals liked the loss of an earning opportunity this would entail.

ITV nevertheless pulled the plug on the doubles and told the WPBSA that they would be interested in a Masters-type event for the top 16. However, ITV's contract with WPBSA stipulated that 13 of the top 16 must enter, whereupon Hearn intimated that four of his top sixteeners would not. The WPBSA had to cave in to avoid losing a plum ITV slot for snooker, salvaging only the concession of a 12- rather than eight-man field.

On the boxing model of several world-title sanctioning bodies, each allied to powerful television interests, Hearn, Warren and Sinrich admitted that they 'went a long way down that road'. Doyle, holding a key card in Hendry, declined to join them.

The WPBSA would have had only itself to blame since its insularity, champagne lifestyle and mishandling of one issue after another were eroding its credibility. Had the Hearn-Warren-Sinrich alliance been a little more interested in structure and a little less in commercial opportunism, it could have relegated the WPBSA to an insignificant role as a players' trade union. As it was, the moment passed.

While Hearn v WPBSA was in full swing, Davis lost by the amazing margin of 0-5 in the third round of the British Open to Ray Reardon, now 38th in the rankings and trying to accustom himself to contact lenses, in place of the spectacles to which he had never fully adapted. Hendry beat White 5-4 on the final black in the quarter-finals, and Thorburn 9-5 in the semis. Hallett beat Parrott only 9-8 from 7-3 up in the other semi-final, but to ITV's mortification Hendry's 13-2

drubbing of Hallett provided only 11 minutes' play for their plum-slot final session.

The outcome of one backstage occurrence at Derby, a drug test, brought snooker unwelcome publicity. With the Embassy World Championship only a few weeks away, it was leaked to the *Sun* that Thorburn had tested positive for cocaine. Hearn, who had recently signed him, engaged lawyers who won a High Court injunction to postpone the disciplinary hearing until after the championship. When Gavin Lightman, QC, did adjudicate on this matter, Thorburn was charged not with any specific drug offence but with 'bringing the game into disrepute', some indication perhaps that the WPBSA's mandatory penalties might not have been legally enforceable. Thorburn was fined £10,000, docked two world ranking points and banned from the first two ranking events of the following season, all penalties much less severe than they would have been under the drug rules.

It was another blow to the WPBSA's credibility as a governing body, and Michael Calvin commented in the *Daily Telegraph* that 'the presence of an independent QC on the WPBSA's disciplinary panel could not dispel the suspicion that an uneasy compromise had been reached'.

EMBASSY WORLD CHAMPIONSHIP

Never before had Steve Davis gone to Sheffield having won three ranking tournaments and both the Benson and Hedges Masters and Irish Masters. He never looked like losing and often played to a standard which demoralised at least two of his opponents: Mike Hallett was beaten 13-1, and Tony Drago, whose dashing style had accounted for both Alex Higgins and Dennis Taylor, fell 13-4.

Cliff Thorburn was in Davis's half and as chance would have it drew another

Canadian with cocaine associations, Kirk Stevens. There was a whiff of embarrassment in the air. Thorburn's 10-6 win put Stevens, once No. 4, out of the top 32 and thus no longer guaranteed a place in the last 64 of world ranking events. The fuss had died down by the time Thorburn held off John Parrott 13-10 and Steve James 13-11 to reach the semi-finals where, from 8-6, Davis drew away to beat him 16-8.

In this half, much of the excitement was provided by James, who made breaks of 104 and 140 in his debut session at the Crucible in beating Rex Williams 10-6. He was fortunate to be there at all. Only ten days before the championship, he had turned his BMW over at high speed and escaped with a few bruises.

In his 13-9 second-round win over Joe Johnson, James took 14 red-blacks only to overhit position for his 15th red with the £90,000 jackpot for a 147 a distinct possibility. A place in the semi-finals appeared within his compass when he held Thorburn to 9-9 but at 9-10, having made a 67 break, he lost the frame after Thorburn had needed a snooker. Twice he reduced the gap to a single frame but was beaten 11-13.

The match of the championship came early in the other half when Jimmy White beat Stephen Hendry 13-12 to reach the quarter-finals. This supreme potting and

Jimmy White (left) and Stephen Hendry focus mentally for the deciding frame of their superb second-round match in the 1988 Embassy World Championship

Terry Griffiths has the world in his arms, but only after accidentally knocking the ornamental globe from its moorings during his unsuccessful 1988 final against Steve Davis

beat him, an obvious enough sentiment for the uninvolved observer, but less easy to accept for a champion who has dedicated his whole life to remaining champion. Without that period of contemplation, Davis felt, he would probably not have won. Even so, he struggled desperately in the first couple of frames on the resumption, the crucial period of the match as it turned out.

In the opening frame, Davis missed two very easy blacks, one quite unbelievable, and also a yellow when it was over a pocket. Griffiths led by 45 but somehow could not manoeuvre himself into a clinching position and Davis, with a mighty effort, cleared the colours to win on the black. He went on to take six of the afternoon's eight frames to lead 14-10, two centuries, 118 and 123, featuring as he concluded the proceedings at 18-11.

'Every time you win the world championship, you've got to be delighted,' commented Davis. 'It might be your last.'

breakbuilding contest produced 26 breaks over 40 in 25 frames. Hendry led 10-7 but White overtook to 11-10 and 12-11. At 12-12, from what Hendry described as 'a tremendous shot under pressure', White ran 86 for his place in the quarter-finals.

From 9-1, White then beat Tony Knowles 13-6 and from 9-9 Terry Griffiths beat Neal Foulds 13-9 to reach the semi-finals, the stage of the competition when the Crucible becomes a one-table arena. Somewhat contrary to popular expectation, Griffiths beat White 16-11. The psychological crusher came at 13-11 when White, having tied the frame with red, pink and all the colours, lost it to the 1979 champion's tie-break black.

Griffiths then split his first day with Davis 8-8, and awoke next morning feeling lively and optimistic that the tide could be running in his favour. Davis, subdued, even morose, after losing six of the previous evening's nine frames, felt ill at ease.

After play, he had driven round Sheffield contemplating his situation and the enormity of possible defeat. He concluded that there was really no shame in losing if someone played well enough to

1988 EMBASSY WORLD CHAMPIONSHIP

FIRST ROUND: S. Davis beat J. Virgo 10-8; M. Hallett beat R. Chaperon 10-2; T. Drago beat A. Higgins 10-2; Dennis Taylor beat B. Werbeniuk 10-8; J. Johnson beat C. Wilson 10-7; S. James beat R. Williams 10-6; J. Parrott beat W. King 10-4; C. Thorburn beat K. Stevens 10-6; N. Foulds beat W. Jones 10-7; D. Mountjoy beat B. West 10-6; W. Thorne beat P. Francisco 10-6; T. Griffiths beat S. Longworth 10-1; T. Knowles beat D. Fowler 10-8; E. Charlton beat S. Francisco 10-7; S. Hendry beat D. Reynolds 10-6; J. White beat J. Campbell 10-3

SECOND ROUND: Davis beat Hallett 13-1; Drago beat Taylor 13-5; James beat Johnson 13-9; Thorburn beat Parrott 13-10; Foulds beat Mountjoy 13-1; Griffiths beat Thorne 13-9; Knowles beat Charlton 13-7; White beat Hendry 13-12

QUARTER-FINALS: Davis beat Drago 13-4; Thorburn beat James 13-11; Griffiths beat Foulds 13-9; White beat Knowles 13-6

SEMI-FINALS: Davis beat Thorburn 16-8; Griffiths beat White 16-11

FINAL: Davis beat Griffiths 18-11

Although snooker's viewing figures remained highly satisfactory, it was not enough. For a decade, the game had been on honeymoon with the public, with television, and in its way, the press, who had been presented with a new cast list of television stars who could generate a regular supply of news stories. 'Dallas with balls' was how Barry Hearn neatly summed up its soap opera appeal.

Snooker, and the WPBSA in particular, behaved as if human fickleness and fashion would never make for tougher times. There was a backlash of cultural snobbery. *Spitting Image* lampooned the BBC's Michael Grade as obsessed by snooker, a dozen screens behind him all showing it. Perhaps this was a factor, though certainly not the only one, in his decision to show no snooker the following season when he moved to Channel 4.

'Snooker helps boost our viewing figures but it damages the image of the channel,' he explained. 'We will replace it with programmes for people who hate snooker.' There was some rivalry between Channel 4 and ITV, and Channel 4 did not care to be cast in the role of helping ITV fulfil its contract. In 1987, Channel 4 had transmitted 51 hours of snooker to ITV's 89 and there was no way that the shortfall could be made up. MIM Britannia, concluding that television coverage of the British Open would be reduced, decided not to renew its sponsorship.

Over the next five years ITV's snooker coverage was to be steadily eroded, and in 1989 the season's domestic curtain-raiser, the Fidelity International, was dropped; in the 1992-93 season the Mercantile Classic's early January slot was also consigned to oblivion, and for the 1993-94 season the WPBSA had no ITV contract at all.

Snooker's status as a mainstream sport, grudgingly conceded in some quarters, received a boost when Davis was awarded the MBE, but there was still the impression of the sport being embroiled in a civil war which the WPBSA had little idea how to deal with. While money was poured into public relations and accountancy services, policy still remained no more than reaction to each issue as it arose. Credibility was lost by the refusal to ban all categories of beta blocker, which kept the WPBSA beyond the pale of the Sports Council.

Guerrilla warfare between Hearn and the WPBSA intensified. He declined to support the WPBSA's annual dinner and awards evening, an event which John Bromley, a senior ITV sport figure, had described in 1984 as 'a unique occasion. Players, sponsors, officials, press and TV all in one room, all having a good time. Snooker is the only sport where everyone is this friendly.' He was commenting, of course, before the occasion had degenerated into an expensive public relations exercise and an attempt to cover the cracks which had developed.

When Rothmans decided not to sponsor Hearn's league for a third year, his reaction put his players in line for retribution: he sued Rothmans and his players agreed not to give press interviews during the Rothmans Grand Prix. This legal action was eventually settled to Hearn's satisfaction, but he had put himself in a bad light with the interview boycott – which was in any case ineffective – and his players were hit hard in the pocket.

Dennis Taylor, who declined five press and two television interviews, was fined £8,000, Jimmy White and Terry Griffiths were fined £4,000 each, Neal Foulds £3,000, Tony Meo £2,000 and Willie Thorne £1,000. Steve Davis, who declined five press and two television interviews, the same as Taylor, was fined £4,000 more – £12,000. This looked suspiciously like fining on the principle of the offender's wealth: Davis had won the £65,000 first prize by beating Higgins 10-6 in the final, having already taken £45,000 for beating Jimmy White 12-6 in the final of the Fidelity International. In that match he made breaks of 108, 101 and 104 in consecutive frames, the first such hat-trick in tournament play.

Another £50,000 came his way for winning Matchroom's in-house championship by beating Taylor 10-7. The event was televised by Super Channel and, in what was then a contravention of WPBSA rules, the finalists sported logos on their waistcoats, marking another initially modest extension of the sport's commercial boundaries.

A newcomer to the circuit, Alain Robidoux, fresh from winning the Canadian Championship, extended Davis to 5-4 in the Fidelity, made a 147 maximum in the qualifying competition

Alain Robidoux made a brilliant start to his professional career

of the new European Open at Blackpool and steamed through to the semi-finals of the Rothmans Grand Prix. He trailed Higgins 0-7 and 1-8 but recovered to 7-8 before an untimely kick let in Higgins with 55 to clinch the match 9-7. He was to become, as Davis predicted at this early stage, a top 16 player, although his early inspiration was quenched after a few years of living so far from home and by the unremitting slog the circuit entailed.

Another Canadian career was drawing to a close. Bill Werbeniuk, having disclosed before drug testing that he was still taking the non-cardio-selective beta blocker Inderal, was suspended and fined £2,000. His inability to pay this effectively terminated his membership.

In another drugs imbroglio, Higgins was fined a lenient £1,500 (suspended) plus £500 costs. Having initially refused to give a urine sample after losing 4-5 to Gary Wilkinson in the final of a non-ranking event in Glasgow, Higgins agreed to do so only in the public toilet, not the test cubicle. He also insisted that the press should be present. Ian Doyle, by now a WPBSA director as well as Hendry's manager, reported that Higgins had sported a black eye for his first match. The following day he had two black eyes. 'According to Alex, he had an accident in a revolving door – twice,' said Doyle.

Bridges were rebuilt between the WPBSA and IMG, who became its representatives in sponsorship and television negotiations for overseas world ranking tournaments. IMG's own financial commitment was about half the £925,000 the WPBSA had earlier turned down. Hearn promoted the Dubai Duty Free Masters for his eight players, Foulds beating Davis in the final, but was outraged to discover that IMG had persuaded the sponsors to switch their support to a WPBSA event the following year. This escalated the warfare between Hearn and the WPBSA.

The WPBSA also came under fire from a threatened 'Peasants' Revolt', led by Geoff Foulds, whose twin thrusts were that the rank and file members were given too few opportunities and that too much of the members' cash was being frittered away on expensive lawyers, accountants, PR men and such indulgences as a box at Goodwood.

An unlikely alliance was formed: Hearn, the élitist, and Geoff Foulds, whose son was a top player but who was himself typical of the game's infantry of journeymen pros. Hearn declared his intention to see an independent governing body in snooker, in which the actual power would rest with professional people who have no direct financial interest.

The WPBSA, increasingly beleaguered, attracted more criticism when the Canadian Masters proved to be a failure on such a scale as to cast away all the progress professional snooker had quietly made in Canada in the previous two years. Two eight-man events, staged in CBC's studios in the heart of Toronto, had been well received. However, the decision was disastrously taken, as the event became world-ranking, to take 32 qualifiers across the Atlantic. These were reduced to 16 through matches played in a high-class dungeon in a hotel situated half an hour out of Toronto amidst a patchwork quilt of freeways. Audiences ranged from a handful to considerably more than the official 250 capacity on the night that Davis, Hendry and White played simultaneously.

The tournament then adjourned to the Minkler Auditorium, an hour out of Toronto by public transport and anything up to 90 minutes by car. Attendances were generally so poor that CBC's coverage could not help but emphasise row upon row of empty seats. Reared on more noisy and athletic sports than snooker, the young Turks who came to power in CBC's sports department around this time decided forthwith that CBC did not want any more snooker.

For Davis, the final was 'the day the rubber band came off'. Having won the first two ranking events of the season in such emphatic fashion that a clean sweep of all eight was not to be ruled out, he lost 4-9 to White, whose reaction was characteristically realistic. 'Not much of a game was it? We both missed a lot of balls.'

At the Tennents UK Championship, the WPBSA announced that Hearn was banned from the press and hospitality room, whereupon the sponsors icily responded that he was welcome.

Hendry had started the season indifferently, still relatively inexperienced and labouring under the illusion that three hours' practice a day was as effective a preparation for the new season as six. Having lost to Steve James in the Fidelity International and to Doug Mountjoy in the Rothmans Grand Prix, he had shown improved form in reaching the Canadian Masters semi-finals, where he led 5-4 before losing 9-5 to Davis. At Preston, his game peaked. He led Davis 8-1, beat him 9-3 and was so clearly favourite for the title that he perhaps underestimated Mountjoy, his final opponent.

At Sheffield in the spring, Mountjoy's 13-1 defeat by Foulds had left him 24th in the rankings. 'It's difficult on your own to find out what you're doing wrong. I went to Frank Callan. Without that guy I'm nothing.' This erstwhile fishmonger from Fleetwood, whose own amateur career had been ended by a back injury, had advised Davis and coached Griffiths, John Parrott and sundry other professionals who asked his advice. He was the first coach to gain credibility with top-class players and was later signed by Ian Doyle to advise his Cuemasters group.

Mountjoy's technique was comprehensively rebuilt and bolted into place by a relentless practice regime. His early-season results, including a 5-1 Rothmans win over Hendry, were encouraging. At Preston, he avenged himself on Foulds, 9-4, beat Joe Johnson 9-5 and led John Virgo 8-3 before his own residual insecurity and Virgo's inspired resistance brought the match level at 8-8. Once he had come through 9-8, his nerves settled. Leading Griffiths 5-2, he felt so relaxed that he fell asleep during the interval of their semi-final before going on to win 9-4.

Doug Mountjoy is presented with the Tennents UK trophy by Dennis Urquhart of Bass, ten years after winning his other UK title. John Virgo, then the WPBSA chairman, applauds in the background. Mountjoy celebrates later (top) with Frank Callan, the coach whose help rescued his career

The final caught the imagination of the viewing public. BBC's audience for the final session was a mammoth 13.2 million, but the key session was the third, in which Mountjoy won six of the seven frames to lead 14-7. Having ended the afternoon with two centuries, 131 and 106, he began the evening with a third, 124, equalling Davis's record hat-trick in the Fidelity final, as he went seven up with eight to play. Although Hendry retrieved five of them, Mountjoy had the belief to ward off panic and ran out the winner at 16-12.

Euphoric as he was, Mountjoy was sober enough to reflect on the fate of Patsy Fagan, the first UK champion 11 years

earlier: 'He beat me in the final. Now he's on the dole. His game went. My game went. But I had Frank.'

As if this was not enough, Mountjoy also won the next world ranking tournament, the Mercantile Classic, beating Wayne Jones 13-11 in a gruelling final. The finalists had known each other since Mountjoy was a star in the crack Abertysswg team in the Rhymney Valley and Jones a mustard-keen promising youngster. They had practised together hundreds of hours and stopped only a year or so earlier when Mountjoy 'didn't want reminding that Wayne plays the way I used to'.

Playing to a lifetime peak, Jones beat Jimmy White, John Parrott and Willie Thorne and led 11-9 in the final before Mountjoy came through with a four-frame winning streak. 'It was terrible out there. People don't realise how close we are. Wayne is like a son really,' said Mountjoy. It had, in fact, been a great tournament for Wales; Tony Chappel put out Davis 5-3 in the third round.

Mountjoy's two titles were separated by Davis winning the inaugural Everest World Matchplay championship at International Hall in Brentwood, the event being restricted to the top 12 ranking-points earners of the previous season. Parrott beat Hendry 9-6 in their semi-final, but lost the first six frames to Davis and was beaten 9-5.

At its AGM, the board of the WPBSA narrowly survived what amounted to a vote of no confidence from its membership, chiefly orchestrated by Hearn. When financial details were reluctantly disclosed, the membership was not pleased to hear that the annual dinner at the Park Lane Hilton had cost £47,000, a junket to Goodwood Races £6,376 and a disastrous public relations operation £15,000.

A loss of £120,000 (a conservative estimate) was admitted on the Canadian

Alex Higgins copes with a media request after hobbling to an uncomfortable victory

Masters and Hearn sought details of the IMG contract in the light of WPBSA's contingent liability of £1.3 million over three years. Nevertheless, the board survived in its entirety, largely because of the proxy votes wielded by two managers on it, Ian Doyle and Howard Kruger.

Davis, who had been voted BBC TV's Sports Personality of the Year, won the Norwich Union Grand Prix on Canal Plus, another Hearn incursion into the burgeoning satellite market, but withdrew from the European Open, pleading the need to conserve his energies. This was widely interpreted as a Hearn retaliation against IMG, the WPBSA's partner in overseas ranking events.

Higgins, having been out of the limelight for a while, recaptured it in unorthodox fashion. An epic row with his girlfriend, Siobhan Kidd, a psychology graduate whom he had met while she was working as a waitress, ended with her locking him inside her flat. Attempting to crawl round the outside of the building, he plunged 25 feet to the ground, breaking bones in his foot.

A couple of weeks later, on crutches, unable to put any weight on his left leg and with his weight distribution therefore all awry, he won a match in the European Open in Deauville and in much the same condition incredibly won the Irish championship in Antrim, battling against imminent exhaustion to beat Jack McLaughlin 9-7 in the final.

There was a farcical courage in his efforts but only farce at Deauville Casino, the venue chosen by IMG for reasons of their own for the inaugural European Open. Snooker in France was in its infancy

and it struck even the most unreflective competitors that it was somehow disproportionate to undertake long and complicated journeys of several hundred miles by bus, ferry and bus again or flights to Paris and a two-hour train trip, to perform for a tiny audience consisting largely of each other. It was like setting down a cricket match in Yankee Stadium. At least the TV packages which TWI sold to Eurosport looked all right. Both semi-finals finished 5-4 – Parrott over Hallett, Griffiths over White – and Parrott beat Griffiths 9-8 in the final.

In the week that Hendry won the Masters title on his Wembley debut, the game's bedrock, its on-table integrity, was challenged. Griffiths beat Silvino

John Parrott clinched his first world ranking title, the European Open, at Deauville Casino

Francisco 5-1, not a surprising score on their current form, but Ladbrokes were unhappy that a punter, or group of punters, had placed seven £90 bets at the generous odds of 6-1 at closely grouped Ladbroke shops in north London. Some guile appeared to have been used by someone who knew that only bets of £100 or more were routinely referred to head office. The problem with snooker betting, several punters had complained, often lay in getting a large bet accepted at the advertised odds. Ladbrokes grew nervous, rang the WPBSA without reply and suspended betting 40 minutes before break-off.

It only takes a bookmaker and a friendly journalist eager for a scoop to write a betting coup story. The *Daily Mirror* ran it big; ITN sent a news crew to follow it up. Other bookmakers leapt on the bandwagon – Coral were an honourable exception – and Francisco, unpopular with the WPBSA's authorities, did not receive the support he might have expected. A black cloud of suspicion hung over him for more than a year. Incredibly, he was even arrested, but only one derisory piece of evidence was produced. Although he was released, without charge, the damage to his reputation and the game had been done.

Hallett beat Parrott 9-7 to win the English Championship, though the event was somewhat devalued by the absence of Hearn's two leading players, Davis and White. John Rea made a 147 break in winning the Scottish title, which was also devalued by the absence of Hendry. In the Matchroom League, sponsorless since Hearn's rift with Rothmans, Thorburn made a 147 at Crawley, emulating Meo's 147 in the league the previous season.

Meo was nevertheless 31st in the ranking by the time he went to the British Open, sponsored this time by Anglian Windows, as a 200-1 outsider. Like Theodore in the 1822 St Leger, he came

Tony Meo's safety first tactics helped him win the 1989 Anglian British Open as a 200-1 outsider. He is here preparing to make his entrance with Dean Reynolds (left), his opponent in a dour final at Derby Assembly Rooms

home to win it. As the Hearn management stable had expanded, so the emotional Meo had slipped further and further to the margins from the No. 2 position in which he had started. He had had his moments, winning two English titles and, with Davis, four world doubles titles, but somehow his confidence had deserted him, so that while his technique had remained in good order, his capacity to use it under stress had largely left him

'It's funny,' he said once. 'When I had nothing, I never used to worry about anything. But now I've got plenty of money and a fantastic lifestyle, I worry all the time.'

It was in his favour that no-one expected him to beat Hendry in the last 16. 'One of the best balls I've ever potted', the match-ball blue, took him through 5-3, but his run seemed about to end in the semi-finals, when he was two down with three to play and needing two snookers against Hallett. He won 9-8. After seven defeats, Parrott at last beat Davis 5-1 in the quarter-finals but from two up with three to play he lost 8-9 to Dean Reynolds in the other semi. The final had little to offer as a spectacle as Meo pulled steadily away to win 13-6, and the loser, apparently unable to appreciate that winning was the point of the whole exercise, criticised Meo's careful approach.

The unlikely achievement of Meo was followed by the equally unlikely triumph of Higgins – no longer hopping but limping – in the Benson and Hedges Irish Masters, in which he beat Thorburn, Foulds and Parrott to reach the final. Hendry beat Davis 6-4 in the semi-finals and led 8-6 in the final before Higgins, roared on by an emotional Irish crowd, won 9-8.

Higgins was certainly playing well enough to succeed at Sheffield. Unfortunately, he never got there. At two o'clock on the day after his exhausting Irish Masters triumph, he had to be in Preston for his Embassy World Championship qualifying match against Darren Morgan, winner of the 1987 world amateur title in Bangalore and doing well in his first professional season. The young Welshman's break of 143, the highest ever made in the qualifying competition, put him 8-7 up, and although Higgins, flagging as he was, levelled at 8-8, Morgan prevailed 10-8 to earn his Crucible debut.

Concurrently with the qualifying competition came the last of the undignified play-offs for full professional status between players ranked 119 to 128 and ten challengers – the world and English amateur champions and the top eight finishers in the series of four professional ticket events the WPBSA ran in conjunction with various holiday camps. Not all those in the relegation zone chose to play, so James Wattana, the

outstanding Thai prospect who had won the 1988 world amateur title in Sydney, was spared this last impediment to a place on the professional circuit.

EMBASSY WORLD CHAMPIONSHIP

Steve Davis had defined the special apprehension of playing on the opening day at the Crucible: 'The first surprise hasn't happened yet. It could be you.' This year, it was not. He beat Steve Newbury 10-5 and went on to win his sixth title.

In truth, it was difficult to concentrate on snooker that first day, for only two miles away the unbelievable horror of Hillsborough was unfolding. Within minutes of kick-off in the Liverpool v Nottingham Forest FA Cup semi-final, a crush behind one of the goals had led to tragedy. The sponsors, Imperial Tobacco, and the WPBSA announced a special collection for the Hillsborough Disaster Fund and started it with a donation of £20,000. John Parrott, a Liverpudlian who had grown up on the terraces at Anfield and Goodison Park, was deeply moved and wore a black armband the following day.

Emotions ran high in the arena, with Parrott receiving much sympathetic support and the followers of Steve James also having their vociferous say before Parrott, having led 9-7, won 10-9. 'I hope that the people of Liverpool will enjoy my victory,' declared Parrott solemnly. 'I'm going to get my head down and do the damnedest I can to take this back to Liverpool, although I know no silverware or amount of money can replace human life.'

Three other first-round matches went the distance. Wayne Jones, runner-up in the Mercantile Classic, produced the highest break of a dour struggle, 61, to beat Neal Foulds, who thus plummeted from third to 20th in the rankings in one season.

Eddie Charlton, one byword for durability, beat another, Cliff Thorburn,

10-9 in a match which ran to an unscheduled third session. After two, only 14 frames had been completed and Charlton had to sit on his 8-6 lead until the evening match on that table had been completed. Little delay was expected, as Tony Meo, fresh from winning the British Open, resumed 8-0 up on Joe Johnson, but Meo was able to clinch victory only at 10-5. So it was 11.25 before Charlton and Thorburn returned to the arena, and 2.40 a.m. with hardly anyone in the place before Len Ganley, the referee, did not have to set them up again. At 9-9, having led 9-7, Charlton had looked demoralised, but the 50 or so discerning patrons who remained saw the veteran Australian make

50 at the right time to win the decider. The 19 frames had taken ten hours 24 minutes. It would not do if every snooker match was like this, but every sport thrives on its variety of character and style. There will always be a place for the unrelenting hard men.

A very different style of match saw Hendry hold off Gary Wilkinson 10-9. One of seven Crucible debutants, Wilkinson, who had reached 38th in the rankings, performed with a spirit and flair which he was subsequently not always to show when carrying the responsibility of a much higher ranking. To an enormous roar, he won a black-ball frame to reach 9-9, but from his break-off shot in the

A minute's silence at the Crucible on the middle Saturday of the 1989 championship in remembrance of the Hillsborough disaster, which occurred elsewhere in Sheffield a week earlier. Pictured (from left) are: Len Ganley (referee), Dennis Taylor, John Parrott, Terry Griffiths, Silvino Francisco and John Street (referee)

decider Hendry drilled in a long red and made a match-winning 67 from it.

Hillsborough again cast its shadow on the middle Saturday of the championship as a minute's silence was observed at 3.06, the time the tragedy occurred. This delayed the start of the afternoon's play, which included Parrott resuming 9-7 up on Dennis Taylor. Parrott trailed 9-10, but crucially won the last frame before the intermission and played much more freely on the resumption to add the three he needed to win 13-10.

This round saw two matches go the full 25 frames. White, whose form had been disappointing for almost six months, trailed John Virgo 11-9 and at 11-11 went one down with two to play to Virgo's break of 86. In the next frame, Virgo was in play with 26 and in position to make a substantial break to clinch the match, when his cue grazed a ball on its follow through. To his great credit, Virgo declared a foul on himself that the referee had not spotted, whereupon White scrambled out of that frame and made 61 to take the decider.

Mike Hallett beat David Roe 13-12 from two down with three to play, Roe having celebrated his Crucible debut by beating Tony Knowles 10-6. This reverse put Knowles out of the top ten for the first time since the heady days of his 10-1 Crucible win over Davis in 1982. He had no difficulty in pinpointing where the rot had set in: his co-operation in a three-part extravaganza of sexual reminiscence for the *Sun*. Realising he could get things so wrong had opened up the first big crack in his self-confidence.

A day's television coverage was lost through a strike by technical and engineering unions. Fortunately, it coincided with a mundane day's play.

From the quarter-finals onwards, there was not a single close finish. Davis had prevailed over Hallett by a frames aggregate of 45-10 in their last five

meetings and now overwhelmed him 13-3, Hallett again demonstrating his incapacity to sustain a tactical game. Hendry made a total clearance of 141 and ousted Griffiths 13-5, while Parrott, gathering authority all season as White struggled, beat him for the third consecutive time, 13-7. In a repeat of the British Open final, Meo beat Reynolds 13-9.

Most of Meo's matches had become dour affairs because he lacked the confidence to be enterprising, his 13-8 second-round win over Charlton having been no exception. Reynolds did what he could to defuse a potentially acrimonious situation by admitting before the match that his criticism of Meo's style of play in their British Open final had been 'totally out of order'.

It was therefore ironic that Meo should escape any caution for slow play while Reynolds did not. Meo had been given such a warning in the 21st and last frame of his match against Charlton, but since this was scarcely distinguishable in tempo from virtually every other frame, it was difficult to understand why he had not been warned before and why Charlton, who was, if anything, a worse offender, had not been warned at all.

Meo led Reynolds 9-7 and won two arduous black-ball games to go four clear. In the second of these, Reynolds was in play with 28 when he was told by the referee, John Williams: 'The first frame took 53 minutes. Come on Deano. Buck your ideas up.' Reynolds, beaten 9-13, began his press conference: 'The decision I had today. . .' and broke down in tears.

He said that only once before in his professional career, in his debut year at the Crucible as a 19-year-old, had he been warned for slow play – by the same referee. 'It all came thudding back to me. I couldn't concentrate. Every time I was down I was conscious of how long I was taking. I was playing some shots without studying them properly.'

John Williams
cautions Dean
Reynolds for slow
play at the Crucible

Meo thus reached his first world semi-final, but he still could not let himself go and was on the verge of tears as he left the arena 2-6 down after the first session of his semi-final with Parrott, who went on to win comfortably 16-7.

Davis, having lost to Hendry in three major semi-finals earlier in the season, was psyched up to the full and hardly made a mistake as he led him 10-2 in the other semi-final. Hendry recovered to 9-12, making a 139 break *en route*, but Davis potted an awkward last red and cleared to the pink to win the last frame of the penultimate session, completing his 16-9 win the following morning.

There was no more drama. 'I had nothing left, nothing at all,' said Parrott, drubbed 18-3 with a session of the final to spare. The cumulative fatigue of all the matches he had played since Christmas caught up with him and the championship petered out in anticlimax.

For Davis, the satisfaction lay in putting right marginal imperfections of technique which had blighted his game in mid-season. 'I know I'm nowhere near as far in front as these scores suggest,' he admitted, having won the title by the frames aggregate of 70-23. Over these 17 days he was, but as the events of the following season were to show, there was something in what he said.

1989 EMBASSY WORLD CHAMPIONSHIP

FIRST ROUND: **S. Davis beat S. Newbury 10-5; S. Duggan beat C. Wilson 10-1; M. Hallett beat D. Mountjoy 10-7; D. Roe beat A. Knowles 10-6; T. Griffiths beat R. Chaperon 10-6; S. Francisco beat J. O'Boye 10-6; W. Thorne beat P. Browne 10-5; S. Hendry beat Gary Wilkinson 10-9; W. Jones beat N. Foulds 10-9; D. Reynolds beat P. Francisco 10-7; T. Meo beat J. Johnson 10-5; E. Charlton beat C. Thorburn 10-9; J. Parrott beat S. James 10-9; Dennis Taylor beat E. Hughes 10-3; J. Virgo beat D. Morgan 10-4; J. White beat D. O'Kane 19-7**

SECOND ROUND: **Davis beat Duggan 13-3; Hallett beat Roe 13-12; Griffiths beat Francisco 13-9; Hendry beat Thorne 13-4; Reynolds beat Jones 13-3; Meo beat Charlton 13-8; Parrott beat Taylor 13-10; White beat Virgo 13-12**

QUARTER-FINALS: **Davis beat Hallett 13-3; Hendry beat Griffiths 13-5; Meo beat Reynolds 13-9; Parrott beat White 13-7**

SEMI-FINALS: **Davis beat Hendry 16-9; Parrott beat Meo 16-7**

FINAL: **Davis beat Parrot 18-3**

Steve Davis's completion of a hat-trick of world titles and six in all emphasised his domination of the game when the chips were down, so much so that in terms of the uncommitted public it was seen as 'bad for the game'.

When the BBC instituted daily coverage of the championship in 1978, snooker went on honeymoon with a vast new audience. Honeymoons do not last forever, although this one had lasted longer than most. During it, as the number of hard-core snooker followers had increased, so some of the more fickle had drifted away and the feelings of many turned from the passionate to the steadily affectionate, except for matches which specifically stimulated dormant appetites.

It was already apparent that the WPBSA had not done enough in the years of plenty to guard against the years when a downturn would surely come. *Marketing Week* reported that, with 15.39 per cent, snooker commanded far and away a larger share of Britain's total sports television audience than any other sport, double football's share and three times that of cricket. Snooker's participation levels, both in quality and and quantity, were higher than ever before.

Yet in summer 1989, the WPBSA contemplated the loss of Tennents, sponsors of the £400,000 UK championship and Anglian Windows, sponsors of the £350,000 British Open, the latter, like their immediate predecessors, MIM Britannia Unit Trusts, after only one year. Overseas, the Canadian Masters had been such a disaster that it was lost from the calendar and the débâcle in Deauville had been an inauspicious debut for the WPBSA-IMG partnership in overseas world ranking events.

There was worse to come. ITV decided to cut back from four events to three, whereupon Fidelity Unit Trusts immediately terminated the sponsorship of a ranking event, to which they had

contributed in 1988 a prize fund of £225,000 plus a substantial back-up budget. Trevor East, ITV's executive producer in charge of snooker, claimed that ITV's withdrawal was 'nothing to do with ratings or a drop in interest, but it's been patently obvious since the withdrawal of Channel 4 from snooker that we have had major scheduling problems.' His negotiations with the ITV network broadly meant dropping one tournament to ensure reasonable exposure for the other three.

IMG did not cover themselves with glory in assigning the promotion rights of their proposed new Australian Open to Ian Robertson, a Sydney man about snooker whose resignation from the New South Wales committee had been demanded a year earlier.

While the WPBSA and IMG believed there would be four days' television coverage and that there was sponsorship in the offing from the Bond Organisation, Qantas and other blue-chip concerns, ABC 2's head of sport, David Salter, claimed there was not and never had been any contract to cover the event. When Ian Anderson, chairman of the Australian Players Association, travelled to Britain to express his scepticism, he was hardly listened to. The truth dawned at last that there was no viable basis for an event in Australia and it was hastily re-assigned to Hong Kong. Davis, who had been fined £200 for scratching from Deauville, entered neither of the WPBSA-IMG events in Australia/Hong Kong or Bangkok, thus endangering his top place in the world rankings. None of Hearn's eight players, some of whom could ill afford the loss of money or ranking points, played in the next WPBSA-IMG promotion, the Dubai Classic.

IMG, fearing Hearn's voting power (nine votes in all) within the WPBSA's small electorate, acquired the contracts of six players from Howard Kruger – Steve

Newbury, Martin Clark, Peter Francisco, Dean Reynolds, David Roe and Tony Drago – to form a players' group of its own and gain some voting power. It soon transpired that they had bought a pig in a poke as Kruger's labyrinthine snooker empire began to receive extensive press scrutiny. The first snooker company of which Kruger was in day-to-day control, Framework Management Ltd, was wound up in the High Court on the application of Higgins, who claimed that the firm owed him £51,536, including £16,000 in back maintenance payments to his ex-wife which should have arrived through the firm.

Humble pie was also on the menu for the WPBSA over the UK Championship, as a Tennents press release announcing that they would not be renewing their 1988 sponsorship pointedly thanked everyone for their efforts – except snooker's governing body. Despite the deployment of the sophisticated marketing technique of placing a 'sponsor wanted' advert in *Sponsorship News*, the WPBSA, having no replacement, had to turn to Hearn. He had Stormseal, a double-glazing concern, in tow with a £2 million package comprising a three-year deal for the UK, one of two years for the Matchroom League and a personal contract for Davis.

The WPBSA had little alternative but to agree to pay all expenses for the qualifying competition and allow Hearn, without paying any sanction fee, to take the whole of the gate from Preston Guild Hall. As it was to turn out 18 months later, though, the Stormseal deal, which also embraced some of Hearn's boxing promotions, was a timebomb, certainly one which initiated Hearn's first serious commercial difficulty when Stormseal abruptly went into liquidation.

Doyle, the most commercially intelligent man remaining on the WPBSA board, resigned after 21 months' service, a warning that the WPBSA had either to become more efficient or degenerate into a rump. He pointed out that his future plans with the WPBSA and Barry Hearn would result in a major conflict of interests. One of these plans was a revival of world series; one of the implicit threats was that Hearn, with a group of eight leading players, and Doyle, now with five, could rob any tournament of credibility if they chose to boycott it. Meanwhile, RTE's four-man curtain-raiser to the season successively sponsored by Carling, Carlsberg and Fosters, was dropped in a welter of complaints of unreasonable demands by some players or their managements.

The WPBSA board had aroused derision at their AGM by increasing the travelling allowance for board members from 50p to £1 a mile. Some players could not understand why this should take a higher priority than the withdrawal of the entire subsidy of £1,000 an entrant, which effectively meant the end of those national championships without a sponsor (i.e. all but the Welsh, which continued until 1992). Geoff Foulds pointed out that new payments of £250 for first-round losers and £400 for second-round losers in world ranking events had been financed only at the expense of national championships. In what is normally thought of as the close season, 13-year-old Ronnie O'Sullivan made his mark by winning the British under-16 title; Gary Hill made a 147 maximum in the world under-21 championship in Reykjavik, won by Ken Doherty, who was also to become world amateur champion in Singapore at the end of the year; Peter Ebdon defeated Doherty 7-4 for the £2,500 first prize in the Pontins Open and beat Darren Clarke 4-3 on the black to take the £7,500 winner's cheque in a Rothmans sponsored amateur event. All these players were still struggling to get on to the professional circuit, which was effectively limited to 128 players. Ray Reardon, down to 54th in the rankings, said he preferred to play exhibitions for Pontins rather than slog through the summer qualifying competitions at the Norbreck Castle Hotel, Blackpool.

Mike Hallett won the Hong Kong Open, beating Hendry 5-4, White 5-2 and, from two down with three to play, Dene O'Kane 9-8. He celebrated by buying some expensive trinkets, several suits and no fewer than 72 shirts. Doyle, his manager, doubted that he could afford to win another £40,000 first prize and threatened to nail his credit cards to his desk. The WPBSA admitted that it expected to lose £120,000 on the event.

Having won the 1988 world amateur title in Sydney, James Wattana delighted his home town crowd in Bangkok by

reaching the final of the 555 Asian Open, with defeats of Mountjoy, Silvino Francisco and Griffiths, all ranked in the top ten, before losing 6-9 to Hendry in the final. At least BAT contributed £90,000 to the £200,000 prize fund. Hendry also won the Scottish Masters, revived by Doyle under the sponsorship of Regal and covered by BBC Scotland.

The Fidelity International, hastily renamed the BCE International in the light of a token last-minute replacement sponsorship, saw Davis take the £40,000 first prize by beating Hendry 9-4. Nigel Bond, the 1989 English amateur champion, made his first professional impact there by beating Steve James 5-0 and John Parrott 5-2, and was nearing a semi-final victory over Hendry when he missed an easy ball and eventually lost 5-6.

In the Rothmans Grand Prix at the Hexagon, Reading, Danny Fowler stepped out from the chorus to play a starring role, beating Hallett, Alain Robidoux and, with a 113 break in the decider, Joe Johnson, before losing 9-2 to Davis in the semi-finals. Hendry lost to Mountjoy for the third time in succession, while the finalist from the other half was Dean Reynolds, who beat Parrott and Dennis Taylor. James Wattana, attracting heavy publicity as the circuit's first notable Asian, beat Willie Thorne and Mountjoy and led Reynolds 7-3 in the semi-finals before losing six of the last seven frames to go under 8-9. Exhausted by this, Reynolds lost 10-0 to a fresh and rested Davis at the final.

At the Dubai Classic, Fowler again reached the semi-finals, only to see Hendry fluke the match-ball brown out of a snooker to win 5-4. Mountjoy beat Parrott 5-4 in the other semi, but Hendry, making seven breaks over 60, trounced him 9-2 in the final.

Both at Reading and in Dubai, Higgins was involved in incidents which, in retrospect, appear the start of a decline to

Mike Hallett, winner of the 1989 Hong Kong Open

his lowest personal ebb. It was an old, old story, almost par for the course, that he should complain, quite unjustifiably, that Johnson, who beat him at Reading, had distracted him while he was down on his shot. Unpleasant verbal abuse of WPBSA officials and members of the snooker press followed in a hotel bar that night. One press man was grabbed round the neck, another threatened with a glass ashtray. When hostilities flared again in a bar in Dubai, Dave Armitage of the *Daily Star* struck him. Jim Chambers, a middle-ranking professional, who had intervened the previous day when Higgins was forcibly ducked in the swimming pool by someone he had upset, now leapt in again. Unfortunately, Chambers the peacemaker then slipped down a short flight of stairs, tearing ligaments in his ankle. He was taken in agony to hospital and returned in a wheelchair.

Two factors may have sent Higgins over the edge: he was distraught at the ending of his relationship with Siobhan Kidd and extremely angry over the way he had been managed by Howard Kruger, a member of the WPBSA board. When Higgins brought disrepute charges against him, Kruger resigned just before the hearing. The only practicable penalty was a reprimand when Gavin Lightman, QC, found him guilty on two counts.

It did not look good that the WPBSA chairman, John Virgo, played an exhibition to open Kruger's new snooker club in Brighton, another commercial failure, on the very night when Kruger had been found guilty. Neither had a sweet odour emanated from the WPBSA's appointment, out of all the thousands of travel agents in Britain, of a Kruger company, International Travel Bureau of Worthing, to handle its travel arrangements for overseas world ranking tournaments. ITB shortly afterwards crashed with debts of £470,000.

The 1989 AGM of the WPBSA was again effectively a vote of confidence in the board. Submitting himself for re-election, its chairman, Virgo, was defeated 30-11, as was another long-serving board member, David Taylor. The auditors, the distinguished city firm of Coopers & Lybrand, were cross-questioned by the disaffected membership and ousted 23-17, widely perceived as protectors of the board rather than servants of the membership. Much as blood is extracted from a stone, disturbing information was elicited, largely by Hearn, aghast that the inefficiency of the WPBSA was endangering the financial basis of the circuit, and Foulds, leader of the 'Peasants' Revolt', whose own bid to join the board succeeded, 30-9.

Some disproportion was perceived between an operating loss of £553,408 – compared with a surplus of £429,553 the previous year – and its primary executive, Del Simmons, being paid more than £80,000. A new £23,000 Toyota had been purchased for his use and Foulds discovered that his previous car, a Mercedes, had been sold to him for £1. Some £80,000 had been spent on new marketing aids without conspicuous success, with £57,000 invested in a new WPBSA supporters' club, another heavy loser. Board members' expenses amounted to £110,000, the annual dinner had cost £42,000, and administrative costs had risen by £400,000, of which £80,000 was attributable to legal and professional costs. Worst of all, in some eyes, £17,983 had been paid in overdraft charges.

WPBSA Ltd was heading for the rocks. Immediate action was needed and the only practical solution seemed to be to co-opt Hearn and Doyle to the board. However honourably they might have tried to resolve it, this would leave them, as snooker entrepreneurs, with the inherent conflict of interest which had occasioned their earlier resignations from the board, Hearn in September 1988, Doyle in July

Gary Wilkinson in play against Steve Davis in their 1989 semi-final at the Stormseal UK Open. A crucial miscount by Wilkinson in the penultimate frame cost him a famous victory

1989. John Spencer was elected chairman but the most committed figures on the new board, Doyle and Foulds, tended to dominate.

As only time would confirm, Davis had begun a 27-month spell in which he would win no ranking title. He had an incredible escape in the Stormseal UK when Gary Wilkinson, having beaten Jimmy White 9-0 to reach his third semi-final of the season, led him 8-7, only to misread the scoreboard. Believing that Davis did not need a snooker, Wilkinson attempted a needlessly fine edge safety from distance to give Davis the penalty points he needed. From the play again, Wilkinson left the pink for Davis to level at 8-8 prior to sailing through the decider.

Hendry beat Davis for the first time over a long distance, 16-12, for the £100,000 first prize. He led 11-10 after three sessions and made two centuries, 123 and 112, in the first two frames of the evening. At 10-14, Davis responded with

a 138 but, from 14-12, the Scot added the remaining two frames he needed.

Having beaten Reynolds 10-0 in the Rothmans final, Davis lost to him 7-9 in the quarter-finals of the Everest World Matchplay at Brentwood; White, having led 8-3, then scraped past Reynolds only 9-8 in the semis. Parrott, beaten 9-6 by Wilkinson in the UK after a 0-7 opening session, beat Hendry 9-8 from 0-5 down to reach the final, but from 5-8 White romped home 18-9 to win the £100,000 first prize.

None of the game's foremost names featured in the Mercantile Classic final at Blackpool. O'Kane beat Hendry 5-2; James beat Parrott 5-3 in the last 16 and Davis 6-4 in the semis. Warren King became the first Australian for 15 years to reach a ranking final, beating Silvino Francisco 6-5 in a marathon lasting six hours five minutes, but James, scoring more heavily in the balls, beat him there 10-6.

Steve James, winner of the 1990 Mercantile Classic

4-1, only for the world No. 1 to win 5-4. Next round, Davis made mistake after mistake as he went out 5-2 to Steve Newbury.

There was surprise after surprise and eventually Bob Chaperon, a Canadian based at Gainsborough and ranked 29th, won the £75,000 first prize with a 10-8 victory over Higgins, whose £45,000 second prize was the highest of his career. Chaperon survived an incredible 5-4 finish against his best friend and fellow-Canadian Alain Robidoux in the last 32, winning the decider from 47 behind with only one red remaining.

Parrott, beaten in eight of his nine previous major finals, retained the European Open at La Maison du Judo, Lyon, recovering from 5-6 to record a 10-6 victory over Hendry, who had beaten Davis in the semis. Higgins, defeated in the last 32 by Steve James, complained in familiar fashion about anything that came to mind and was the subject of an 'ungentlemanly conduct' report from the referee, Len Ganley.

This was a mere aperitif to his conduct at the British Car Rental World Cup at Bournemouth, in which Canada (Robidoux, Chaperon and Thorburn) beat Northern Ireland (Higgins, Dennis Taylor

Hendry retained the Benson and Hedges Masters by beating Parrott 9-4, after Parrott's 6-2 semi-final win over Davis had revealed the six-times world champion to be in deep disarray, tending to overcut when potting to his left and undercut when potting to his right. Davis had lost his trueness of cueing and it was several months before he realised, after following several false trails, how he could put it right. He had days when he played like his old self, others when his game was in tatters.

The British Open, newly sponsored by Pearl Assurance, changed to an 'all in the hat' type of draw with no seeding. Darren Morgan, fresh from winning the Senator Welsh championship, restricted to Welsh players, beat Hendry 5-4 and led Davis

Bob Chaperon, surprise winner of the 1990 Pearl British Open

Alex Higgins (left) and Dennis Taylor exchange a distant and glacial handshake before they commence 'the grudge match of all time' at the Benson and Hedges Irish Masters in 1990

and Tommy Murphy) 9-5 in the final. At the semi-final victory press conference Higgins hinted at what was to come when he mumbled, 'If I'm not captain tomorrow, I'm not playing,' the sort of childish threat which he had uttered so often during his career that it tended to be ignored. Taylor was the designated captain, but in order to keep the peace, he went along with Higgins's suggestion as to their order of play. However, when Higgins lost his second frame to Robidoux, he insisted, despite Taylor being dressed and ready to play, that he play the remaining two frames of the afternoon himself. Higgins lost them both to leave Northern Ireland 2-6 down.

A furious row ensued in the WPBSA room in which Higgins threatened to have Taylor shot and let fly a volley of personal abuse. After the match, Taylor made an official complaint.

As chance would have it, Higgins and Taylor had to meet in the quarter-finals of the Benson and Hedges Irish Masters, 'the grudge match of all time' as Davis put it. The contrast between Northern Ireland's two former world champions was poignant: Taylor surrounded by family, friends and well-wishers, Higgins, give or take minders and hangers-on, spiritually alone.

When he had called on his former wife, Lynn, a few weeks earlier with presents for their children, she had refused to let him in. Hurt and angry, he had thrown a skateboard through the window, for which he had been fined £50 for criminal damage. Even between beating James Wattana 10-6 on the Tuesday to qualify for the Crucible and this match against Taylor on the Friday, Higgins had maintained his defiant front.

With all seats taken and standing

accommodation full on all three tiers of what is at the best of times a cockpit of an arena, the atmosphere would not have been out of place at a bare-knuckle prize fight. Taylor won 5-2 and Higgins ended the evening a pitiable figure, wild eyed, heavy with drink.

Emotionally drained as he was after beating Higgins, Taylor went on to defeat White 6-5, but in the final Davis beat him 9-4, despite playing to what Taylor assessed was only 60 per cent of his best form.

EMBASSY WORLD CHAMPIONSHIP
That Stephen Hendry should become the first Embassy world champion of the nineties was not all that surprising, in view of the way he had dominated the season, winning three world ranking titles and two major invitation events on his way to the Crucible.

Steve Davis made a colossal effort in defence of his title; at times he played superbly but at others it seemed he had to make a prodigious effort to concentrate, instead of being able to do so automatically and leave all his mental energies free for the quality of his play.

Jimmy White produced a fine performance to beat Davis in the semi-finals but his defeat by Hendry in the final, particularly in the closing stages, revealed a safety game not good enough to contain the quality of the Scot's long potting. Hendry thus superseded Alex Higgins, 1972 vintage, as the youngest world champion ever. Sadly, it was a championship which saw Higgins reduced to new depths of despair and even, it seemed, illness.

His 10-5 defeat in the first round was marked by a '16 red' clearance of 135, James being awarded a free ball with all reds remaining in the 11th frame and clearing the table. Ordinarily, this would have been news, but this time it was overtaken by the behaviour of Higgins.

At the mid-session interval, he remained

in his chair in the arena rather than going off to his dressing room. When he had lost, he stayed several more minutes while the table was being covered, as if unwilling to relinquish the limelight, and ripped the head off Antrim, his leprechaun mascot.

Much worse, on his way to the press conference he punched Colin Randle, the WPBSA's press officer, in the stomach, an unprovoked attack which was immediately added to the list of official complaints already standing against the twice world champion. Without waiting for press questions he launched into a rambling diatribe against all and sundry. His old adversary, Gavin Lightman, QC, was later to suspend him for the whole of the following season.

Although it did not go the distance, Hendry's victory over Alain Robidoux was perhaps the most dramatic of the other first-round matches. At 7-7, the referee, John Street, called a controversial push shot against the Canadian, which left Hendry in for 58 to lead 8-7, and two more frames completed his 10-7 victory.

John Parrott trailed Mark Bennett by two with only three to play, but at 0-59 in the decider produced a mighty 69 clearance to win on the pink; Mike Hallett was another 10-9 winner at the expense of Steve Newbury.

Darren Morgan required an intensive course of treatment, plus the issuing of a certificate that he was free of infectious diseases and could therefore perform in public, after an attack of chicken-pox had threatened his participation. He beat Joe Johnson 10-8, the margin by which Neal Foulds prevailed over Dennis Taylor and Tony Meo over Wayne Jones. Peter Francisco, down 2-4 to Dean Reynolds, potted blacks with his first seven reds in the seventh frame. In striving to maintain red-black position, he chose a more difficult red than he needed to, Reynolds replied with 58 and won the frame on the

Alex Higgins alone in
his corner

Stephen Hendry
becomes the
youngest-ever world
champion in 1990

pink. 'I shouldn't have gone for the 147, but when there's £100,000 staring you in the face it's hard not to be tempted,' said Francisco, after losing 10-7.

The surprise of the round saw John Virgo produce his best form of the season to close out Gary Wilkinson 10-6 after his 7-2 interval lead had been reduced to 7-6.

Only three of the eight second-round matches ended in close finishes. Neal Foulds trailed Willie Thorne 9-7 going into the final session but beat him 13-11; Cliff Thorburn battled for 12 hours 37 minutes to beat Doug Mountjoy 13-12; and Parrott beat Reynolds 13-11, fluking the match-ball pink from a safety shot when the match ran into an unscheduled fourth session.

The four quarter-finals produced no close finishes, though a closer margin than 13-8 certainly appeared likely when Davis's 6-2 first-session lead over Foulds became 8-8 after two sessions. Davis laboured dreadfully in the middle session, but on the last morning played virtually flawlessly to reel off five frames for the match, Foulds aggregating only 12 points in the first three.

From 4-5, Terry Griffiths subsided to a 13-5 defeat by Jimmy White and from 4-4 Hendry progressed to a 13-6 win over Morgan. Parrott made the highest break of the championship, 140, to lead Thorburn 8-4. The Canadian then closed to 6-8 and opened the scoring with 64 in the next frame, but Parrott cleared with 65 to win on the black and completed a 13-6 victory without further loss.

White's 16-14 semi-final win over Davis hinged on the third session, in which he improved from 6-8 to 13-9. Davis reduced his arrears to 13-14 by winning the 27th frame on the black after needing a snooker. Rather than being distracted, White regained his concentration and, from 0-40, White went two up with three to play, clinching his 16-14 victory in the next frame but one.

The balance of power shifted in extraordinary fashion in the other semi-final. Parrot led 4-0 and should have led at least 6-2 overnight, instead of 5-3. Next day, Hendry won six straight frames to lead 9-5, before Parrott won the following six to lead 11-9. Strangely, he did not win another frame as Hendry, taking the last two of the third session and the first five of the fourth, completed the seven-frame winning streak which carried him into the final, 16-11.

The final itself required only six hours three minutes playing time for its 30 frames, an average of barely 12 minutes each. Hendry was five times two frames in front on the opening day, which he ended with a 108 break to lead 9-7. Crucially, he added the first four frames next afternoon in only 45 minutes to open up a six-frame gap, which White was never able to reduce to fewer than four.

Beaten 18-12, White admitted that while he was disappointed with his safety play, he was pleased for Hendry, who had 'played tremendous snooker. You could count his misses on one hand.' So deeply had Hendry psyched himself up that he appeared eerily cool in the aftermath of victory.

1990 EMBASSY WORLD CHAMPIONSHIP

FIRST ROUND: S. Davis beat E. Charlton 10-1; S. James beat A. Higgins 10-5; W. Thorne beat T. Drago 10-4; N. Foulds beat Dennis Taylor 10-8; T. Griffiths beat N. Gilbert 10-4; A. Knowles beat T. Chappel 10-4; S. Hendry beat A. Robidoux 10-7; T. Meo beat W. Jones 10-8; D. Morgan beat J. Johnson 10-8; M. Hallett beat S. Newbury 10-9; C. Thorburn beat C. Wilson 10-6; D. Mountjoy beat B. Gollan 10-8; D. Reynolds beat P. Francisco 10-7; J. Parrott beat M. Bennett 10-9

SECOND ROUND: Davis beat James 13-7; Foulds beat Thorne 13-11; Griffiths beat Knowles 13-6; White beat Virgo 13-6; Hendry beat Meo 13-7; Morgan beat Hallett 13-8; Thorburn beat Mountjoy 13-12; Parrott beat Reynolds 13-11

QUARTER-FINALS: Davis beat Foulds 13-8; White beat Griffiths 13-5; Hendry beat Morgan 13-6; Parrott beat Thorburn 13-6

SEMI-FINALS: White beat Davis 16-14; Hendry beat Parrott 16-11

FINAL: Hendry beat White 18-12

The age of Hendry had begun and the era of open snooker was about to. It had long been obvious that the WPBSA had been operating a restrictive entry policy which was not in the game's best interests. By restricting full tournament-playing rights to 128 players, with a maximum of ten newcomers replacing the stragglers each year, it was clear that many more were propped up by mutual mediocrity.

Various limited expansion schemes were put forward, including an illogical and unsatisfactory package which was put to a WPBSA EGM, the irony of which was that the existing members were expected to vote in a threat to their livelihoods. The greatest furore was created by the suggestion that the women's world champion, Allison Fisher, be granted full playing rights as a special case.

Fisher's case was strongly argued by Barry Hearn, who was poised to become her manager. A little later, he also became the manager of two other leading women, Stacey Hillyard and Karen Corr, and negotiated a contract with the World Ladies Billiards and Snooker Association giving him exclusive rights to promote the women's world championship for the next five years. There was no undertaking, incidentally, that any future women's world champion would be invited into the WPBSA.

Just about everyone in snooker was in favour of women having equal

Three women's world champions: Allison Fisher (left), Stacey Hillyard (above) and Karen Corr

incorporate minor ranking events at lower points tariffs. For once, virtually everyone was in favour of a brave new world, although there proved to be many difficulties in implementing it in time for the following 1991-92 season.

In summer 1990, an Irishman, Joe Swail, beat a Scotsman, Alan McManus, 13-11 for the English amateur title; Peter Ebdon won the world under-21 title in Brisbane; and Alex Higgins's latest series of grave disciplinary offences was punished by depriving him of 25 world ranking points – taking him from 14th to 120th – a fine of £5,000 and a ban for the whole of the 1990-91 season.

World Series II, under the joint auspices of Hearn and Doyle, began at the Hong Kong Hilton with Wattana beating Davis and White for the £20,000 first prize. Doyle put the Regal Scottish Masters, won by Hendry, into World Series and Parrott won the Humo Masters in Antwerp, yet once again World Series did not finish the course. All the tournaments were well received individually but, with no overall prize funds or bonuses, they did not hang

opportunity: the objection was to giving them preference. Fisher had competed in the professional ticket series and one year had finished 16th, but there was extensive opposition to her being favoured simply on the grounds of gender.

The WPBSA's second thoughts were refreshing in their simplicity: open up membership to anyone, regardless of ability, who was prepared to pay a £500 enrolment fee, £100 annual subscription and £100 per tournament entry fee. This scale of fees, it was calculated, would enable the necessary pre-qualifying and qualifying competitions for world ranking events not to be run at a loss. The new intake totalled an astonishing 443.

In turn, this involved revising the ranking points system, not only to accommodate larger fields but also to

The name is Bond. Nigel Bond. He eliminated several top-class adversaries to reach the final of the 1990 Rothmans Grand Prix

credibly together.

With ITV's September slot gone, the first ranking tournament of the season was the Rothmans Grand Prix at Reading. Hendry was almost put out of contention before striking a ball when his cue was stolen from the practice room. After much panic and promise of reward it was returned at a press conference, to an emotional reception from Hendry.

At 3-4, he trailed Silvino Francisco by 34 with only two reds remaining in the eighth, but the South African missed an eminently pottable penultimate red to allow Hendry to scrape into the last 16, 5-4. He was not seriously threatened again until the final, in which he beat Bond 10-5.

Bond, having beaten Davis in qualifying for the 16-man final phase of the Asian Open, beat him again at Reading and had further wins over Eddie Charlton, Willie Thorne, Neal Foulds and, in the semi-finals, Jimmy White, 9-8 on the final black. A four-frame winning streak in

which he made breaks of 100, 65, 139 and 85 helped him lead Hendry 5-3, but the Scot then won all seven evening frames.

Hendry took two more titles in style – the Asian Open and the Dubai Classic. In Guangzhou, in mainland China, up-river from Hong Kong, he beat Dennis Taylor 9-3 in a final which television scheduling required to start at 9 a.m. This was unfortunate for Taylor, who had laboured until 11.36 the previous evening for his 6-5 win over Tony Chappel, who had earlier put out John Parrott. In the Dubai Classic, the new world champion dropped only three frames in four matches, crushing Davis 9-1 in the final.

Hendry threatened to overwhelm Davis again in the Stormseal UK final, taking the opening session 6-1, but eventually had to take the last two frames to win 16-15. In his 57 clearance to win the penultimate frame on the black, Hendry's blue for pink was one of the best rest shots ever played under pressure. He took the decider with a break of 98. Much as he would like to have won, Davis took pleasure in the renewal of his form and confidence, commenting, 'It's very hard to keep up the charade of being a top player when you don't feel like one.'

Alan McManus made his first notable professional showing, beating White 9-6 in the quarters and holding Hendry to 5-5 before the world champion seized his 9-5 victory with breaks of 61, 109, 69 and 108. Undeterred, McManus dashed through the night to Glasgow in time to play his first match in the Benson and Hedges satellite event the following morning. By winning it, he earned one of the two wild cards which were on offer for the Benson and Hedges Masters at Wembley.

However, the UK Championship provided Hearn with a serious problem as Stormseal went into receivership, leaving him, as the promoter, to find a shortfall of £299,000 in prizemoney. He also upset the snooker press by omitting to inform them that the prize fund for his Coalite World Matchplay had been reduced from the advertised £250,000 to £200,000 and that White had earned not £100,000 but £70,000 for beating Hendry 18-9. Hendry's ten-month unbeaten run in Britain ended in anticlimax as the head cold which had troubled him during his 9-6 semi-final win over Davis worsened steadily through the two-day final.

This initiated a £330,000 hat-trick of first prizes for White, who led Hendry 9-0 and beat him 10-4 in the Mercantile Classic final. Hendry did not appear to have marshalled his mental resources for a needlessly early 11 a.m. start, after his 6-4 semi-final win over Neal Foulds had kept him in the building until nearly midnight the previous evening.

To complete his hat-trick, White won the £200,000 first prize, a record for snooker, in the Mita World Masters which Hearn promoted at the National Exhibition Centre, Birmingham, with the aid of a £2.5 million budget agreed by Rupert Murdoch on behalf of BSkyB, who then controlled Eurosport. The event was designed as a special attraction, not only for the channel's existing viewers, but to stimulate satellite dish sales for new ones.

This was a prodigious coup by Hearn. The format was uncannily similar to that which the Hearn-Warren-IMG triumvirate had envisaged for their World Open, never staged. In fact, so similar was it that IMG threatened legal action. Hence, it became the World Masters with men's and women's singles and doubles, a mixed doubles and a junior event. The top 64 in the WPBSA rankings were invited, with the result that every country with even the faintest snooker tradition was represented by at least one player. All former world champions were invited and here lay the first source of conflict between Hearn the promoter and Hearn the WPBSA board member.

Higgins was suspended and rightly so. The WPBSA board – Hearn naturally dissenting – thought its credibility as a governing body would be damaged if he was allowed to play, even though it was not a WPBSA event. A boycott was threatened by certain players and there appeared to be an impasse, which Higgins resolved by declining the invitation. Next day, the WPBSA sanctioned the tournament.

Hearn also felt the need to jazz up the event by introducing a gratuitous tie-break, the two elements of which had no compatible logic. On the one hand, he decided that matches must have a two frame winning margin; on the other, he stipulated that after a maximum number of frames, a tie-break should be played, involving only one red and all the colours. The event would have been successful without these extraneous gimmicks, neither of which have been repeated.

Wattana celebrated his 21st birthday by making a 147 maximum, but

Jimmy White, in play, brought Stephen Hendry's ten-month unbeaten run in Britain to a close by beating him in the Mercantile Classic final in January 1991

unfortunately Sky's interesting technical innovation, a mobile crane camera to cover the 'outside' tables to supplement the full camera coverage on the two show tables, proved unequal to the occasion. The mobile was parked two tables away and, short of charging heedlessly across the intervening table, there was nothing that could be done in the eight minutes it took Wattana to make what would have been only the fourth televised maximum. Asked to describe his feelings as the last black went down, Wattana replied: 'I feel very happy. I am thinking of a big money.' He was disappointed to learn there was no jackpot prize for a maximum.

Much of the flavour of the event came from the supporting cast, which included Rui Chapeu, a Brazilian who played in all white from shoes to cap, Juan Castaneda of Panama, who had never played snooker but creditably made a 50 break, and Gotfried Kotzinger, an Austrian who had mostly played billiards on pocketless tables.

The event also produced the first notable miscarriage of justice inherent in the new guidelines on the miss rule that the WPBSA had issued to referees on 1 January 1990. These were intended to make snooker players give a higher priority to attempting a successful escape. Some had made escaping a low priority in comparison with leaving no breakmaking opportunity for their opponents.

Any professional referee should have been able to read the game sufficiently clearly to enforce the miss rule as it stood but, in attempting written clarification, the situation was created whereby the player, unless he escaped from the snooker or left a pot on, was very likely to be required to play again from the original snookered position. Hence, it became relatively common for snookers to be worth 20 or more points. Most drastic of all was the directive that if a player three times in succession failed to connect with

a ball he could hit direct, the frame would be awarded to his opponent.

To make matters worse, in the quarter-finals of the World Masters this directive was imperfectly understood. Terry Griffiths was leading Tony Drago 3-2 when, snookered, he four times attempted a two-cushion escape to a group of reds, conceding 21 in penalties. After the third attempt, the referee, Alan Chamberlain, warned Griffiths that he risked disqualification if he offended again. He was as good as his word and Griffiths farcically forfeited the frame without a ball potted.

The referee had exceeded his powers, not entirely inexcusably since the guidelines were in their infancy and not crystal clear, but this was no consolation to Griffiths, who eventually lost on a tie-break shoot-out 9-8. Drago went on to reach the final before losing to White, 10-6.

Hendry and Hallett (men's doubles), Karen Corr (women's singles), Allison Fisher and Stacey Hillyard (women's doubles) and Steve Davis and Fisher (mixed doubles) were the other champions, while a 15-year-old Scot, John Higgins, won the junior event, in which a 13-year-old Australian, Quinten Hann, made a break of 100 on television.

White's winning streak ended in the semi-finals of the Benson and Hedges Masters at Wembley, where he was beaten 6-1 by Hendry, aggregating only 59 points in the last six frames. Next afternoon, it was Hendry's turn to be drubbed as Hallett led him 7-0 at the interval. He missed the pink for 8-0, led 8-2, but missed the pink for victory at 9-2 and the match was still alive at 8-3 at the intermission. Hallett had chances in most frames, but knowing that he should already have won put more pressure on him than he could take. Hendry, knowing he should have lost, buckled down coolly to win 9-8.

Hendry also regained the Pearl British

Open, recording his sixth consecutive tournament win over Davis 9-7 in the semi-finals. Gary Wilkinson, having led 8-5, stumbled over the line a 9-8 semi-final winner over White, and was level at 8-8 before Hendry beat him 10-9 in the final.

Having won seven major titles and £595,000 in official prizemoney in seven months, Hendry inexplicably lost in the last 16 of the European Open in Rotterdam, going down 5-0 to Mark Johnston-Allen, who was then ranked 55 in the world. Cliff Thorburn, feeling his brightest since having been seriously ill with a poisoned appendix in the autumn, beat Davis 5-4 in a 3.11 a.m. finish. Tony Jones, 36th in the rankings, beat

Tony Jones was the surprise winner of the 1991 European Open

Johnston-Allen 9-7 in the final, the capacity crowds in the Imax Centre indicating the appetite of the Dutch public for top-class snooker. Davis renewed his hopes of a seventh world title by retaining the Benson and Hedges Irish Masters, with wins over White and Parrott in the last two rounds.

EMBASSY WORLD CHAMPIONSHIP

John Parrott, a racing man, appreciates the importance of timing a run to perfection. After a run-of-the-mill season, he discovered a new dimension of

temperament to add to the skill he had long possessed – and came home the winner of the Embassy World Championship stakes by a considerable distance. His triumph, as emphatic as it was unexpected, laid to rest the canard that he was a first-class player but a fatally flawed competitor.

Having lost seven major finals in Britain, it seemed that he could withstand pressure until it became the climactic pressure of a final. Perhaps there had been less pressure in winning two European Opens in the comparative obscurity of Deauville and Lyon than in winning ranking events on BBC or ITV in Britain. While he had always been an impressive front runner, this year he was much more resolute, particularly in responding positively to an opponent's comeback. He was less inclined to blame external factors, having come to realise that, while luck can be important, a player's attitude to it is more important still. 'I've grown up,' he said, within minutes of this triumph at Sheffield.

The most dramatic match of the opening round saw Steve Davis turn a 6-8 deficit into a 10-8 win over a Crucible debutant, Ken Doherty. Alan McManus also made an impressive Crucible debut by beating Willie Thorne 10-8 and there were two other 10-8 finishes. Despite these close scores, though, the opening round produced comparatively few moments of drama.

One of them saw Gary Wilkinson pot 15 reds and 15 blacks, before missing a straightforward yellow with a 147 – and the £100,000 jackpot it carried – very much in sight.

Three second-round matches went the full distance. Steve James won the last two frames for his 13-12 win over Dean Reynolds, as did Jimmy White, having trailed Neal Foulds 8-11. Terry Griffiths, 7-10 down against McManus, levelled at 10-10 and swapped frame for frame before

calling deeply on his vast reserves of experience and resolve to take the decider.

Parrott showed a title contender's form in crushing Tony Knowles 13-1, with 138 as his top break. He felt that a new, specially made cue had made a great deal of difference.

The quarter-finals saw the exit of the defending champion as Steve James, trailing 7-9 going into the final session and 9-11 halfway through it, seized a 13-11 victory with a run of four straight frames. As runs of 69 and 88 gave James the lead for the first time at 12-11, Hendry could not take advantage of his only chance in what proved to be the last frame. James's achievement was all the more remarkable in the light of his diabetes, diagnosed eight months earlier, and thus his suspect stamina.

White brushed Wilkinson aside 13-3, concluding the match with a break of 138, and Davis, unruffled by a 400-mile round trip the day before the match to the Essex hospital where his wife, Judy, was giving birth to their first child, pressed home a 9-7 advantage to beat Dennis Taylor 13-7. Parrott had his 11-8 lead over Griffiths reduced to 11-10 but prevailed 13-10.

White held a comfortable 8-3 lead over James in their semi-final, before James recovered to 8-9, helped by three centuries

in four frames – 102, 106 and, in the first frame of the last morning, 135. White nevertheless led 13-9 after three sessions and clinched victory without further loss at 16-9.

Parrott was even better placed at 11-4 before Davis, by taking the last frame of the second session and the first three of the third, presented him with a major test of character. Davis won the first two frames of the final session, but Parrott had plenty left and responded with breaks of 86 and 64, to clinch his 16-10 win and his second final appearance in three years.

It is hard to imagine a better first-session performance than the one which gave Parrott a 7-0 lead in the final. He began the session with a break of 97 and ended it with one of 117, to aggregate 634-80 for the afternoon.

Although White narrowed the gap to four at 11-7, this was the nearest he could get as Parrott ended the match at 18-11, with the seven-frame advantage he had earned that first afternoon.

1991 EMBASSY WORLD CHAMPIONSHIP

FIRST ROUND: S. Hendry beat W. King 10-4; A. Robidoux beat S. Newbury 10-5; S. James beat I. Graham 10-3; D. Reynolds beat R. Marshall 10-8; Gary Wilkinson beat D. Mountjoy 10-2; M. Clark beat M. Bennett 10-6; N. Foulds beat E. Charlton 10-7; J. White beat N. Dyson 10-3; J. Parrott beat N. Gilbert 10-6; T. Knowles beat J. Virgo 10-8; A. McManus beat W. Thorne 10-8; T. Griffiths beat B. Pinches 10-3; T. Jones beat M. Hallett 10-4; Dennis Taylor beat J. Johnson 10-6; T. Meo beat C. Edwards 10-7; S. Davis beat K. Doherty 10-8

SECOND ROUND: Hendry beat Robidoux 13-8; James beat Reynolds 13-12; Wilkinson beat Clark 13-9; White beat Foulds 13-12; Parrott beat Knowles 13-1; Griffiths beat McManus 13-12; Taylor beat Jones 13-8; Davis beat Meo 13-6

QUARTER-FINALS: James beat Hendry 13-11; White beat Wilkinson 13-3; Parrott beat Griffiths 13-10; Davis beat Taylor 13-7

SEMI-FINALS: White beat James 16-9; Parrott beat Davis 16-10

FINAL: Parrott beat White 18-11

On a tide of hope and expectation, David Harrison had been appointed the WPBSA's chief executive in April 1991, with Del Simmons, previously its key executive, receiving a generous severance payment totalling £270,000.

Harrison had worked intermittently in snooker for almost a decade and had five years' experience as tournaments director and contracts negotiator for the World Indoor Bowls Council. He understood snooker's internal politics without being bogged down in them; he had experience of television and sponsorship negotiations; he was personable and articulate. He was to spend two years in the £60,000-a-year post before his unwillingness to abandon commercial work in bowls, contrary to his WPBSA agreement, forced his resignation.

Harrison was the first WPBSA executive to have a vision of a mutually productive relationship between the amateur and professional games, which came as a refreshing contrast to the closed minds of most amateur and professional officials in this respect. While the B&SCC, founded in 1885, had originally been the sole governing body, the WPBSA had declared its autonomy to run the professional game in 1971 and the one nation one vote International Billiards and Snooker Federation, founded in 1971, was effectively the world amateur governing body long before the B&SCC officially conceded this in 1984.

The B&SCC thus became an English amateur association which also ran some British tournaments, but when the Sports Council withdrew its grant on grounds of limited efficiency in 1989, it could generate little in the way of funds and respect on its own. Clapped out and cashless, it arrived at the knacker's yard in the summer of 1991, when Harrison instigated not only the WPBSA's purchase of its assets, including a highly arguable copyright of the rules, but a new body, the English Association for Snooker and Billiards, to carry out its English domestic functions. He also encouraged closer relationships with the fledgling European Amateur Association and the IBSF, which was starting to feel the pinch of financial and political problems.

The world amateur championship had been put on an annual basis in 1984, but the more players who joined the WPBSA the more amateur titles became devalued. While Harrison envisaged a structure for snooker, with the WPBSA at its apex, whereby the whole of the amateur and professional games could hang together from top to bottom, the amateur officials, jealous of their perks, positions and authority, tended not to agree with this. At least, though, Harrison initiated contact and debate across the barricades of prejudice.

There were more immediate problems to deal with. The board's answer to the need for a new ranking system to accommodate the influx of new players and the establishment of minor ranking events was to try to force through a heated EGM its proposal to re-rank players retrospectively on a new tariff, on the basis of results already known. This naturally provoked fury from those who were disadvantaged, yet surprisingly this ludicrous proposal failed only by a single vote. It also exacerbated the distrust between board and membership.

The much expanded summer qualifying school required and received meticulous organisation. Three first-class snooker clubs at Aldershot, Bolton and Sheffield were used for the pre-qualifying stage and a specially set-up arena at Trentham Gardens, Stoke for the qualifying. It was immediately apparent that the professional game had acquired overnight a large number of high-quality players. Centuries were commonplace and a maximum 147 came from Peter Ebdon in the very first frame of pre-qualifying for the new

John Parrott's capture of the 1991 world title made him Merseyside's Sportsman of the Year, ahead of all its famous footballers

Mick Price equalled the world record by making centuries in three consecutive frames in the Benson and Hedges satellite tournament in Glasgow in 1990

pad with events in Bangkok (won by Davis), Hong Kong and Delhi (won by Hendry), plus the Regal Scottish Masters and the Humo Masters, both won by Hallett. Hearn, increasingly occupied with boxing, had admitted a shift in emphasis from management to promotion and Taylor, Meo, White, Thorne and Foulds had already left his fold, none without later expressing certain dissatisfactions. Hearn had been joined by Ronnie O'Sullivan, the 15-year-old who had made a 147 break in the southern final of the English Amateur Championship, lost the national final to Steve Judd, but won the world under-21 title in Bangalore. However, Griffiths and Thorburn also left him, so that by 1993 his stable comprised only Davis, O'Sullivan and the three leading women, Allison Fisher, Stacey Hillyard and Karen Corr.

The mundane functionalism of even the latter stages of the Stoke qualifying extravaganza, in contrast to the exotic venues and relatively pressure-free World Series events, helped to account for the failure of some distinguished practitioners to qualify for the final phases of world ranking events. Hendry lost to Warren King in the Dubai Classic, 5-0 to Joe Swail in the Asian Open, and to Mark Johnston-Allen, for the second year in succession, in the European Open.

Parrott, playing much as he had in

Strachan Open. Paul Dawkins, twice Welsh amateur champion, made breaks of 115, 102 and 134 in consecutive frames in the UK Open, a hat-trick previously achieved only by Steve Davis, Doug Mountjoy and, in the Benson and Hedges satellite tournament in Glasgow in 1990, by Mick Price.

There was limited success for Alex Higgins, back from his year's suspension but ranked 120 and condemned to a long hot summer in the qualifying school. Recovering to 72nd by the end of the season, he bore some of his defeats better than others and qualified for the 64-man final phase of the UK Championship at Preston Guild Hall, scene of 'some of my tumultuous occasions, good and bad'.

While the hopefuls slogged through the qualifying, World Series III left the launch

Mark Johnston-Allen twice eliminated Stephen Hendry from the European Open

winning the world title, won the first ranking tournament of the new season, the Dubai Classic, by beating an at least partly rejuvenated Tony Knowles 9-3. Paul Davies, a rookie Welshman, won ten matches to reach the semi-finals before losing 6-0 to Parrott; Martin Clark beat Davis 5-3 before losing to Davies.

The good ship Hendry needed to be steadied and achieved just that by retaining the Rothmans Grand Prix title. His closest match was his first, a recovery from 2-4 to beat Mark Rowing, the 1989 English amateur champion, 5-4. Parrott, reacting to his Dubai triumph, lost 5-4 to Brian Morgan, a former world under-21 champion who had won only one match in the whole of the previous season. Joe Johnson, who had almost died from a heart attack six months earlier, reached the quarter-finals, as did a rookie professional, Dave Finbow, who won nine matches to get there.

Hendry drubbed Davis 7-1 in the opening session of the final and although Davis closed to 6-8, winning the 14th frame on the black with a titanic 71 clearance, a break of 106 completed Hendry's 10-6 victory.

At Brighton County Court, a venue not usually associated with snooker, Howard Kruger, former WPBSA board member and manager of a group of players who had all suffered financial bruising, was disqualified from holding any company directorship for five years.

Britain's economic recession was starting to bite on the snooker world. With no suitable replacement for Stormseal to sponsor the UK Open, the WPBSA made a prize fund of £250,000 available from its own resources. Hearn's three-year promotion of a one-night-a-month dinner and black tie tournament at London's Café Royal ended when his sponsors, Continental Airlines, went into receivership and could not be replaced. Many of the commercially run clubs which

had opened in the boom of the 1980s closed in the recession of the 1990s.

Parrott achieved his third world ranking title in four attempts by beating White 16-13 in the UK final. Wattana beat Davis 9-6 in the last 16 to establish himself further as a serious contender for major titles, before losing 9-7 to Parrott in the semis.

Hendry, beaten 9-2 by White in the other semi-final, gave only glimpses of his quality after being involved in a distressing encounter with Higgins, whom he had beaten 9-4 in the last 64. There were two versions of what was said as the players shook hands. Higgins claimed he said: 'Well done, Stephen, you were a little bit lucky.' Hendry heard this as: 'Up your **** you ****.' For such remarks after the match and his behaviour during the day, official complaints against Higgins were filed by Hendry, Ian Doyle, the referee John Street, and the tournament director Ann Yates. Higgins counter-complained against Doyle, a member of the board as well as Hendry's manager, on the grounds that such remarks as 'He is a demented raving lunatic who has to be removed from the game' were inappropriate to a board member and prejudicial to a fair hearing of the case.

Although the case against Higgins appeared cut and dried, the WPBSA made some baffling procedural errors in the eight months it took to resolve it, and neither Doyle nor Hendry chose to appear in person at the disciplinary hearing. The dismissal of five of the seven charges against Higgins left him with only two reprimands and two £500 fines, which was a flea-bite in view of his previous disciplinary record.

Gary Wilkinson, cast into a negative frame of mind by having started the season fifth in the world rankings, ended a poor run of results by winning the Coalite World Matchplay with victories over Parrott 9-8, White 9-6 and Davis 18-11.

Davis had earlier inflicted a 9-2 drubbing on Hendry, who was still out of sorts. Wilkinson had played to a high level of competence, yet even in victory could not release his emotions, admitting to feeling numb rather than elated.

Despite his defeat by Wilkinson, it was clearly apparent that Davis was regaining form and confidence, through his unremitting application. Three consecutive first prizes in December 1991 and January 1992 were to confirm this, and he did not disguise his elation after beating Hendry 10-9 to win the sixth and last World Series event in Antwerp. Hendry had looked invincible all through the tournament, to the point where he led Davis 4-0 in the final. (Hearn, too, could take satisfaction in having, at his third attempt, piloted World Series through to its advertised conclusion, largely through three events being sponsored by 555. However, this satisfaction was not to be repeated the following year.)

A 9-8 victory over Hendry in the final of the Mercantile Classic gave Davis his first ranking title for 27 months. Hendry had played some deadly spells during the tournament, scoring 353, 315 and 291 points without reply in three of his matches, but Davis's tactical acumen and all-round consistency did not allow Hendry to flow in this way during their encounter.

Davis completed his hat-trick by winning the Asian Open in Bangkok with a 9-3 defeat of Alan McManus, who confirmed that he had become a rising force in the game.

Davis's winning streak came to an end when he was beaten 5-4 by Neal Foulds in the quarter-finals of the Benson and Hedges Masters, but Hendry's unbeaten run at Wembley continued as he took the title for the fourth time. This came in February and was

Hendry's first title since October. White and Parrott, who had both been struggling, also did better at Wembley, but Hendry beat White 6-4 in their semi and Parrott 9-4 in the final.

Hendry immediately added the inaugural Regal Welsh Open to his portfolio of success. Darren Morgan, who had won the corresponding event for the two previous years when it was still restricted to Welsh players, drew on patriotic support to beat Parrott 6-3 in the semi-finals, before a capacity crowd of 1,400 saw a 9-3 victory for Hendry in the final.

At the Pearl British Open White, needing to re-establish his world title credentials, beat Davis 9-8 in the semis and Wattana 10-7 in the final – but not before his 7-0 lead had been reduced to 8-7. The young Dubliner, Ken Doherty, reached his first ranking semi-final by beating Hendry 5-2 and led Wattana 6-5 only to go down 9-6.

Wattana, for reasons within and beyond his control, was the star of the tournament. Told just before his fifth-round match with Tony Drago that his father had been shot in Bangkok – over gambling debts as it transpired – he went on to make a 147 maximum and won 5-1. Minutes later, he learned that his father

Darren Morgan drew on patriotic Welsh support to reach the final of the 1992 Regal Welsh Open

James Wattana made a 147 break in the Pearl British Open shortly after learning that his father had been shot in Bangkok. Minutes after his 5-1 victory over Tony Drago, he was told that the wounds had proved fatal

had died of his wounds. Perhaps his Buddhist faith enabled him to accept this tragedy more readily than most players would have done. In any event, he buckled down not only to reach the final but to win the circuit's next tournament, the untelevised Strachan Open at Bristol, by swamping Parrott 9-3 in the final. Doherty, who had beaten Parrott 5-4 in the British Open, led him 5-0 in the semi-finals only to lose 9-7, while Nigel Bond made his fourth unsuccessful semi-final appearance of the season, beaten 9-5 by Wattana.

Neither Davis nor White, who at the time of entry had also been under Hearn's management, had competed in the Strachan Open – to the detriment of their world rankings. Both had qualified for the eight-man concluding phase of the European Open in Tongeren, where White beat Davis 5-1, Terry Griffiths 6-0 and triumphed 9-3 in the final against Mark Johnston-Allen, a 6-2 semi-final winner over Parrott. White, whose capacity for sociable enjoyment has never been in doubt, informed the press that he had resolved to live more sensibly and soberly on the run up to Sheffield.

Doherty, though beaten 9-6 by Hendry, became the first Republic of Ireland player to reach the Irish Masters final in its 14-year history, although the event was chiefly memorable for Davis forfeiting their deciding ninth frame after a triple miss in their quarter-final. At 4-4, Davis led 37-36 with three reds, all lying on the top cushion, remaining. He three times attempted a thin edge return to baulk safety shot but three times failed to make contact. Under the guidelines, John Street awarded frame and match to Doherty.

Doherty had the form to do well at the Crucible. Unfortunately, he did not produce enough of it at Preston for the world qualifying, in which he lost 10-7 to Peter Francisco. It was again a miss rule decision that proved decisive, at 7-9, and this time Doherty was less than happy with the referee's interpretation. He felt it was getting out of hand.

Alan McManus qualified for the Crucible by beating Mark Bennett from three down with four to play, Bennett having led 63-0 in the penultimate frame, while Wattana scraped through to a Crucible debut 10-9 over a temporarily rejuvenated Kirk Stevens.

EMBASSY WORLD CHAMPIONSHIP
A vintage championship and a final turning on the mother of all comebacks was just what snooker needed to combat the niggling negativity of some journalists, notably Patrick Collins in the *Mail on Sunday*, a persistent and longstanding enemy of the game who had even argued on television that snooker should not be covered on the sports pages. A peak audience of 11.6 million viewers for the climax of the final, in which Stephen Hendry overtook Jimmy White to win the title for the second time, emphasised the prominent place the best of snooker could earn in the affections of the British public.

The audience for this match was less than one million fewer than the 12.3 million average maintained through the

90 minutes' play in the FA Cup final, the daddy of all Britain's traditional sporting events. Despite the erosion of all audiences through the growing strength of Channel 4 and the satellite stations, it was the highest for a world final for six years.

From the outset, this championship also succeeded in attracting many of the more marginal followers of the game, who become involved only if they sense something special is happening. This year the marginals were captured by a build-up of factors: the emergence of Peter Ebdon, who made a striking debut at the Crucible by eliminating Steve Davis and reaching

the quarter-finals at his first attempt; a number of interesting matches between established players and relative newcomers; and White's 147 in the context of his continuing quest for the elusive title.

This was a championship in which several dogs had their day, be they well-liked old dogs like Terry Griffiths, a semi-finalist, or unknown new dogs like Chris Small, an 18-year-old Scot who made it all the way from the first pre-qualifying round to the last 16 at the Crucible.

The opening day brought the Crucible's first whitewash, 10-0 for John Parrott over

Peter Ebdon beat Steve Davis on his Crucible debut and went on to reach the world quarter-finals

Eddie Charlton. The opening round brought another landmark, with its second 147 by Jimmy White in the course of his 10-4 victory over Tony Drago. 'If I can handle that kind of pressure, I know my nerve will stand up to anything thrown at me for the rest of the championship,' was his reaction to having secured not only the £14,000 highest break prize but the £100,000 bonus.

Peter Ebdon was inspired rather than daunted by the prospect of making his Crucible debut against Steve Davis, and set about proving it with a break of 92 at his first scoring visit. Davis led 4-3 and 43-0 but his failure at an easy pink set off the seven-frame winning streak with which Ebdon put him out. Davis had gone into the arena lacking nothing in preparation or desire, yet somehow without the emotional charge which activates high form in response to circumstances.

Dene O'Kane trailed Steve James 0-5 before pulling up to 4-5 overnight. He fell 6-9 in arrears next afternoon, but snatched a 10-9 victory from three down with four to play, leaving James to wonder how or why he'd lost his habitual calm under pressure.

Small, a Leith bank clerk until the preceding August, became one of the few Crucible debutants to make a century, 110, in his first session on snooker's most famous stage. He trailed Doug Mountjoy 5-4 overnight, but in a series of close finishes committed fewer unforced errors than the Welsh veteran as he got through 10-7. It was his ninth win in the event, his earlier victims in the qualifying competition having included women's

Chris Small won eight pre-qualifying and qualifying matches to reach the Crucible in his first professional season and also beat Doug Mountjoy on snooker's most famous stage

world champion Allison Fisher, Cliff Thorburn and Danny Fowler.

Terry Griffiths, from 9-5, held off Bob Chaperon 10-8 and Neal Foulds, from 6-2, was a 10-8 winner over Jason Ferguson, another Crucible newcomer.

A 10-8 win for Alan McManus sent Mike Hallett out of the top 16, while Willie Thorne celebrated his appearance at that stage by beating Gary Wilkinson 10-6. Mick Price, making his Crucible debut, beat Dennis Taylor 10-6, as the 1985 champion produced one of his poorest displays at the venue.

Jim Wych, on only his third return to the Crucible since reaching the quarter-finals in his debut year, 1980, beat Dean Reynolds 10-7 in a match which provided one item for students of snooker trivia: Reynolds's winning total of 38 in the eighth frame was the lowest ever recorded in a frame of professional snooker in which all balls were potted. Wych went on to secure a cheque for £22,500, the largest of

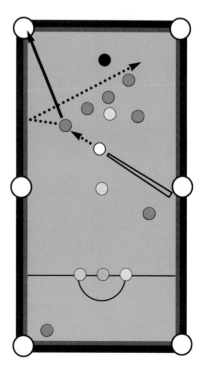

JIMMY WHITE'S 147: 1992 EMBASSY WORLD CHAMPIONSHIP

Shot 1
9th red
Position had to be retained by striking the cue-ball right off centre to spin it off the side cushion and avoid a kiss on other reds.

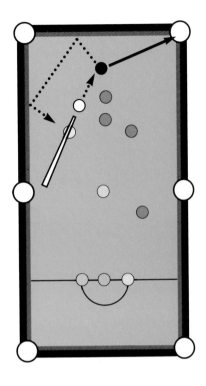

Shot 2
11th black
White, a left-hander, had to use the rest for a delicate fine cut, dropping the black in at pocket weight to hold position for his next red. This required him to screw the cue-ball off a thin edge of the black.

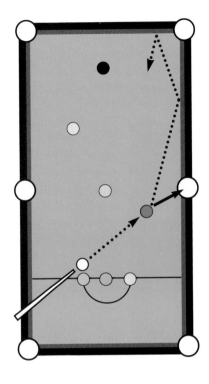

Shot 4
15th red
White had left a natural angle to pot the last red and take the cue-ball off two cushions to finish on the black. The skill of the shot lay in leaving the ideal angle on the black.

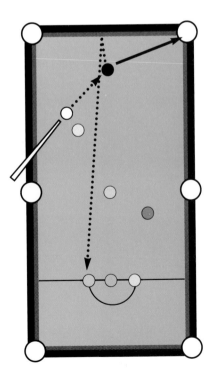

Shot 3
14th black
Slightly out of ideal position to be sure of potting the black, White had to make sure that the cue-ball finished near enough the baulk line to leave the requisite angle on the last red from which to gain position on the 15th black.

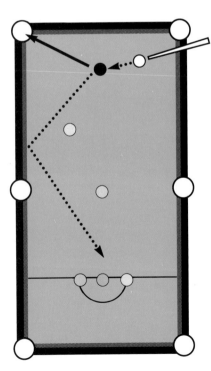

Shot 5
15th black
A straightforward positional shot from black to ideal position for yellow with the colours ideally situated for the clearance.

his career, by beating Thorne 13-6 to reach the quarter-finals.

Parrott, a 13-1 winner over Tony Knowles at the corresponding stage of the 1991 competition, beat him again 13-4, though only after a highly controversial incident in the 11th frame had knocked the stuffing out of Knowles's resistance.

At 4-6 he was still competing keenly when he was undone by an application of the miss rule which was surely never envisaged by its originators. With the last four colours remaining, Parrott attempted to play the cue-ball through a narrow gap between pink and blue to hit the brown. He snicked the fine edge of the pink and Knowles exercised his option to have the balls replaced with Parrott to play again from the original position. Television replays showed conclusively that the cue-ball was inaccurately replaced. When Parrott swerved it through the gap between pink and blue, he potted the

brown and cleared to lead 7-4.

Knowles was adamant that he would never have called for the balls to be replaced had he not been certain that Parrott could not pot the brown, although he admitted he did not check the re-set position. Annoyed as he was, Knowles directed the blame much less at the referee than at the miss rule guidelines, confirming the view of many that 'It's putting referees under pressure and it's annoying the players'. He did not win another frame.

McManus overturned 6-2 arrears at the first interval to beat Price 13-10; White beat Alain Robidoux 13-11, despite a patchy performance which was perhaps a reaction to his 147 in the previous round. Ebdon produced a nine-frame winning streak to beat Martin Clark 13-4 and Griffiths clinched his ninth consecutive appearance in a Crucible quarter-final by beating Foulds 13-7.

John Parrott's reign as world champion ends at the hands of Alan McManus

Terry Griffiths was the victim of one of Stephen Hendry's most devastating displays in the semi-final

Alan McManus, mentally exhausted from reaching the semi-finals for the first time, offered dwindling resistance to Jimmy White

O'Kane, transparently feeling all the pressure of a player who would never forgive himself if he lost to someone provisionally ranked 338th with a world quarter-final place at stake, eventually nailed the tenacious Small 13-10. Hendry's 13-10 win over Wattana was not the classic widely expected, and with Hendry off form, Wattana was disappointed at his own failure to snatch some of the chances he had.

Parrott's reign as champion ended in the quarter-finals at the hands of McManus, who had taken himself into the top 16 after only two professional seasons. The Scot led 11-7 at one stage but eventually had to win the last two frames to go through 13-12.

White won his opening session against Wych 6-2 and always appeared to have

something in hand as he reached the finishing line at 13-9; Hendry, held to 5-5 by O'Kane, pulled away to win 13-6. Despite losing 13-7 to Griffiths, Ebdon nevertheless made three centuries and impressed his opponent, who felt the young Londoner was 'good news for the game'.

The semi-finals saw Griffiths overwhelmed 16-4 by Hendry, in the Crucible's most crushing semi-final victory margin, and a result that extended Hendry's career record over Griffiths to 13-0. Hendry made two centuries and 11 other breaks over 50 in racing to victory with a session to spare after leading 10-0. From 4-4, White drew away from a mentally exhausted McManus to win the other semi-final 16-7, and for three of the four sessions looked the winner of the marvellous final.

For the first time in a world final, the opening frame produced a century, 105 by Hendry, but White led 4-3 at the first interval and 10-6 overnight. Making breaks of 40, 50 and 134, White added the first two frames of the third session, thus completing a run of 294 points without reply, to lead 12-6. However, Hendry settled into an unhurried occupancy of the table in the following frame, which yielded an 86 break, and after taking the next frame as well, he trailed only 8-12 at the intermission.

White left the arena looking thoughtful. He had hit Hendry with two heavy punches, but still the Scot's form and belief had remained unshaken. Again, White spurted six frames clear through a framewinning 65 and a 63 clearance which gave him victory on the pink. A scrappy frame went to Hendry and the turning point of the match came in the last frame of the afternoon.

Leading by 52, White missed a red with the rest. The balls were far from ideally placed for a winning clearance, but Hendry made 64 to the pink to trail only 10-14, instead of the 9-15 which had seemed likely, going into the final session.

The key shot came after Hendry had potted the last red down the cushion to a baulk pocket and screwed back, intending to leave an angle on the blue from which it would have been convenient to play position for the yellow, which lay a few inches away from the baulk cushion. Instead, the cue-ball finished in the jaws of the middle pocket. He could have rolled in the straight blue and played safe on the yellow. With incredible nerve, he chose instead to roll the brown from its spot at dead weight to the corner pocket, a choice of shot which would certainly have presented White with a six-frame lead had the brown not dropped.

Refusing to be demoralised into not thinking positively, Hendry had shown himself to be far from intimidated by the score, his opponent, or the occasion. He had been thinking primarily about how to win the frame rather than how to avoid losing it.

Four frames was still a large gap. Indeed, in no Crucible final had such a lead going into the final session proved insufficient. Yet Hendry had sown the seed of doubt in White's mind; he had absorbed White's very best and still was far from done.

The first frame of the evening saw White cruelly punished for the cardinal error of not making sure of the last red, a short-range pot which would have left Hendry needing two snookers. At his next visit but one, Hendry cleared to win on the black and narrow the gap to three. A green to pink clearance made it 12-14 and White was unfortunate in the following frame when, screwing into the bunch with

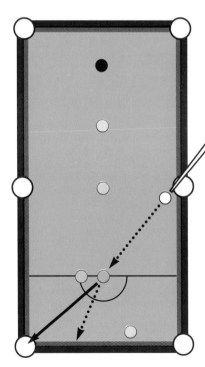

THE SHOT THAT TURNED THE TIDE

Trailing Jimmy White 9-14 in their best-of-35-frames final of the 1992 Embassy world championship, Stephen Hendry had finished straight on the blue after potting the last red. He could have rolled the blue in and played safe. Instead, he took on a very much more difficult brown, knowing that if he missed it White would be left a simple chance to pot the yellow and clinch a 15-9 lead. Hendry potted the brown and completed a 64 clearance to the pink to trail only 10-14, going on to win the first eight frames of the evening session to take the title.

Stephen Hendry in play as Jimmy White remains seatbound in their 1992 world final

power, he unluckily went in-off. Had the cue-ball not crept into a middle pocket, a 60-70 break and a three-frame lead would have beckoned. As it was, he did not score again in this frame, nor in the next, which featured Hendry's break of 128.

Clearly and indeed understandably, White had now 'gone'. Although he could have tied the next frame, his blue from near the pink spot stopped an inch short of the middle pocket. Hendry was full ball snookered by the pink but played coolly off the side cushion to pot the frame ball and lead 15-14. A break of 52 put him two frames in front, and like a tidal wave he finished off the match with breaks of 134 and 112 to complete his ten-frame winning streak.

Hendry had been fuelled by the irresistible confidence of a player reprieved from the very brink of defeat; White had been demoralised through the threat of having his heart's desire, for so much of the match almost within his grasp, snatched away. In winning the title for the second time, Hendry left White runner-up for a fourth. Icy self-discipline had kept Hendry afloat when the going was rough – six down and with 13 to play – before his best form burst forth like champagne from a bottle when it was most needed.

1992 EMBASSY WORLD CHAMPIONSHIP

FIRST ROUND: J. Parrott beat E. Charlton 10-0; T. Knowles beat M. Johnston-Allen 10-4; M. Price beat Dennis Taylor 10-6; A. McManus beat M. Hallett 10-8; W. Thorne beat Gary Wilkinson 10-6; J. Wych beat D. Reynolds 10-7; A. Robidoux beat N. Bond 10-7; J. White beat T. Drago 10-4; P. Ebdon beat S. Davis 10-4; M. Clark beat P. Francisco 10-7; T. Griffiths beat B. Chaperon 10-8; N. Foulds beat J. Ferguson 10-8; D. O'Kane beat S. James 10-9; C. Small beat D. Mountjoy 10-7; J. Wattana beat T. Jones 10-5; S. Hendry beat S. Murphy 10-3

SECOND ROUND: Parrott beat Knowles 13-4; McManus beat Price 13-10; Wych beat Thorne 13-6; White beat Robidoux 13-11; Ebdon beat Clark 13-4; Griffiths beat Foulds 13-7; O'Kane beat Small 13-10; Hendry beat Wattana 13-1

QUARTER-FINALS: McManus beat Parrott 13-12; White beat Wych 13-9; Griffiths beat Ebdon 13-7; Hendry beat O'Kane 13-6

SEMI-FINALS: White beat McManus 16-7; Hendry beat Griffiths 16-4

FINAL: Hendry beat White 18-14

Even before the 1992 championship had been completed, the draw for 1993, involving 542 entrants, was known, and while hordes of young hopefuls prepared themselves for the summer qualifying school, the Forte Hotels Matchroom league was completed. Allison Fisher excelled herself by beating Neal Foulds, Mike Hallett and Tony Drago and drawing with Tony Meo, while Hendry made a 147 before going on to beat White 9-0 and Davis 9-2 in the play-offs to take the £50,000 first prize. He thus completed his season with nine titles, grossing £645,360 in prizemoney to add to the £646,000 he had earned the previous year.

The star of the summer qualifying school was Ronnie O'Sullivan, now aged 16. He won his first 38 matches, thereby superseding – albeit against less exalted opposition – Hendry's record run of 36 victories in world ranking events, from the 1990 Embassy World Championship to the 1991 Mercantile Classic. In three months at Blackpool, O'Sullivan won 70 matches out of 72, his 5-1 win over Jimmy White helping him to the 16-man final phase of the European Open.

Sanity at last prevailed on one front when the board accepted the recommendations of a nine-and-a-half-hour meeting of leading players, chaired by Terry Griffiths, to return largely to the miss rule guidelines which had been operative prior to 1 January 1991, when all misses were called at the sole discretion of the referee.

However, sanity failed to prevail in the board's inexplicable decision to allow *Pot Black* to be played on a 'Timeframe' version of the game, a trivialising and undignified experience for the players, which fortunately they were never called upon to repeat.

ITV's decision to network only two rather than three tournaments in the coming season meant the demise of the Mercantile Classic, although this pill was sweetened by BSkyB's agreement to be host broadcaster for a new ranking event at Plymouth in April.

A serious rift developed between Barry Hearn and Ian Doyle, always uneasy bedfellows despite their frequent mutual self-interest. They were indeed an odd couple: Doyle a fanatic for detail, Hearn an exponent of the instinctive broad brush technique.

Parrott beat Hendry 6-5 to win the Kent Cup in Peking, the first event of World Series IV, but late payment for this event from Hearn and an unedifying guerrilla skirmish over wild cards for the Humo Masters in Antwerp, won by James Wattana, provided elements of the background against which Doyle resigned as Hearn's co-director of World Series Ltd.

Ronnie O'Sullivan turned professional as world under-21 champion and won 70 of his first 72 professional matches

The co-operation of Doyle's stable of ten players was highly desirable for the events which Hearn wished to promote, so that Hendry's decision not to play in Hearn's Matchroom League, won by White, was taken as an escalation of the warfare between the two camps. Several of Hearn's former players – Dennis Taylor, Neal Foulds, Tony Meo, Willie Thorne and Jimmy White – also spoke unkindly of the quality of management he had given them, although Terry Griffiths, Cliff Thorburn and, naturally enough, Steve Davis defended him strongly.

Neal Foulds won the Regal Scottish Masters, supposed to be a World Series event but never in its entire history appearing to the public to be anything other than a high-grade, self-contained invitation tournament. Astonishingly, Gary Wilkinson came from 1-5 down to beat Hendry 6-5 in the quarter-finals, going on to dispose of Davis 6-4, before losing 10-8 in the final to Foulds, who thus took his first title for four years.

John Parrott recorded his second consecutive victory in the Dubai Classic in 1992

The WPBSA's summer qualifying school at Blackpool

There were further early-season disappointments for Hendry. Let off the hook in the penultimate frame, he beat Wattana 6-5 in the semi-finals of the Dubai Classic, only for Parrott to beat him 9-8 in the final, clearing up with 63 to win the decider on the black.

Hendry was then the object of a series of death-threats from a woman, later convicted, who also sent him a copy of a play she had written, entitled *Daggers in the Billiard Room*, in which he is killed in the last act. Unsettled and unable to concentrate, he failed to take his defence of the Rothmans Grand Prix title beyond his first match, losing 5-3 to the world No. 53, Tony Chappel.

Jimmy White, who had spent the summer in deep depression and without the heart to practise after his third consecutive world final defeat, won the £80,000 first prize, as much to his own surprise as anyone else's. 'It's a total bonus to me,' he said, after beating Ken Doherty 10-9 in the final.

In the previous season Doherty, a former world under-21 and world amateur champion, had reached two world ranking semi-finals and the final of the Irish Masters. Having beaten Davis 5-2 in the quarters and Griffiths 9-5 in the semis, he was inspired by a full house at the Hexagon to lead 5-3 at the interval. White, still tending to play in bursts as he had all tournament, nevertheless had the skill and the temperament to lead 9-8. Having levelled with a break of 117, Doherty then trailed 0-51 in the decider before missing his first chance, a difficult one, which signalled the end.

Earlier John Higgins had become the youngest player ever to reach the last 16 in a world ranking tournament. At 17 years four months, eclipsing Hendry's record by four months, he made consecutive centuries, 100 and 127, in beating Dene O'Kane 5-2 and accounting also for the world No. 8, Gary Wilkinson, 5-4. Parrott was beaten 5-3 by an old favourite, Cliff Thorburn, who had borne an extended spell in the wilderness with dignity and wry humour. It had been almost two and half years since he had last qualified to play on television, largely because he had been unable to discover how he came to be striking the cue-ball marginally left of centre almost every time. Defeat by Alan McManus in the next round ended his season, for attempts to qualify in all other ranking events had perished in the anonymity of the Blackpool qualifying school at the Norbreck Castle Hotel.

It was the point of farewell for Rothmans. A change of company policy meant its withdrawal from domestic sports sponsorship, thus bringing to an end their eight-year snooker sponsorship.

As they left, Royal Liver Assurance came in to sponsor the UK championship won by White. His 6-1 opening session in the

final against Parrott proved the key to his 16-9 victory and the title which filled an important gap in his c.v. In the third round, Peter Ebdon made a 147 maximum but lost to Doherty, and in the quarter-finals McManus achieved his first win over a below-par Hendry, 9-8. The semi-finals brought a 9-5 victory for Parrott over Davis while White, 7-3 up on McManus, was relieved to beat him 9-7.

James Wattana receives an enthusiastic media welcome in Bangkok on his return with the Coalite World Matchplay title

Going straight from a fortnight-long tournament, second only to the world championship in the strain and stress it imposes, to another week of best-of-17s at the Coalite World Matchplay at the Dome, Doncaster, White and Parrott both lost their opening matches. Meanwhile, Wattana was on the way to the most important first prize of his career as he beat Parrott 9-3, McManus 9-3 and Davis 9-4, Davis having uniquely compiled three total clearances – 141, 123, 135 – in the opening session of his 9-4 semi-final win over Martin Clark.

The young Thai received a tremendous Michael Jackson-style welcome at Bangkok airport on his return home with the trophy, as well as being awarded a diplomatic passport and the honorary title of Sports Ambassador. The Thai author-ities also promised to make moves towards legalising snooker for under-18s in Thai-land, a restriction Wattana himself had evaded only through being able to play as a teenager in his mother's snooker hall.

Having lost again to McManus, 9-6 in

the World Matchplay, Hendry began his rehabilitation by winning a minor event, the Canal Plus European Challenge in Epernay, but in defence of his Regal Welsh Open title, he lost 5-3 to Bond in the last 16. Doherty, clearly a rising force, captured his first world ranking title by beating McManus 9-7 in the final.

If Hendry had needed any further motivation, it came with the announcement by Benson and Hedges that he would be given permanent possession of the trophy if he won the Masters for a fifth consecutive time. He duly took his un-beaten record at Wembley to 20 matches, drawing away from 4-3 at the interval to beat Wattana 9-5 in the final. It was nevertheless a hard-earned triumph. Down 3-4 to Doherty in the first round, he made breaks of 105 and 131 to win 5-4, and his 6-4 semi-final over McManus, a 5-4

winner over Davis, was one he needed to reassert himself as Scotland's No.1.

White, unable to fire on all cylinders, gave one of the relatively ragged displays which was to feature on his rocky road to Sheffield this season, and went down 6-3 to Wattana in the semi-finals. Wattana had followed his defeat of Parrott in two 1992 finals, the Strachan Open and the Humo Masters, by beating him again 5-3 in the quarters.

At this stage of the season there was no clear world title favourite, although one emerged when Davis won both the European and British Opens, the latter sponsored by Wickes Home Improvements. His 10-4 victory over Hendry in Antwerp evoked memories of his heyday. In Derby he beat Doherty 5-4 in the quarter-finals after his 4-0 lead had become 4-4; he showed himself the master

Stephen Hendry has held the Benson and Hedges Masters trophy aloft on final night on each of the five occasions he has competed in the tournament

Ken Doherty's capture of the Regal Welsh Open was his first world ranking title

breakbuilder in beating White 6-3 in the semi-finals, including a break of 139; then in the final he became the master tactician as he froze out Wattana 10-2. Wattana had scored a 6-4 victory over Hendry in the semi-finals, but against Davis he was nowhere.

Davis's defence of the Asian Open foundered in humid conditions, as he was beaten 5-4 on the final black in the fourth round by Fergal O'Brien, a Dubliner standing 192nd in the world rankings. Hendry also qualified for an early flight home, beaten 5-2 by Dave Harold, a second-season professional from Stoke, who amazingly went on to take the £30,000 first prize. Another to be in pocket was the brother of the world's No. 93, who had invested £10 with a bookmaker prepared to offer 500-1.

'All the shocks just go to prove the strength in depth in our game at the moment,' commented Parrott, himself a

2-5 quarter-final loser to Paul Davies, the world No. 48, who in turn lost 5-2 to Harold. Darren Morgan looked the title favourite when he beat White 5-4 in the semis, but Harold beat him comfortably 9-3 in the final.

Davis shrugged off his Bangkok setback to win the Benson and Hedges Irish Masters for the seventh time, beating Hendry 6-3 in the semi-finals and then posting a 9-4 win over McManus, who had ousted Parrott 6-5 in the semis.

With his world title defence looming up, Hendry's 10-6 victory over Davis in the final of a new world ranking event, the Sky Sports international at Plymouth Pavillions, was therefore a timely boost to his confidence. It was not just the result, but the manner of it. His total of ten centuries was a record for a ranking tournament, superseding the eights of Davis and Parrott in the Embassy World Championships of 1986 and 1991 respectively. His 6-0 semi-final despatch of Harold, who had brought much of his Bangkok form back to Plymouth, took him only 71 minutes. Having trailed Davis 5-4 at the interval, he turned the match by reeling off the first five frames of the evening in only 54 minutes, and thus departed for Sheffield with his confidence fully restored.

Sky's first snooker event as host broadcasters brought evening viewing figures which they described as 'good' and afternoon figures recorded as 'very good'. Having already taken either live or delayed coverage from other host broadcasters for the Regal Scottish Masters, the Dubai Classic, the Regal Welsh Open, the Asian Open and the Benson and Hedges Irish Masters, they decided to attack the snooker market in a big way.

This coincided with ITV's loss of interest, which had come about largely because snooker had become progressively harder to schedule. It was difficult enough to persuade 15 ITV schedulers to take a football match lasting less than two hours, but eight or nine days' coverage of a snooker ranking event was invariably being pushed, except for Saturday afternoons, into obscure afternoon and late-night slots.

BSkyB had, if anything, the opposite problem: countless hours to fill and not enough high-quality sport to fill it. Following the success of Plymouth, their negotiations with the WPBSA resulted in their acquiring the British Open – from ITV – and the European Open, which had been shown on Eurosport. The demise of Screensport, acquired by Eurosport, substantially reduced coverage for Hearn's Matchroom League, which was won by White. Screensport, for whom Hearn had made himself the sole supplier of snooker programming, had shown many matches live, several in prime Sunday lunchtime slots, but Eurosport, whose programmes tended to be aimed more at continental preferences, showed much less snooker and in inferior slots.

EMBASSY WORLD CHAMPIONSHIP

Stephen Hendry's third world title in four years brought him £175,000, took his official career prize money to £3,048,001 and confirmed the position at the top of the world rankings he had held since becoming the youngest ever champion three years earlier.

He dominated the championship so thoroughly that it was easy to forget the inconsistency which had plagued him for most of the season. Perhaps he had needed the threat of losing his No. 1 position in the rankings, or the sting of losing to players he had become accustomed to beating, to remotivate himself after a 1991-92 campaign which had yielded him nine titles.

His defence of the title began with a 10-1 drubbing of Danny Fowler, which brought his total of centuries to 200 in only eight years on the professional circuit, seven years fewer than it had taken Davis.

The first week of the championship suffered from an unduly high proportion of runaway wins, partly because the WPBSA had scheduled world qualifying

Dave Harold won the Nescafé Asian Open as a long-shot outsider

Doug Mountjoy won a match at the Crucible under the shadow of a malignant tumour. His left lung was removed six weeks later and he recovered from surgery in time to start the 1993-94 season

as early as September. This had created the situation whereby relatively inexperienced players could become match hardened in the summer qualifying school and then catch cold many established players just outside the top 16 in the rankings, which would have exempted them from the qualifying competition. In this way, such well-known players as Silvino Francisco, Joe Johnson, Dene O'Kane, Mike Hallett, Tony Knowles and Ken Doherty, not to mention Alex Higgins, failed to make it to the Crucible.

Among the eight who earned debut appearances on snooker's most famous stage were three first-season professionals, John Giles, Spencer Dunn and Ronnie O'Sullivan, each of whom had negotiated 11 rounds to reach the televised stage.

Dunn, the only snooker player sponsored by the Prince's Youth Business Trust, whose £40 a week grant enabled him to turn professional, was beaten 10-4 by Nigel Bond at Sheffield, but could nevertheless reflect that it was quite a journey from the third division of the Stourbridge League to the Crucible in only three years.

Although O'Sullivan became the youngest player to qualify for the Crucible, by the time he actually appeared there he was two months older than Hendry had been on his 1986 debut.

O'Sullivan had made a record 30 centuries in his rookie season and had generally been expected to deliver more extended runs in world ranking tournaments, of which that to the quarter-finals of the European Open was his best. He led Alan McManus 6-5 at the Crucible but, for all his maturity and poise, pressure appeared to affect his fluency. Brilliant pots were negated by unforced errors as McManus beat him 10-7.

Peter Ebdon, the hero of the first weekend in 1992 when he put out Steve Davis 10-4, was this time a 10-3 loser to the same player. Ebdon had come to Sheffield a second time not having quite lived up to the expectations raised by his first professional season, while Davis was in his best form for years. Joe Swail, having won the Irish Championship the previous May, had enjoyed a season in which he reached two quarter-finals and a semi in major ranking events. Now, however, he was one of the debutants who did not do himself justice, falling 4-10 to Jimmy White.

Dennis Taylor kept the cooler head in the deciding frame to beat Tony Drago 10-9, while Doug Mountjoy's 10-6 win over Alain Robidoux provided a story whose full significance was unappreciated at the time. As Mountjoy had not won a match since November and Robidoux only four all season, a classic was not expected. Nor did one ensue.

Although Mountjoy, one of snooker's most familiar television faces for more than 15 years, had felt weak and ill all season, it was not diagnosed until the week following the championship that he had a malignant tumour on his left lung. This was removed in June. In the circumstances, his dogged professionalism was all the more to be applauded.

Two other members of Mountjoy's generation, Dennis Taylor and Terry Griffiths, battled for 13 hours 19 minutes in the second round before Taylor achieved a 13-11 victory. Their match was three

Alan McManus beat Steve Davis in reaching the world semi-finals for the second consecutive year

frames behind schedule as Taylor led 9-4 after two sessions. Griffiths closed to 8-10 only for his momentum to be broken by a highly controversial miss decision in the following frame as Taylor pushed on to 12-8. Griffiths recovered three frames, but Taylor fluked the decisive blue in the 24th frame to earn a quarter-final place that had scarcely been indicated by his pre-championship form, affected by the breakup of his 23-year-old marriage.

Hendry crushed Darren Morgan 13-4 to earn his quarter-final place and there were also relatively comfortable second-round wins for Nigel Bond, Neal Foulds, White, James Wattana and John Parrott, who thus reached his fifth consecutive world quarter-final.

The match of the round saw Alan McManus beat Davis 13-11. Davis's 144 total clearance in the third frame was to stand as the highest break of the championship and the fourth-highest in the 66-year history of the event, yet he still trailed 4-1 before levelling at 4-4 overnight.

At 9-5 McManus threatened to take a commanding lead into the final session, before he inexplicably faltered, permitting Davis to limit the damage to 7-9 at the close. On the last morning, McManus led 10-7 and 11-8, and the intermission was taken at 11-9, with Davis responding grittily and McManus starting to feel the pressure of clinching such an important victory.

McManus missed his first chance to clinch 12-9, but an outstanding long yellow from tight under the baulk cushion gave him the opportunity to go three up with four to play. Even so, Davis threatened to take the contest the full distance until, at 11-12, he missed a blue which would have left McManus needing a snooker. McManus cracked a yellow to the far corner and cleared up for a famous victory.

The strain of this match and his previous one against O'Sullivan began to tell in his quarter-final against Foulds, whom he just managed to nail 13-11 after leading 12-8. Apprehensively, he noted that his next opponent, Hendry, was very much fresher. 'I've lost almost as many frames in one match as he has in three,' he observed. Hendry's 13-7 win over Bond, who made breaks of 139 and 101, prompted the loser to say that he couldn't see anyone stopping him on that form.

Parrott failed to take his appointed place in the semi-finals, beaten 13-6 by Wattana, who won six frames in succession from 5-5. White beat Taylor 13-8 but didn't feel he was playing particularly well.

Just as he had in 1992, McManus understandably ran out of mental steam and from 4-4 after the opening session was well beaten by Hendry 16-8. White's 16-9 win over Wattana in the other semi-final also appears a comfortable margin, though this had hardly seemed likely when the Thai led 5-0 and 6-2. Wattana appeared burdened with a colossal weight of national expectation, from a personal message from Thailand's prime minister to the support of 13 million Thai viewers of BBC's live coverage by satellite.

Wattana's lack of a fine edge of self-belief interacted with White's innate

James Wattana became the first Thai to reach the world semi-finals but wilted under heavy pressure of national expectation

Stephen Hendry won the world title for the third time in four years

visit to the table was a portent of a ruthlessly brilliant display, which left White the 18-5 loser of his fourth consecutive world final and fifth in all. Long before the end, which arrived a session early, it had become not so much a contest as a prolonged lap of honour. During it, Hendry equalled the Davis-Parrott joint record of eight centuries in a Crucible championship as he increased his total of Crucible centuries to 36, four more than Davis, the previous record holder. His frames tally of 70-25 was only one frame worse than Davis's 1989 record.

Hendry regarded his own form as 'of a higher quality than my previous two world championship wins', and reflected on how radically his season had changed from disappointment – by his standards – to triumph. 'It felt awesome,' he said of the championship. 'From the first frame to the last I was totally focused.' Moreover, he had dominated the 1990s thus far as thoroughly as Davis had dominated the 1980s.

determination and match playing qualities. Two bouts of flu and a stomach virus in Bangkok, patchy form since Christmas and miscellaneous off-table concerns meant that White's concentration had not been in its best shape. Four consecutive frames, albeit not in his most convincing mode, allowed him to level at 6-6 before 13 reds, 13 blacks brought the 104 break with which he led for the first time at 7-6. The remaining two reds, clinging awkwardly together, evaded his attempt at disturbance from the 13th black, thus forestalling his bid for a repeat of his 147 in 1992, but he was by now perfectly in stroke as he extended his winning streak to 12 frames to lead commandingly 14-6.

So it was that after 542 entrants had played a total of 4,944 frames, Hendry and White disputed their third final in four years. Historical factors might have constituted some psychological barrier to victory if White had got anywhere near it, but as it turned out he could hardly have been more comprehensively defeated.

Hendry's 136 total clearance at his first

1993 EMBASSY WORLD CHAMPIONSHIP

FIRST ROUND: S. Hendry beat D. Fowler 10-1; D. Morgan beat L. Dodd 10-5; N. Bond beat S. Dunn 10-4; Gary Wilkinson beat D. Reynolds 10-4; M. Clark beat K. Payne 10-6; N. Foulds beat B. Morgan 10-5; A. McManus beat R. O'Sullivan 10-7; S. Davis beat P. Ebdon 10-3; J. White beat J. Swail 10-4; D. Mountjoy beat A. Robidoux 10-6; Dennis Taylor beat T. Drago 10-9; T. Griffiths beat D. Roe 10-6; J. Wattana beat T. Jones 10-7; S. James beat J. Giles 10-2; W. Thorne beat S. Mellish 10-6; J. Parrott beat S. O'Connor 10-1

SECOND ROUND: Hendry beat Morgan 13-4; Bond beat Wilkinson 13-7; Foulds beat Clark 13-7; McManus beat Davis 13-11; White beat Mountjoy 13-6; Taylor beat Griffiths 13-11; Wattana beat James 13-7; Parrott beat Thorne 13-9

QUARTER-FINALS: Hendry beat Bond 13-7; McManus beat Foulds 13-11; White beat Taylor 13-8; Wattana beat Parrott 13-6

SEMI-FINALS: Hendry beat McManus 16-8; White beat Wattana 16-9

FINAL: Hendry beat White 18-5

TOURNAMENT WINNERS AND PRIZEMONEY

1976   Benson and Hedges Masters – Ray Reardon (£2,000) beat Graham Miles (£1,000) 7-3
Embassy World Championship – Ray Reardon (£3,500) beat Alex Higgins (£2,000) 27-16

1977   Benson and Hedges Masters – Doug Mountjoy (£2,000) beat Ray Reardon (£1,000) 7-6
Embassy World Championship – John Spencer (£6,000) beat Cliff Thorburn (£2,000) 25-21
Super Crystalate UK Championship – Patsy Fagan (£2,000) beat Doug Mountjoy (£1,200) 12-9

1978   Benson and Hedges Masters – Alex Higgins (£3,000) beat Cliff Thorburn (£1,500) 7-5
Benson and Hedges Irish Masters – John Spencer (£2,000) beat Doug Mountjoy (£1,000) 5-3
Embassy World Championship – Ray Reardon (£7,500) beat Perrie Mans (£3,500) 25-18
Champion of Champions – Ray Reardon (£2,000) beat Alex Higgins (£1,000) 11-9
Coral UK Championship – Doug Mountjoy (£3,500) beat David Taylor (£1,750) 15-9

1979   Benson and Hedges Masters – Perrie Mans (£3,000) beat Alex Higgins (£1,500) 8-4
Benson and Hedges Irish Masters – Doug Mountjoy (n.a.) beat Ray Reardon (n.a.) 6-5
Embassy World Championship – Terry Griffiths (£10,000) beat Dennis Taylor (£5,000) 24-16
Coral UK Championship – John Virgo (£4,500) beat Terry Griffiths (£2,250) 14-13

1980   Wilsons Classic – John Spencer (£3,000) beat Alex Higgins (£1,500) 4-3
Benson and Hedges Masters – Terry Griffiths (£4,500) beat Alex Higgins (£2,500) 9-5
British Gold Cup – Alex Higgins (£4,000) beat Ray Reardon (£3,000) 5-1
Benson and Hedges Irish Masters – Terry Griffiths (£2,500) beat Doug Mountjoy (£1,500) 9-8
Embassy World Championship – Cliff Thorburn (£15,000) beat Alex Higgins (£7,500) 18-16
Champion of Champions – Doug Mountjoy (none) beat John Virgo (none) 10-8
Coral UK Championship – Steve Davis (£6,000) beat Alex Higgins (£3,000) 16-6

1981   Wilsons Classic – Steve Davis (£5,000) beat Dennis Taylor (£2,500) 4-1
Benson and Hedges Masters – Alex Higgins (£6,000) beat Terry Griffiths (£3,000) 9-6
Yamaha Organs Trophy – Steve Davis (£10,000) beat David Taylor (£5,000) 9-6
Benson and Hedges Irish Masters – Terry Griffiths (£5,000) beat Ray Reardon (£2,500) 9-7
Embassy World Championship – Steve Davis (£20,000) beat Doug Mountjoy (£10,000) 18-12
Jameson International – Steve Davis (£20,000) beat Dennis Taylor (£10,000) 9-0
Langs Scottish Masters – Jimmy White (£8,000) beat Cliff Thorburn (£3,500) 9-4
Northern Ireland Classic – Jimmy White (£5,000) beat Steve Davis (£3,500) 11-9
Coral UK Championship – Steve Davis (£10,000) beat Terry Griffiths (£5,000) 16-3

1982   Wilsons Classic – Terry Griffiths (£5,000) beat Steve Davis (£3,000) 9-8
Benson and Hedges Masters – Steve Davis (£8,000) beat Terry Griffiths (£4,000) 9-5
Yamaha Organs Trophy – Steve Davis (£10,000) beat Terry Griffiths (£5,000) 9-7
Benson and Hedges Irish Masters – Terry Griffiths (£6,666) beat Steve Davis (£3,333) 9-5
Embassy World Championship – Alex Higgins (£25,000) beat Ray Reardon (£12,500) 18-15
Langs Scottish Masters – Steve Davis (£9,000) beat Alex Higgins (£4,500) 9-4
Jameson International – Tony Knowles (£22,000) beat David Taylor (£12,000) 9-6
Professional Players Tournament – Ray Reardon (£5,000) beat Jimmy White (£2,500) 10-5
Coral UK Championship – Terry Griffiths (£11,000) beat Alex Higgins (£6,000) 16-15
Hofmeister World Doubles Championship – Steve Davis and Tony Meo (£24,000) beat Terry Griffiths and Doug Mountjoy (£12,000) 13-2

1983   Lada Classic – Steve Davis (£16,000) beat Bill Werbeniuk (£10,000) 9-5
Benson and Hedges Masters – Cliff Thorburn (£16,000) beat Ray Reardon (£8,000) 9-7
Yamaha International Masters – Ray Reardon (£12,000) beat Jimmy White (£6,000) 9-6
Benson and Hedges Irish Masters – Steve Davis (£10,680) beat Ray Reardon (£5,340) 9-2
Embassy World Championship – Steve Davis (£30,000) beat Cliff Thorburn (£15,000) 18-6
Winfield Australian Masters – Cliff Thorburn (£11,760) beat Bill Werbeniuk (£5,880) 7-3
Langs Scottish Masters – Steve Davis (£10,000) beat Tony Knowles (£5,000) 9-6
Jameson International – Steve Davis (£24,000) beat Cliff Thorburn (£12,000) 9-4
Professional Players Tournament – Tony Knowles (£12,500) beat Joe Johnson (£7,500) 9-8
Coral UK Championship – Alex Higgins (£12,000) beat Steve Davis (£6,500) 16-15
Hofmeister World Doubles – Steve Davis and Tony Meo (£25,000) beat Tony Knowles and Jimmy White (£10,000) 10-2

1984   Lada Classic – Steve Davis (£18,000) beat Tony Meo (£12,000) 9-8
Benson and Hedges Masters – Jimmy White (£35,000) beat Terry Griffiths (£16,000) 9-5
Yamaha International Masters – Steve Davis (£12,000) beat Dave Martin (£8,000) (final a 3-man round-robin with John Dunning)
Benson and Hedges Irish Masters – Steve Davis (£12,295) beat Terry Griffiths (£7,377) 9-1
Embassy World Championship – Steve Davis (£44,000) beat Jimmy White (£22,000) 18-16

Winfield Australian Masters – Tony Knowles (£11,000) beat John Virgo (£5,500) 7-3
Langs Scottish Masters – Steve Davis (£10,000) beat Jimmy White (£6,000) 9-4
Jameson International – Steve Davis (£30,000) beat Tony Knowles (£18,000) 9-2
Rothmans Grand Prix – Dennis Taylor (£45,000) beat Cliff Thorburn (£27,000) 10-2
Coral UK Championship – Steve Davis (£20,000) beat Alex Higgins (£12,000) 16-8
Hofmeister World Doubles – Alex Higgins and Jimmy White (£34,500) beat Cliff Thorburn and Willie Thorne (£18,750) 10-2

1985 Mercantile Classic – Willie Thorne (£40,000) beat Cliff Thorburn (£24,000) 13-8
Benson and Hedges Masters – Cliff Thorburn (£37,500) beat Doug Mountjoy (£21,000) 9-6
Dulux British Open – Silvino Francisco (£50,000) beat Kirk Stevens (£30,000) 12-9
Benson and Hedges Irish Masters – Jimmy White (£17,250) beat Alex Higgins (£10,000) 9-5
Embassy World Championship – Dennis Taylor (£60,000) beat Steve Davis (£35,000) 18-17
Winfield Australian Masters – Tony Meo (£12,500) beat John Campbell (£8,000) 7-2
Langs Scottish Masters – Cliff Thorburn (£10,500) beat Willie Thorne (£6,500) 9-7
Goya Matchroom Trophy – Cliff Thorburn (£35,000) beat Jimmy White (£21,000) 12-10
Rothmans Grand Prix – Steve Davis (£50,000) beat Dennis Taylor (£30,000) 10-9
BCE Canadian Masters – Dennis Taylor (£15,000) beat Steve Davis (£9,000) 9-5
Coral UK Championship – Steve Davis (£24,000) beat Willie Thorne (£14,400) 16-14
Hofmeister World Doubles – Steve Davis and Tony Meo (£40,000) beat Tony Jones and Ray Reardon (£22,000) 12-5

1986 Mercantile Classic – Jimmy White (£45,000) beat Cliff Thorburn (£27,000) 13-12
Benson and Hedges Masters – Cliff Thorburn (£45,000) beat Jimmy White (£25,000) 9-5
BCE Belgian Classic – Terry Griffiths (£12,000) beat Kirk Stevens (£7,000) 9-7
Dulux British Open – Steve Davis (£55,000) beat Willie Thorne (£33,000) 12-7
Benson and Hedges Irish Masters – Jimmy White (£20,089) beat Willie Thorne (£11,607) 9-5
Embassy World Championship – Joe Johnson (£70,000) beat Steve Davis (£42,000) 18-12
Hong Kong Masters – Willie Thorne (£34,800) beat Dennis Taylor (£17,400) 8-3
Langs Scottish Masters – Cliff Thorburn (£13,000) beat Alex Higgins (£8,000) 9-8
Matchroom Trophy – Willie Thorne (£50,000) beat Steve Davis (£20,000) 10-9
BCE International – Neal Foulds (£35,000) beat Cliff Thorburn (£21,000) 12-9
Rothmans Grand Prix – Jimmy White (£55,000) beat Rex Williams (£33,000) 10-6
BCE Canadian Masters – Steve Davis (£18,750) beat Willie Thorne (£11,250) 9-3
Tennents UK Open – Steve Davis (£60,000) beat Neal Foulds (£36,000) 16-7
Hofmeister World Doubles – Steve Davis and Tony Meo (£50,000) beat Mike Hallett and Stephen Hendry (£25,000) 12-3

1987 Mercantile Classic – Steve Davis (£50,000) beat Jimmy White (£30,000) 13-12
Benson and Hedges Masters – Dennis Taylor (£51,000) beat Alex Higgins (£28,000) 9-8
Dulux British Open – Jimmy White (£60,000) beat Neal Foulds (£36,000) 13-9
Benson and Hedges Irish Masters – Steve Davis (£22,500) beat Willie Thorne (£13,005) 9-1
Embassy World Championship – Steve Davis (£80,000) beat Joe Johnson (£48,000) 18-14
Matchroom League – Steve Davis (£53,600)
Winfield Australian Masters – Stephen Hendry (£22,222) beat Mike Hallett (£13,333) 371-226 (aggregate score)
Hong Kong Masters – Steve Davis (£30,000) beat Stephen Hendry (£12,000) 9-3
Langs Scottish Masters – Joe Johnson (£16,000) beat Terry Griffiths (£10,000) 9-7
Fidelity International – Steve Davis (£40,000) beat Cliff Thorburn (£24,000) 12-5
Rothmans Grand Prix – Stephen Hendry (£60,000) beat Dennis Taylor (£36,000) 10-7
BCE Canadian Masters – Dennis Taylor (£25,000) beat Jimmy White (£12,000) 9-7
Matchroom Trophy – Dennis Taylor (£50,000) beat Willie Thorne (£25,000) 10-3
Tennents UK Open – Steve Davis (£70,000) beat Jimmy White (£42,000) 16-14
Fosters World Doubles – Mike Hallett and Stephen Hendry (£60,000) beat Cliff Thorburn and Dennis Taylor (£35,000) 12-8

1988 Mercantile Classic – Steve Davis (£50,000) beat John Parrott (£30,000) 13-11
Benson and Hedges Masters – Steve Davis (£56,000) beat Mike Hallett (£32,000) 9-0
MIM Britannia British Open – Stephen Hendry (£60,000) beat Mike Hallett (£36,000) 13-2
Benson and Hedges Irish Masters – Steve Davis (£26,080) beat Neal Foulds (£15,650) 9-4
Embassy World Championship – Steve Davis (£95,000) beat Terry Griffiths (£57,000) 18-11
Matchroom League – Steve Davis (£70,000)
Lion Brown New Zealand Masters – Stephen Hendry (£12,000) beat Mike Hallett (£7,200) 6-1
Hong Kong Masters – Jimmy White (£30,000) beat Neal Foulds (£12,000) 6-3
Fidelity International – Steve Davis (£45,000) beat Jimmy White (£27,000) 12-6
Dubai Duty Free Masters – Neal Foulds (£25,000) beat Steve Davis (£12,000) 5-4
LEP Matchroom Championship – Steve Davis (£50,000) beat Dennis Taylor (£25,000) 10-7
Rothmans Grand Prix – Steve Davis (£65,000) beat Alex Higgins (£39,000) 10-6
BCE Canadian Masters – Jimmy White (£40,000) beat Steve Davis (£24,000) 9-4
Tennents UK Open – Doug Mountjoy (£80,000) beat Stephen Hendry (£48,000) 16-12
Everest World Matchplay – Steve Davis (£100,000) beat John Parrott (£40,000) 9-5

1989   Mercantile Classic – Doug Mountjoy (£55,000) beat Wayne Jones (£33,000) 13-11
Benson and Hedges Masters – Stephen Hendry (£62,000) beat John Parrott (£36,000) 9-6
European Open – John Parrott (£40,000) beat Terry Griffiths (£24,000) 9-8
Anglian Windows British Open – Tony Meo (£70,000) beat Dean Reynolds (£42,000) 13-6
Benson and Hedges Irish Masters – Alex Higgins (£27,242) beat Stephen Hendry (£16,764) 9-8
Embassy World Championship – Steve Davis (£105,000) beat John Parrott (£63,000) 18-3
Rothmans Matchroom League – Steve Davis (£70,000)
Lion Brown New Zealand Masters – Willie Thorne (£11,000) beat Joe Johnson (£7,000) 7-4
Hong Kong Open – Mike Hallett (£40,000) beat Dene O'Kane (£22,500) 9-8
555 Asian Open – Stephen Hendry (£40,000) beat James Wattana (£22,500) 9-6
Regal Scottish Masters – Stephen Hendry (£32,500) beat Terry Griffiths (£16,000) 10-1
BCE International – Steve Davis (£40,000) beat Stephen Hendry (£24,000) 9-4
Rothmans Grand Prix – Steve Davis (£70,000) beat Dean Reynolds (£42,000) 10-0
Dubai Duty Free Classic – Stephen Hendry (£40,000) beat Doug Mountjoy (£22,500) 9-2
Stormseal UK Championship – Stephen Hendry (£100,000) beat Steve Davis (£48,000) 16-12
Everest World Matchplay – Jimmy White (£100,000) beat John Parrott (£40,000) 18-9

1990   Mercantile Classic – Steve James (£60,000) beat Warren King (£36,000) 10-6
Benson and Hedges Masters – Stephen Hendry (£70,000) beat John Parrott (£38,000) 9-4
Pearl Assurance British Open – Bob Chaperon (£75,000) beat Alex Higgins (£45,000) 10-8
European Open – John Parrott (£40,000) beat Stephen Hendry (£22,500) 10-6
Benson and Hedges Irish Masters – Steve Davis (£37,000) beat Dennis Taylor (£23,000) 9-4
Embassy World Championship – Stephen Hendry (£120,000) beat Jimmy White (£72,000) 18-12
Matchroom League – Steve Davis (£70,000)
555 World Series Challenge (Hong Kong) – James Wattana (£20,000) beat Jimmy White (£10,000) 9-3
Regal Scottish Masters – Stephen Hendry (£35,000) beat Terry Griffiths (£17,500) 10-6
Humo Belgian Masters – John Parrott (£30,000) beat Jimmy White (£15,000) 9-6
Rothmans Grand Prix – Stephen Hendry (£75,000) beat Nigel Bond (£40,000) 10-5
Norwich Union Grand Prix – John Parrott (£25,000) beat Steve Davis (£15,000) 4-2
555 Asian Open – Stephen Hendry (£35,000) beat Dennis Taylor (£22,000) 9-3
Dubai Duty Free Classic – Stephen Hendry (£35,000) beat Steve Davis (£22,000) 9-1
Stormseal UK Open – Stephen Hendry (£110,000) beat Steve Davis (£60,000) 16-15
Coalite World Matchplay – Jimmy White (£70,000) beat Stephen Hendry (£30,000) 18-9

1991   Mercantile Classic – Jimmy White (£60,000) beat Stephen Hendry (£36,000) 10-4
Mita World Masters – Men's Singles: Jimmy White (£200,000) beat Tony Drago (£70,000) 10-6
Mita World Masters – Men's Doubles: Stephen Hendry and Mike Hallett (£50,000) beat Jim Wych and Brady Gollan (£20,000) 8-5
Benson and Hedges Masters – Stephen Hendry (£100,000) beat Mike Hallett (£50,000) 9-8
Pearl Assurance British Open – Stephen Hendry (£75,000) beat Gary Wilkinson (£44,000) 10-9
European Open – Tony Jones (£35,000) beat Mark Johnston-Allen (£22,000) 9-7
Benson and Hedges Irish Masters – Steve Davis (£36,000) beat John Parrott (£21,600) 9-5
Embassy World Championship – John Parrott (£135,000) beat Jimmy White (£80,000) 18-11
Matchroom League – Stephen Hendry (£50,000)
Canal Plus European Challenge – Jimmy White (£20,000) beat Steve Davis (£10,000) 4-1
Continental Airlines London Masters – Steve Davis (£30,000) beat Stephen Hendry (£12,500) 4-0
Thai Masters – Steve Davis (£15,000) beat Stephen Hendry (£7,500) 6-3
555 Hong Kong Challenge – Stephen Hendry (£20,000) beat James Wattana (£10,000) 9-1
555 Indian Challenge – Stephen Hendry (£20,000) beat John Parrott (£10,000) 9-5
Regal Scottish Masters – Mike Hallett (£37,000) beat Steve Davis (£18,500) 10-6
Dubai Duty Free Classic – John Parrott (£40,000) beat Tony Knowles (£25,000) 9-3
Humo Belgian Masters – Mike Hallett (£30,000) beat Neal Foulds (£15,000) 9-7
World Seniors Championship – Cliff Wilson (£16,000) beat Eddie Charlton (£8,000) 5-4
Rothmans Grand Prix – Stephen Hendry (£75,000) beat Steve Davis (£40,000) 10-6
UK Open – John Parrott (£35,000) beat Jimmy White (£20,000) 16-13
Coalite World Matchplay – Gary Wilkinson (£70,000) beat Steve Davis (£25,000) 18-11
555 Belgian Challenge – Steve Davis (£20,000) beat Stephen Hendry (£10,000) 10-9

1992   Mercantile Classic – Steve Davis (£60,000) beat Stephen Hendry (£36,000) 9-8
Asian Open – Steve Davis (£30,000) beat Alan McManus (£19,000) 9-3
Benson and Hedges Masters – Stephen Hendry (£105,000) beat John Parrott (£54,000) 9-4
Regal Welsh Open – Stephen Hendry (£25,000) beat Darren Morgan (£13,500) 9-3
Pearl Assurance British Open – Jimmy White (£75,000) beat James Wattana (£45,000) 10-7
Strachan Open – James Wattana (£12,500) beat John Parrott (£6,700) 9-3
European Open – Jimmy White (£25,000) beat Mark Johnston-Allen (£14,000) 9-3
Benson and Hedges Irish Masters – Stephen Hendry (£40,375) beat Ken Doherty (£24,225) 9-6
Embassy World Championship – Stephen Hendry (£150,000) beat Jimmy White (£90,000) 18-14

Matchroom League – Stephen Hendry (£50,000) beat Steve Davis (£35,000) 9-2
Kent Classic – John Parrott (£25,000) beat Stephen Hendry (£15,000) 6-5
Regal Scottish Masters – Neal Foulds (£40,000) beat Gary Wilkinson (£20,000) 10-8
Dubai Duty Free Classic – John Parrott (£40,000) beat Stephen Hendry (£25,000) 9-8
Rothmans Grand Prix – Jimmy White (£80,000) beat Ken Doherty (£43,000) 10-9
Humo Belgian Masters – James Wattana (£15,000) beat John Parrott (£10,000) 10-5
Royal Liver UK Open – Jimmy White (£70,000) beat John Parrott (£35,000) 16-9
Coalite World Matchplay – James Wattana (£70,000) beat Steve Davis (£25,000) 9-4

1993   Nescafé Extra Challenge – Ronnie O'Sullivan (£10,500) (round-robin format)
Canal Plus European Challenge – Stephen Hendry (£20,000) beat Tony Drago (£10,000) 5-3
Regal Welsh Open – Ken Doherty (£27,500) beat Alan McManus (£15,000) 9-7
Benson and Hedges Masters – Stephen Hendry (£110,000) beat James Wattana (£56,000) 9-5
European Open – Steve Davis (£25,000) beat Stephen Hendry (£14,000) 10-4
British Open – Steve Davis (£50,000) beat James Wattana (£25,000) 10-2
Nescafé Asian Open – Dave Harold (£30,000) beat Darren Morgan (£17,500) 9-3
Benson and Hedges Irish Masters – Steve Davis (£45,000) beat Alan McManus (£27,000) 9-4
Sky Sports International Open – Stephen Hendry (£25,000) beat Steve Davis (£16,000) 10-6
Embassy World Championship – Stephen Hendry (£175,000) beat Jimmy White (£105,000) 18-5
Matchroom League – Jimmy White (£25,000) beat Alan McManus (£10,000) 10-7

WORLD AMATEUR CHAMPIONSHIP

1963 **(Calcutta)**	Gary Owen (England) round-robin
1966 **(Karachi)**	Gary Owen (England) round-robin
1968 **(Sydney)**	David Taylor (England) beat Max Williams (Australia) 8-7
1970 **(Edinburgh)**	Jonathon Barron (England) beat Sid Hood (England) 11-7
1972 **(Cardiff)**	Ray Edmonds (England) beat Mannie Francisco (South Africa) 11-10
1974 **(Dublin)**	Ray Edmonds (England) beat Geoff Thomas (Wales) 11-9
1976 **(Johannesburg)**	Doug Mountjoy (Wales) beat Paul Mifsud (Malta) 11-1
1978 **(Malta)**	Cliff Wilson (Wales) beat Joe Johnson (England) 11-5
1980 **(Launceston)**	Jimmy White (England) beat Ron Atkins (Australia) 11-2
1982 **(Calgary)**	Terry Parsons (Wales) beat Jim Bear (Canada) 11-8
1984 **(Dublin)**	O.B. Agrawal (India) beat Terry Parsons (Wales) 11-7
1985 **(Blackpool)**	Paul Mifsud (Malta) beat Dilwyn John (Wales) 11-6
1986 **(Invercargill)**	Paul Mifsud (Malta) beat Kerry Jones (Wales) 11-9
1987 **(Bangalore)**	Darren Morgan (Wales) beat Joe Grech (Malta) 11-4
1988 **(Sydney)**	James Wattana (Thailand) beat Barry Pinches (England) 11-8
1989 **(Singapore)**	Ken Doherty (Republic of Ireland) beat Jon Birch (England) 11-2
1990 **(Colombo)**	Stephen O'Connor (Republic of Ireland) beat Steve Lemmens (Belgium) 11-8
1991 **(Bangkok)**	Noppadon Noppachorn (Thailand) beat Dominic Dale (Wales) 11-8
1992 **(Malta)**	Neil Mosley (England) beat Leonardo Andam (Philippines) 11-2

DENNIS TAYLOR
(Northern Ireland)

BORN: 19.1.49
RANKING: 15
TURNED PROFESSIONAL: 1971
BEST PERFORMANCES OF CAREER:
Winner 1984 Rothmans
Grand Prix; world champion
1985; winner 1987 Benson
and Hedges Masters

KEN DOHERTY
(Republic of Ireland)

BORN: 17.9.69
RANKING: 11
TURNED PROFESSIONAL: 1990
BEST PERFORMANCES OF CAREER:
Winner 1993 Regal Welsh
Open; runner-up 1992
Rothmans Grand Prix; runner-
up 1992 Benson and Hedges
Irish Masters

WILLIE THORNE
(England)

BORN: 4.3.54
RANKING: 7
TURNED PROFESSIONAL: 1975
BEST PERFORMANCES OF CAREER:
Winner 1985 Mercantile
Classic; runner-up 1985 UK
Championship

JOHN PARROTT
(England)

BORN: 11.5.64
RANKING: 2
TURNED PROFESSIONAL: 1983
BEST PERFORMANCES OF CAREER:
World champion 1991; UK
champion 1991; 6 world
ranking titles in all

THE EMBASSY COLLECTION

NIGEL BOND
(England)

BORN: 15.11.65
RANKING: 9
TURNED PROFESSIONAL: 1989
BEST PERFORMANCE OF CAREER:
Runner-up 1990 Rothmans
Grand Prix

STEPHEN HENDRY
(Scotland)

BORN: 13.1.69
RANKING: 1
TURNED PROFESSIONAL: 1985
BEST PERFORMANCES OF CAREER:
World champion 3 times; UK
champion twice; winner
Benson and Hedges Masters
5 times; 16 world ranking
titles in all

NEAL FOULDS
(England)

BORN: 13.7.63
RANKING: 14
TURNED PROFESSIONAL: 1983
BEST PERFORMANCES OF CAREER:
Winner 1986 BCE
International; winner 1993
Regal Scottish Masters

JIMMY WHITE
(England)

BORN: 2.5.62
RANKING: 3
TURNED PROFESSIONAL: 1980
BEST PERFORMANCES OF CAREER:
UK champion 1992; winner
1984 Benson and Hedges
Masters; runner-up World
Championship 5 times; 9
world ranking titles in all

ALAN McMANUS
(Scotland)

BORN: 21.1.71
RANKING: 6
TURNED PROFESSIONAL: 1990
BEST PERFORMANCES OF CAREER:
Runner-up 1992 Asian Open;
runner-up 1993 Regal Welsh
Open; semi-finalist 1992
Regal Welsh Open; semi-
finalist 1993 World
Championship

DARREN MORGAN
(Wales)

BORN: 3.5.66
RANKING: 10
TURNED PROFESSIONAL: 1988
BEST PERFORMANCES OF CAREER:
Welsh professional champion
twice; runner-up 1992 Regal
Welsh Open; runner-up 1993
Asian Open

JAMES WATTANA
(Thailand)

BORN: 17.1.70
RANKING: 5
TURNED PROFESSIONAL: 1989
BEST PERFORMANCES OF CAREER:
Winner 1992 Coalite World
Matchplay; winner 1992
Strachan Open; semi-finalist
1992 World Championship

THE EMBASSY COLLECTION

STEVE JAMES
(England)

BORN: 2.5.61
RANKING: 13
TURNED PROFESSIONAL: 1986
BEST PERFORMANCES OF CAREER:
Winner 1990 Mercantile
Classic; semi-finalist 1991
World Championship

GARY WILKINSON
(England)

BORN: 7.4.66
RANKING: 17
TURNED PROFESSIONAL: 1987
BEST PERFORMANCES OF CAREER:
Winner 1991 Coalite World
Matchplay; runner-up 1991
British Open; runner-up 1992
Regal Scottish Masters

ALAIN ROBIDOUX
(Canada)

BORN: 25.7.60
RANKING: 18
TURNED PROFESSIONAL: 1986
BEST PERFORMANCES OF CAREER:
Canadian professional
champion 1988; semi-finalist
1990 Rothmans Grand Prix;
semi-finalist 1989 BCE
International

PETER EBDON
(England)

BORN: 27.8.70
RANKING: 21
TURNED PROFESSIONAL: 1991
BEST PERFORMANCE OF CAREER:
Quarter-finalist 1992 World
Championship

TERRY GRIFFITHS
(Wales)

BORN: 16.10.47
RANKING: 8
TURNED PROFESSIONAL: 1978
BEST PERFORMANCES OF CAREER:
World champion 1979;
winner 1980 Benson and
Hedges Masters; UK
champion 1982

MARTIN CLARK
(England)

BORN: 27.10.68
RANKING: 12
TURNED PROFESSIONAL: 1987
BEST PERFORMANCES OF CAREER:
Semi-finalist 1992 Coalite
World Matchplay; 8 world
ranking quarter-finals

STEVE DAVIS
(England)

BORN: 22.8.57
RANKING: 4
TURNED PROFESSIONAL: 1978
BEST PERFORMANCES OF CAREER:
World champion 6 times; UK
champion 6 times; winner
Benson and Hedges Masters
twice; 26 world ranking
titles in all

MISCELLANEOUS RECORDS

PROFESSIONAL

Record number of consecutive match wins in world ranking tournaments – 38 by Ronnie O'Sullivan, 36 by Stephen Hendry

Record number of consecutive frames won in world ranking tournaments – 33 by Steve Lee

Record number of consecutive frames won in any single world ranking tournament – 25 by Chris Scanlon (1993 Asian Open)

Record number of unbroken points scored in a world ranking tournament – 353 by Stephen Hendry (1992 Mercantile Classic)

Highest points aggregate in a frame during a world ranking tournament – 185 – Sean Storey 93 v Graham Cripsey 92 (1992 Asian Open)

Least number of points scored in a match during a world ranking tournament – 8 – Graham Bradley v Paul Smith (pre-qualifying competition 1992 Regal Welsh Open)

Most century breaks by an individual in a world ranking tournament – 10 by Stephen Hendry (1993 Sky Sports International Open)

Most consecutive century breaks in professional competition – 3 by Steve Davis (1988 BCE International), Doug Mountjoy (1988 UK Open), Mick Price (1990 Benson and Hedges Satellite), Paul Dawkins (1991 UK Open), Paul Davis (1992 DDO Masters), Peter Ebdon (1993 European Open)

Fastest frame during a world ranking tournament – 3 minutes by Tony Drago v Danny Fowler (3rd round 1988 BCE International)

Fastest best-of-nine-frame matches – 34 minutes (unofficial timing) Tony Drago v Sean Lanigan (5th round 1993 Strachan Challenge – 2nd leg); 43 minutes 26 seconds (official) Ronnie O'Sullivan v Jason Curtis (3rd pre-qualifying round 1992 Rothmans Grand Prix); 44 minutes (official) Jimmy White v James Wattana (1992 Nescafé Super League)

Fastest 17-frame match – 81 minutes Tony Drago v Joe O'Boye (3rd round 1990 UK Open)

Longest frames in a world ranking tournament – 88 minutes Cliff Thorburn v Paul Gibson (3rd round 1991 Rothmans Grand Prix); 83 minutes Robby Foldvari v Paul McPhillips (2nd round 1991 Strachan Professional); 75 minutes Matt Gibson v John Lardner (6th pre-qualifying round 1993 Asian Open)

Longest frame on television – 73 minutes 30 seconds (official) Steve Davis v Dene O'Kane (final 1990 World Team Cup)

Longest best-of-nine-frame match in a world ranking tournament – 386 minutes (official) Cliff Thorburn v Paul Gibson (3rd round 1991 Rothmans Grand Prix); 365 minutes (official) Steve Duggan v Paul Medati (3rd round 1992 Mercantile Classic); 351 minutes (official) Rex Williams v Robby Foldvari (3rd round 1992 European Open)

Longest 11-frame match – 434 minutes (official) Paul Tanner v Robby Foldvari (2nd round 1991 UK Open)

Longest best-of-19-frame match – 583 minutes (official) Jack Fitzmaurice v Marcel Gauvreau (2nd qualifying round 1991 Embassy World Championship); 576 minutes (official) Robby Foldvari v Kieran McAlinden (2nd qualifying round 1992 Embassy World Championship); 570 minutes (official) David Greaves v Paul Thornley (1st qualifying round 1987 Embassy World Championship)

AMATEUR

Youngest winner of IBSF World Amateur Championship – 18 years 40 days Stephen O'Connor 1990

Youngest English amateur champion – 16 years 11 months Jimmy White 1979

Youngest player to compile 147 maximum in recognised amateur competition – 15 years 97 days Ronnie O'Sullivan 1991

WOMEN

Highest break by a woman in competition – 137 Stacey Hillyard v Nicola Binden (1992 General Portfolio Women's Classic)

Highest break by a woman in professional competition – 133 Allison Fisher v Joe Swail (2nd round 1992 Dubai Classic)

MAXIMUM BREAKS (IN PROFESSIONAL COMPETITION)

1. John Spencer (Holsten Lager Classic) v Cliff Thorburn, January 1979
2. Steve Davis (Lada Classic) v John Spencer, January 1982
3. Cliff Thorburn (Embassy World Championship) v Terry Griffiths, April 1983
4. Kirk Stevens (Benson and Hedges Masters) v Jimmy White, January 1984
5. Willie Thorne (UK Open) v Tommy Murphy, November 1987
6. Tony Meo (Matchroom League) v Stephen Hendry, February 1988
7. Alain Robidoux (European Open) v Jim Meadowcroft, September 1988
8. John Rea (Scottish Championship) v Ian Black, February 1989
9. Cliff Thorburn (Matchroom League) v Jimmy White, March 1989
10. James Wattana (World Masters) v Paul Dawkins, January 1991
11. Peter Ebdon (Strachan Professional) v Wayne Martin, June 1991
12. James Wattana (British Open) v Tony Drago, February 1992
13. Paul Davies (DDO Masters) v Oliver King, April 1992
14. Jimmy White (Embassy World Championship) v Tony Drago, April 1992
15. John Parrott (Matchroom League) v Tony Meo, May 1992
16. Stephen Hendry (Matchroom League) v Willie Thorne, May 1992
17. Peter Ebdon (UK Open) v Ken Doherty, November 1992

1993 WORLD RANKINGS

1	Stephen Hendry	Scotland
2	John Parrott	England
3	Jimmy White	England
4	Steve Davis	England
5	James Wattana	Thailand
6	Alan McManus	Scotland
7	Willie Thorne	England
8	Terry Griffiths	Wales
9	Nigel Bond	England
10	Darren Morgan	Wales
11	Ken Doherty	Republic of Ireland
12	Martin Clark	England
13	Steve James	England
14	Neal Foulds	England
15	Dennis Taylor	Northern Ireland
16	David Roe	England
17	Gary Wilkinson	England
18	Alain Robidoux	Canada
19	Mike Hallett	England
20	Tony Drago	Malta
21	Peter Ebdon	England
22	Dene O'Kane	New Zealand
23	Tony Knowles	England
24	Mark Bennett	Wales
25	Joe Swail	Northern Ireland
26	Joe Johnson	England
27	Mick Price	England
28	Dean Reynolds	England
29	Tony Jones	England
30	Doug Mountjoy	Wales
31	Mark Johnston-Allen	England
32	Jason Ferguson	England
33	Silvino Francisco	South Africa
34	Eddie Charlton	Australia
35	Danny Fowler	England
36	Paul Davies	Wales
37	Brian Morgan	England
38	Peter Francisco	South Africa
39	Bob Chaperon	Canada
40	Jim Wych	Canada
41	Cliff Thorburn	Canada
42	Jason Prince	Northern Ireland
43	Wayne Jones	Wales
44	Jon Birch	England
45	Rod Lawler	England
46	Les Dodd	England
47	Cliff Wilson	Wales
48	Tony Chappel	Wales
49	Anthony Hamilton	England
50	Dave Harold	England
51	Tony Meo	England
52	Nigel Gilbert	England
53	Nick Terry	England
54	Andy Hicks	England
55	Ian Graham	England
56	Steve Newbury	Wales
57	Ronnie O'Sullivan	England
58	Jack McLaughlin	Northern Ireland
59	Billy Snaddon	Scotland
60	Stephen Murphy	Republic of Ireland
61	Alex Higgins	Northern Ireland
62	Eugene Hughes	Republic of Ireland
63	Dave Finbow	England
64	Drew Henry	Scotland
65	John Campbell	Australia
66	Barry West	England
67	David Taylor	England
68	Brady Gollan	Canada
69	Kirk Stevens	Canada
70	Warren King	Australia
71	Andy Cairns	England
72	John Virgo	England
73	Mark Rowing	England
74	Paul McPhillips	Scotland
75	Nick Dyson	England
76	Colin Roscoe	Wales
77	Troy Shaw	England
78	John Read	England
79	Franky Chan	Hong Kong
80	Tony Wilson	England
81	Paul Tanner	England
82	Steve Campbell	England
83	Karl Broughton	England
84	Robby Foldvari	Australia
85	Shaun Mellish	England
86	Brian Rowswell	England
87	Joe Grech	Malta
88	Paul Gibson	England
89	Craig Edwards	England
90	Anthony Davies	Wales
91	Mark Davis	England
92	Jon Wright	England
93	Robert Marshall	England
94	Karl Payne	England
95	Bill Oliver	England
96	Steve Duggan	England
97	Peter Daubney	England
98	Chris Small	Scotland
99	Ken Owers	England
100	Fergal O'Brien	Republic of Ireland
101	Steve Lee	England
102	Anthony Harris	England
103	Murdo Macleod	Scotland
104	Jimmy Chambers	England
105	David McDonnell	England
106	Jason Smith	England
107	Euan Henderson	Scotland
108	Paddy Browne	Republic of Ireland
109	Barry Pinches	England
110	Shokat Ali	England
111	Peter Lines	England
112	Stefan Mazrocis	England
113	Jamie Woodman	England
114	Stephen O'Connor	Republic of Ireland
115	Steve Longworth	England
116	Paul Medati	England
117	Jason Whittaker	England
118	Jason Weston	England
119	Mark J. Williams	Wales
120	Joe O'Boye	England
121	Ian Brumby	England
122	John Higgins	Scotland
123	Rex Williams	England
124	Bob Harris	England
125	Dave Martin	England
126	Jimmy Michie	England
127	Pat Kenny	England
128	John Rea	Scotland

PICTURE CREDITS